Recovery from Depression
Using the Narrative Approach

Recovery from Depression
Using the Narrative Approach

A Guide for Doctors, Complementary Therapists
and Mental Health Professionals

Damien Ridge

Jessica Kingsley Publishers
London and Philadelphia

First published in 2009
by Jessica Kingsley Publishers
116 Pentonville Road
London N1 9JB, UK
and
400 Market Street, Suite 400
Philadelphia, PA 19106, USA

www.jkp.com

Library of Congress Cataloging in Publication Data
Ridge, Damien.
    Recovery from depression using the narrative approach : a guide for doctors, complementary
therapists, and mental health professionals / Damien Ridge.
        p. ; cm.
    Includes bibliographical references and index.
    ISBN 978-1-84310-575-6 (pb : alk. paper) 1. Depression, Mental--Alternative treatment.
2. Narrative medicine. I. Title.
    [DNLM: 1. Depressive Disorder--therapy. 2. Complementary Therapies. 3. Narration. 4.
Psychotherapy--methods. WM 171 R544r 2009]
    RC537.R533 2009
    616.85'27--dc22
                                                                        2008021119

British Library Cataloguing in Publication Data
A CIP catalogue record for this book is available from the British Library

ISBN 978 1 84310 575 6

Printed and bound in Great Britain by
Athenaeum Press, Gateshead, Tyne and Wear

Contents

List of Boxes

List of Case Studies

Dedication

This book is dedicated to Mark Arber for engaging with my own life narrative, and so ultimately making this book possible.

Acknowledgements

I would first like to thank the participants in this study for so thoughtfully sharing their stories of depression and recovery. Thanks especially to Sue Ziebland for her contributions to the original analysis of the data used to underpin this book, particularly the section on stigma. Thank you also to my supportive colleagues at Oxford University, especially Ann McPherson and Francie Smee for helping in this research, as well as recruiters and advisory panel members who are credited for their vital work on the Depression module on the *Health Talk Online* (formerly DIPEx) website (www.healthtalkonline.org). I would also like to thank those who reviewed the manuscript for providing much helpful and insightful feedback, including Krysia Canvin, Christopher Dowrick, Laurence Gallagher, Andrew Herxheimer, Ian Holder, Hilary Lavender, Stuart Perkins, Karen Pilkington, David Plummer, Robert Reynolds, Sarah Russell and Stephen Jones from JKP. Thanks also to Janice Spurgeon for making late corrections. The research was originally funded by the Mental Health Task Force, Department of Health, UK. I carried out the research for this book as a senior researcher at the University of Oxford, and I further analysed the data and wrote this book while funded by the University of Westminster, London.

Preface: About this Book

The idea for this book for professionals grew out of research on patient[1] experiences of depression which I undertook while I was a researcher in the *Health Talk Online* research group at Oxford University from 2003 to 2004. *Health Talk Online* produces a unique free public access website (www.healthtalkonline.org/mental_health) featuring video and audio clips from interviews with patients discussing the ways they experience and cope with their various health conditions. Each 'module' (or health condition) not only contains video clips, but also around 25 thoroughly researched 'chapters' which discuss in detail the key findings related to the health conditions listed on the website (e.g. choosing treatments, negotiating the health system, self-management). The box below provides an outline of topics discussed on the *Health Talk Online* depression website.

Box 0.1: The 27 topics for patients on the *Health Talk Online* **depression website (www.healthtalkonline.org/mental_health/depression)**

Stories of discovery
- Childhood and life before depression
- Experiencing depression
- Recognition and diagnosis

Negotiating the health system
- Doctors
- Psychiatrists and other professionals
- Newer anti-depressant medication

---

1   Sensibilities over the use of terms to describe clients of health professionals change all the time (e.g. service user, consumer). I have used the term 'patient' to be consistent with other literature in the UK and elsewhere, even though the term is not ideal, as many readers will recognise.

- Other medical treatments
- Attitudes to medication
- Talking therapies – Considering talking therapies
- Talking therapies – Finding a therapist
- Talking therapies – Experiences of talking therapy
- Hospital-based treatment
- Complementary and holistic approaches

Self care
- Managing the mind
- Distraction, activities and creativity
- Limiting and controlling episodes
- Life and money
- Self-help resources
- Spirituality

Supports and challenges
- Support groups
- Friends and family
- Work and education
- Stigma and mental health
- Being different, ethnicity and sexuality

Living with depression and recovery
- Getting better
- Gaining insights
- Hope, advice and wisdom

The idea of *Health Talk Online* is to provide online informational and emotional support, rather like having 'expert patients' available 24 hours a day via the Internet. The resource is mainly designed for patients, although carers and professionals do use the site also. At the time of writing this book there were 46 different modules available on the *Health Talk Online* website, including information on a range of health issues like Black and minority ethnic experiences of mental health (patients and their carers), HIV, chronic pain, young people and sexual health, heart attack and many cancers. Over a dozen more modules were in production in 2009. The *Health Talk Online* site statistics show that in 2007 the site regularly received 1.5 million hits each month, and depression was second only to 'sexual health of young people' as the most popular module. The popularity of the depression module is an indication of the need for patients to find out from other patients' experiences about mental health via the Internet.

While certainly covering a range of patient and carer perspectives that will help professionals gain key insights into their work with patients, the *Health Talk Online* website is specifically written as an independent and trusted website for patients themselves (see Box 0.2: Key facts about *Health Talk Online*). The current book takes a more in-depth look at the data, and was written with a range of professionals in mind, including doctors, nurses, social workers, community psychiatric nurses and talking therapists. An up-to-date look at key issues in the academic literature is included in this book to better contextualise the use of patient narratives. For instance, this book looks at questions like 'How effective is yoga for depression?' 'How much does it matter to patients whether or not there is controlled clinical trial evidence for relatively safe treatments like fish oils or homeopathy for depression?' At the end of each chapter the key issues covered are high-lighted, and some of these issues are dealt with further in the concluding chapter. Chapter 9 surveys the findings, linking them to key insights for professionals in their work with people with depression. It is also hoped that people who experience depression and who are interested in pursuing issues in greater depth after viewing the *Health Talk Online* depression website can also gain deeper insights into depression, self-management, help-seeking and recovery from this book.

Box 0.2: Key facts about *Health Talk Online*

Answering questions and getting support
The *Health Talk Online* research group ultimately aims to cover all major health conditions from patient and carer perspectives. Patient questions collected in the course of constructing each module are answered by identifying links to reliable outside websites that specialise in answering those questions. The modules also list the key support groups, services and organisations for each condition. The information on the *Health Talk Online* website is regularly reviewed and updated.

Awards

Health Talk Online was voted by *The Times* newspaper as one of the top three patient health sites (2006), was in *The Guardian*'s top ten health websites (2004) and was singled out in a recent University of Northumbria study (*The Times*, 7 March 2007) as a favourite, trusted site for patient web users. The *Health Talk Online* website has also won various awards including the BUPA Foundation Communication Award (2004) and the BMA Patient Information Award (2005).

Independence

Health Talk Online has an ethical funding policy, and the impartiality of the website is ensured by the charity trustees and 'no advertising' policy. In contrast to other resources designed for patients on the Internet, all *Health Talk Online* modules are based on a rigorous social science qualitative research methodology. As such, *Health Talk Online* overcomes many of the inadequacies of other Internet resources for health information (e.g. lack of balance).

Chapter 1

Introduction

Moderate to severe depression – as described by the lay people interviewed for this book – is a condition of existential misery (often profound) and personal isolation. As will become clear in this book, depression also raises fundamental questions about people's sense of who they actually are. As a matter of course people tend to recover from depression, although many struggle to feel well again. Depression is often a chronic condition and recovery may be only partial and temporary. Nevertheless, people with depression do make significant and ongoing recoveries. A key perspective put forward in this book is that depression can only be fully appreciated by the person experiencing the condition. This is because depression is experienced as an ailment of *interiority*, i.e. affecting people's internal thoughts, feelings and bodily sensations. No one has full access to the interiority of another person, other than the person concerned. This means that ultimately only the person with depression can ever become the real expert on themselves. Thus I argue that professionals must be content to be 'guardians' or 'allies' of patient-driven self-management, help-seeking and recovery. This is not to say that patients with depression are always able to feel or act as experts. Far from it: depression undermines people, it zaps their confidence and it depletes the spirit. At least until people begin to emerge from their depression, effective professionals may need to be keepers of the ultimate ideal that patients are the experts on themselves and their depression.

An argument that runs throughout this book is that people try to construct meaningful narratives – and assemble recovery 'tools' (such as medication, fish oils, yoga, talking therapies, spirituality) – to make sense of their lives, their depression and their recoveries (Ridge and Ziebland 2006). This narrative and recovery 'tool' approach as described in this book takes the focus away from single treatments (e.g. antidepressants) and their clinical trial evidence for depression, which, after all, are more squarely on the radar for professionals than patients. The focus at all times in this book is on the multitude of strategies and narrative threads that patients must choose from and tailor to themselves and their circumstances to retrieve meaning from the experience of depression. Indeed, I argue that focusing on just one approach, like medication, can put patients at a disadvantage in recovering from depression. Instead, the stories from patients as outlined in this book show that people can benefit from taking as much interest as possible in their depression and recoveries. Additionally, the people I spoke to for this book reported that they were more successful when they found numerous useful (i.e. considered effective within their own narratives) and relatively safe tools to recover with. Moreover, patients benefit if they can take appropriate responsibilities in their recovery, become more expert and ultimately take control of their recoveries.

Finally, a key issue is that patient narratives suggest that many times there is a 'true self' or 'authentic self' to be discovered that can provide strong foundations for recovery. The concept of an authentic self or even an authentic story of the self will be a difficult one for some readers to digest. In using the word 'authentic' in this book, I am not suggesting that a hopeful attitude is more authentic than a despairing one. Rather, despite the relative meanings available to us in our post-modern lives, people do select and tell stories about themselves which attempt to get to the things that feel right or true at the time of the story telling. As Frank (1995, p.22) rightly points out, 'the truth of stories is not only what *was* experienced, but equally what *becomes* experience in the telling and its reception... Stories are true to the flux of experience, and the story affects the direction of that flux.' As outlined by participants in the present study, identifying stories that feel right can reinvigorate people and inspire creativity and feelings of grounding and wholeness. In this way, 'true' selves and stories can provide patients with better foundations for recovering from depression. While I will use words like 'authenticity' in this book, other words that could equally be substituted include 'more useful', 'more helpful', 'more life giving' and 'more functional'. Regardless of the words used, establishing authentically felt selves and stories may provide much joy in life that patients did not expect to exist beyond depression and everyday survival.

Organisation of chapters

In the present chapter I discuss issues to do with depression as a category of mental distress, as well as some of the concepts and theories that underpin the analysis in this book. I outline how arguments used in this book are underpinned by cultural relativism, the consumer-based 'recovery movement', theorising about the 'self' (e.g. from symbolic interactionism and self psychology) and patient narrative approaches. Finally, the qualitative methods used in this book are briefly outlined. In Chapter 2 I investigate the ways in which participants link life events and early life deprivations to their subsequent episodes of depression. One thread that is picked up on in this discussion is how many participants felt different and out of step with others from early on in their lives and how this is linked to narratives of depression. This chapter also discusses the difficulties people had in arriving at a 'depression' label for their condition including the lack of a language to describe depression. Chapter 3 goes into detail about the experience of depression itself. The issues discussed include the downward spiral into depression (depressive interlock), the interior experience of depression (thoughts, feelings, physical sensations), suicide considerations in depression (e.g. suicide logic) and how the ongoing narrative about the self can wobble or even 'crash' in depression with dangerous consequences. Chapter 4 discusses the ways in which, despite the seriousness of depression, depression provides personal opportunities. It outlines how people go about recovering from depression both in the short and the long term. This chapter also discusses how people manage to stay well between depressive episodes (e.g. noticing the warning signs), and how they better manage actual episodes of depression in order to minimise their impact. In terms of longer-term recovery, participants in this chapter discuss the different types of insight they gain. People also discuss how they rewrite their personal narrative more constructively and take increasing responsibility for recovery as they gain increasing experience of dealing with depression.

In Chapters 5 and 6 the multiple medical and non-medical 'tools' that people use to help them shift their existential experience and narrate their recoveries from depression are discussed. Tools discussed in detail include antidepressants, electroconvulsive therapy (ECT), hospitalisation, St John's wort, yoga, bibliotherapy, exercise, omega-3 fatty acids, homeopathy and spirituality/prayer. Chapter 7 discusses ways in which professionals can be better 'recovery allies' and what this specifically entails, including validating interior experiences of patients and promoting recovery attitudes. Issues in working with men who are depressed are explored as a case study. Given that talking therapies were considered so important to participant recoveries, Chapter 8 is dedicated entirely to these therapies. This chapter discusses among other issues the emotional work patients do in therapies, the specific benefits people get from therapy, the styles of therapy they appreciate and the need to eventually end the therapy relationship. This chapter also has a case study looking at cognitive behavioural therapy, a short-term kind of therapy commonly discussed by participants. Finally, Chapter 9 draws together the threads of the narrative and multiple 'tool' approach as elaborated in this book, and the chapter discusses how professionals might begin to distil and integrate the findings from this study of patient perspectives. The chapter also includes a case study about stigma to show how professionals can support patient narratives in concrete and everyday ways.

Diagnosing depression

Depression is common, with one in six people in the community experiencing depression in their lifetime (Ebmeier, Donaghey and Steele 2006). However, less than half of these people will access health services because of their depression. While diagnoses of depression have increased in recent decades, there is some uncertainty about what this rise means: Is it due to increased rates of depression, increased recognition of depression, improved patient help-seeking or a mixture of these explanations? The answer to this question is not clear. Even when people visit health professionals when suffering from depression, often the condition is still missed (Burroughs *et al.* 2006). Patients with depression may not recognise their condition, particularly if they also have physical symptoms making diagnosis more complicated (Murray *et al.* 2006; Shiels *et al.* 2004). Despite some evidence to the contrary (Murphy *et al.* 2000) there is, however, some evidence suggesting that actual rates of depression are increasing in the West (Doris, Ebmeier and Shajahan 1999; Klerman and Weissman 1989). Thus it is predicted that by 2020 depression will move from fourth place to second place as the leading cause of disability in the world (Michaud, Murray and Bloom 2001).

As depression is very much a personal and 'interior' experience, there is no agreed 'objective' way to know if depression is present in a patient or not. Instead, depression is usually diagnosed by counting the presence of certain reported symptoms (e.g. low mood, fatigue, disturbed sleep, poor concentration, guilt, low self-confidence, suicidal thoughts) for a recent time period (e.g. the previous two weeks). The more symptoms present, the more severe the depression is thought to be. Two major classification systems used to diagnose depression are the *Diagnostic and Statistical Manual (DSM)* and the *International Classification of Diseases (ICD-10)*. The ICD-10 uses a list of ten depressive symptoms. Mild depression is considered when a maximum of four symptoms are present, while severe depression requires that seven or more symptoms be present. The DSM works similarly to the ICD, although the DSM groups symptoms into four categories: mood (e.g. sadness, worthlessness), behaviour (e.g. withdrawal from social life), cognition (e.g. difficulty thinking) and physical problems. Different types of depression may also be identified by classification systems including dysthymia (chronic mild depression) and bipolar disorder (where the mood swings between two poles: the low mood of depression and the euphoria of mania).

In practice, classification systems like the ICD and DSM are as much 'political manifesto' as they are scientific documents (Pilgrim 2007, p.538). We only have to briefly survey history to see that this is the case. The medical classification of depression was at least partly driven by the rather urgent need psychiatry had as a young profession in the early twentieth century to mark out its territory and sell its expertise in mental illness so as to become a viable medical specialty (McPherson and Armstrong 2006). Today, the classification of depression reflects the way that the medical profession, researchers, consumers and pharmaceutical companies have historically negotiated a kind of uneasy consensus. While most of the key stakeholders are clear that depression is a diagnosis with some legitimacy, there is still a good deal of debate (Pilgrim 2007), including:

- There is no firm position among psychiatrists on the different types of depression.

- Depression is not easily discernible from other diagnoses, like anxiety.

- Experts put greater emphasis on different aspects of depression, such as mood disturbance or cognitive impairment.

- Experts can disagree on the symptoms that need to be present for a diagnosis of depression.

- There is a spectrum of causal explanations for depression including biochemical, psychological (e.g. early development) and social explanations (e.g. oppression of women).

- It is not clear if depression as a diagnosis is appropriate in certain non-Western cultural circumstances (see discussion of 'culture and depression' below).

There is certainly value in getting a diagnosis of depression for patients who are experiencing misery that is profound. The label of depression validates the experiences of the person, identifies a specific condition, and points people in the direction of some potentially useful treatments (Karp 1994). However, the label can also signal a mental illness, and so it comes with considerable baggage, not least of which is the social stigma attached to such conditions (Dinos *et al.* 2004). It is not surprising then that patients' own stories frequently attempt to 'normalise' their experience of depression, rather than have their depression categorised as a 'mental illnesses' or a type of 'madness' (Kangas 2001).

And so depression is more or less considered a legitimate category by professionals and patients. However, rather than focusing on symptoms for diagnosis, this book takes a slightly different vantage point: how depression as a category of experience is *meaningful* to patients. That is, I am more concerned with the interior experience of the person (the thoughts, feelings and bodily sensations) in their social context, rather than the classic symptoms of depression. So in this book, I will unpack – in considerable detail – the interior suffering involved in depression. The approach in this book is consistent with the many professionals who now understand depression to be determined by psychosocial – rather than just biomedical – factors (Chew-Graham *et al.* 2002; Murray *et al.* 2006). Additionally, many professionals now see depression as comprehensible once social circumstances are taken into account (e.g. abuse, old age, poverty, gender, isolation, loss, ill health) (Burroughs *et al.* 2006; Chew-Graham *et al.* 2002; Matheson *et al.* 2006). Along with patient reports on the interior meanings of depression, I am also interested in exploring how people contextualise their experiences of depression. For example, I explore the role of early family life and health professionals in depression.

Culture and depression

Culture is about the practices, knowledge, symbols and beliefs that give human activities their meaning. Rather than being static, cultures are always dynamic, forever being created and recreated through everyday lived experience (Matsumoto, Kudoh and Takeuchi 1996). However, it can be difficult for people to view their knowledge and ways of living as based on a cultural belief system. A perspective of 'cultural relativism' – respecting the beliefs and practices of other people's cultures while resisting the desire to judge it according to one's own cultural ways – is the approach taken in this book (Fenton and Sadiq-Sangster 1996). From this perspective, medicine itself can be read as a culturally specific health belief system which gained ascendancy over alternative health belief systems for political rather than just scientific reasons (Willis 1989). For instance, despite popular opinion to the contrary, many epidemiologists accept that effective medical treatments (like antibiotics and vaccines) came too late to adequately explain the significant decline in infectious disease in the West since the second half of the nineteenth century (Mackenbach 1996). What really seemed to make all the difference were wider changes in society at the time, including better sanitation, nutrition, increased standards of living and less overcrowding. Similarly, before Western medical approaches, madness was thought of in non-medical ways, including as just being a part of everyday life or even as the opposite of reasonableness (Foucault 2001). The medical approach to 'madness' only began in the late eighteenth century, and 'psychiatry was not approved as a medical specialty' in the US until the 1930s (Anlue 1998, p.104). Psychiatry has gone on to become one of the more controversial areas in medicine. For instance, its early classification of homosexuality as an individual pathology (rather than homophobia being considered a societal pathology) was successfully challenged politically in the 1970s (Plummer 1999; Spitzer 1981). So from a cultural relativist perspective psychiatry and even medicine itself can be thought about as health belief systems that evolve over time, rather than a collection of self-evident universal truths.

Classification systems like the DSM can disguise considerable cultural variation in the way that depression is experienced, expressed, understood and addressed. Again the debate between universalism and relativism is relevant as there are different views on whether the misery of depression cuts across a wide variety of social and cultural contexts, or whether there needs to be a better understanding of the social circumstances underpinning the condition (Fenton and Sadiq-Sangster 1996). In this book, I agree with researchers who argue that some experiences of depression can be similar across different cultural contexts, while there is also the potential for wide cultural variations (Mallinson and Popay 2007). In terms of cultural variations, in some groups (like certain sections of Chinese society), depression tends to be experienced more physically than psychologically (e.g. as discomfort, inner pressure, pain, fatigue) (Kleinman 2004). Other groups (e.g. Somalian and Ethiopian refugees in Australia) may highlight the misery of depression as more of a collective experience, rather than emphasise individual perspectives as Westernised people may do (Kokanovic *et al.* 2008). In terms of what people believe causes depression, Westernised cultures are frequently sympathetic to biomedical and psychological explanations about causality, where outside events are frequently seen to play a role.

On the other hand, some cultural groupings in the West are more inclined to adopt spiritual rather than biomedical or psychological explanations. For instance, some Yorubas and Bangladeshis in the UK believe that magic (e.g. black magic, curses, possession by evil spirits) plays a role in the causality of depression (Lavender, Khondoker and Jones 2006). Indeed, many established cultural groups take it for granted that good and bad 'spirits' exist in the world and can cause problems for people, including depression and psychosis (Bose 1997). Such health beliefs can have profound implications for the ways in which people seek to recover their wellbeing. For instance, some people believe that electroconvulsive therapy (ECT) works by driving malevolent spirits away (Betty 2005).

Given that the present study was mainly among white people living in the UK, the discussion of spiritual causes of depression was much less common than biomedical, psychological and social causes. Nevertheless, even among the relatively white middle-class group of people interviewed for this book, some saw depression as a 'spiritual crisis' and believed that recovery could be positively influenced by spiritual practices (Chiu *et al.* 2005). And these kinds of beliefs are supported by certain studies indicating a positive link between health (physical and mental) and skilled practices of spirituality or religion (Koenig 2000; Koenig, Larson and Larson 2001; Shoshanah Feher 1999; Stanton, Danoff-Burg and Huggins 2002; Thoresen and Harris 2002). Even if metaphysical explanations of mental distress have fallen out of favour with professionals, many lay accounts see it differently, and spiritual approaches to recovery are taken up in Chapter 6.

While the emphasis in this book is on depression experienced as an ailment of the self, this individualistic perspective needs to be understood as emergent from a Western cultural gaze. Many cultural groups talk about their experiences of depression in such a way that the self is not so important and is hidden or even absent (Fenton and Sadiq-Sangster 1996), such as the Somalian and Ethiopian refugees cited above. Clearly then, caution should be exercised when considering how the findings of this book relate to cultural groups outside of the people interviewed for this study.

Recovery in the context of mental health

The notion that people could recover from severe mental illnesses really only took off in the second half of the twentieth century in the aftermath of deinstitutionalisation: i.e. moving people with mental illness from long-term hospital care back into the community, theoretically (but often not in practice) with adequate social supports (Anlue 1998). By this time too, more effective drug treatments for mental illnesses were becoming increasingly available, making community living a real possibility for more and more people. Additionally, narratives about the struggle of mental health 'consumers' to recover were erupting into the public consciousness and being backed up by some hopeful research findings (Anthony 1993; US Department of Health and Human Services 1999). Today, the literature suggests that even in severe conditions like schizophrenia, recovery is possible, although mostly not without considerable difficulties and qualifications (Hopper 2007).

'Recovery' is actually a complex and multifaceted construct, and there are many different definitions of recovery available in the literature. The diversity in the way that 'recovery' is defined is probably largely because the concept inherently elevates lay narratives – with their diverse experiences – as the authoritative accounts (Jacobson 2003). The problems in defining recovery may be uncomfortable for those who desire a more precise definition. However, patients are much more focused on individual and collective recovery narratives, and finding helpful treatments, than ensuring their understanding of recovery fits with professional models. Indeed, in their stories, patients resist 'narrative surrender' to medical narratives (Frank 1995, p.18). Pessimistic professional understandings of mental health are challenged by patient narratives that emphasise human qualities and the empowerment of users of mental health services. As such, it is more useful for the purposes of this book to understand recovery narratives as variably constructed in practice by patients, and possibly in tension with professional narratives. In this book I accept that recovery is a highly personal experience and so it resists being reduced to a single professional definition. While recovery is a contested idea, this is not to say there are not helpful ways of viewing recovery that can get to the heart of patient experience. For instance, recovery is considered by some to be the task of becoming a full citizen with human rights, having good social supports, getting better access to resources and being supported to make choices (Nelson, Lord and Ochocka 2001). Others see recovery as about overcoming dominant social narratives which stereotype and undermine 'sufferers', while finding ways to tell tales of 'joy' rather than misery and 'terror' (Rappaport 2000, p.13). Alternatively, some feminist researchers believe recovery involves disrupting the persuasiveness of 'good woman' narratives in our society that assume that women should put the needs of others before their own (Lafrance and Stoppard 2006, p.316).

Despite the variety of ways of viewing recovery, we still know relatively little about the personal experience of recovery: What does recovery feel like? What are the common experiences? What treatments and circumstances help recovery narratives? Nevertheless, one early and influential construction of recovery resonates well with the stories told in the present study. It is worth summarising this definition by Anthony (1993) to help set the scene for the approach in this book:

> [Recovery is] a deeply personal, unique process of changing one's attitudes, values, feelings, goals, skills and/or roles. It is a way of living a satisfying, hopeful, and contributing life, even with limitations caused by the illness. Recovery involves the development of new meaning and purpose in one's life as one grows beyond the catastrophic effects of mental illness. (p.527)

Anthony (1993) goes on to outline some key issues in how people recover from mental health problems that align well with the findings in this book:

- Professionals can only facilitate recovery; it is clients who must 'recover'.

- An ally – someone who is trustworthy, really believes in the client, and is available in times of need – is a common thread in success stories of recovery.

- For people who recover, symptoms and episodes may not disappear altogether, but may reduce in frequency and severity, and be experienced as less ominous.

- Recovery is not perfect or linear, and so it can feel directionless or even like it is going backwards to patients.

The importance of personal approaches, hope, professionals as allies, personal responsibility and the partiality of recovery are taken up in some depth in this book. Before looking at recovery from depression it is worth briefly considering just how much recovery represents a radical shift in thinking for Western societies. It was not long ago that people considered to have mental illnesses were in effect warehoused in psychiatric institutions with very little in the way of useful treatments available (Foucault 2001). Society has now changed enough so effective treatments are available and the discourses of recovery are capturing the imagination of government health departments (Roberts and Wolfson 2004). Recovery and 'expert patient' training programmes are now being advocated from within health departments both in the UK and the US (National Institute for Mental Health in England 2005; US Department of Health and Human Services 1999).

Depression and recovery

There is still only limited research on how people go about understanding and organising their recoveries from depression. Additionally, the patient-centred research on recovery from depression that does exist tends to focus on women more than men. Nevertheless, this body of research is already important because it has identified ways of understanding the individual transitions, social circumstances and challenges involved in depression and recovery. For instance, as part of recovery, women frequently feel the need to get to know – and care for – themselves better (Lafrance and Stoppard 2006). Schreiber's (1996) North American study of 21 women recovering from depression showed that women re-work their sense of self in phases. Here women attempt to tell their own story, seek social understanding and support, gain insights and thus understand themselves and others with greater clarity. Similarly, in the area of female postpartum depression, a synthesis of 18 studies found that recovery involved a range of challenges, such as having to battle the health system to get appropriate help, adjusting downwards initial high expectations of what it means to be a mother and trying to better understand and take care of the self (Beck 2002). One study of postpartum depression in Taiwanese women summed up recovery as women being 'reborn' whereby they come to identify and better care for their authentic self (Chen *et al.* 2006).

While there are no studies specifically investigating processes of recovery from depression for men other than the present study (Emslie *et al.* 2006), Karp included eight men in his sample of 20 people when he investigated experiences of depression in North America in the early 1990s (Karp 1994). He found that while there were people who view the prospect of depression as something they will always have to cope with, others believed it possible to recover more fully from depression. Karp like other researchers focused on the idea of 'transition' through depression (which he called 'depression career'), and of how people's identities can change during transition. These themes of self, transition and authenticity as described in these earlier studies are taken up in great detail in the present book. Indeed, the starting position for this book is that depression in Western cultural circumstances tends to be constructed by lay people as a problem of the self, where recovery often involves some kind of re-working of the self towards a greater sense of functionality or feelings of authenticity (see section on 'Self' below).

There are also some 'auto-ethnographic' accounts of depression in the academic literature, that is, where researchers study themselves, their life history and circumstances. For instance, Brett Smith focuses on the issue of his own sense of masculinity and how he feels he must battle with his emotions and depression. He also discusses in detail the problems men like himself have in admitting emotional vulnerability (Smith 1999). Smith also questions what he sees as the tendency in the literature to tell stories of triumph over depression, and the problems this might entail in appreciating the full complexity in depression, including the possibility of anti-recovery: 'I see, or feel, no conclusions', he says of himself (p.275). Nevertheless, he notices his 'powerful urge to be heard' (p.276). The issue of 'voice' is also taken up in this book. Again, like other researchers of patient experience, Smith identifies the importance of people (re)constructing their sense of self through the experience of depression, while pointing to the importance of telling (and hearing) personal and collective stories about illness and healing. On a similar note, an auto-ethnographic account of a female depression constructed the future as 'perpetual efforts to keep disintegration at bay' (Jago 2002, p.743). Like others, Jago points to the central role of identity in depression, noting that 'one of the worst aspects of depression is the ability to watch yourself disappear' (p.743). Problems with the self in depression – including the apparent potential for self disorganisation and annihilation – are taken up in Chapter 3.

To summarise then, the patient-centred research focusing on recovery from depression is still in its infancy. Nevertheless, it is clear that depression is experienced by patients (Westernised ones at least) as a disorder that brings the self into question. Individual and social contexts like gender, cultural beliefs and the very human need to tell personal stories (and have these stories heard and validated) play important roles in depression and constructions of recovery. The research on women and depression, for instance, points to the way gendered expectations on women can pull them away from a clear sense of who they are, and so recovery involves a remedy in terms of more authentic story telling about the self. While there is less research with men, the indications are that men also consider depression to be an ailment of self, but they are under different kinds of pressures, such as how to tell stories about depression that are somehow validating of masculinity (Emslie et al. 2006). Additionally, it is clear that recovery involves a phased transition of the self, which may be partial, imperfect, or feel like it is going backwards rather than forwards.

The self-concept

Qualitative research on patient experience suggests that depression is primarily an ailment of the 'self' in the West, that difficulties frequently emerge early on in life, and that the self comes to be viewed as dysfunctional, broken or in need of repair (Beck 2002; Karp 1994). With this focus on 'the self', it is useful to examine a little more deeply what is meant by the self, before moving on to discuss how the self can be influenced by early life experiences, depression and recovery in later chapters. Frequently when we talk about the self in everyday life, we tend to focus only on certain aspects of the self, like 'self-esteem', sense of 'self-worth' or a person's identity (e.g. businessman, mother, gay). This approach, while a useful shorthand for getting through social life, can prevent a fuller appreciation of the self. And understanding depression requires a broader understanding of the self than this. There are four main conceptual frameworks in this book that underpin the discussion about the self.

First, the examination of the self in this book is underpinned by a symbolic interactionist perspective. Symbolic interactionism assumes that human beings behave towards things and events in the world around them according to the meaning they attribute to these things and events (Blumer 1969). In turn, these kinds of meanings emerge out of everyday human life including our interactions with other people. Also, to arrive at the meaning of things and events we need to interpret our social experiences. Second, in addition to being able to reflect and think about things happening around us, our 'selves' are also *active* beings in the world, able to make choices, and thus people can also reflect on themselves (Demo 1992). And so although 'the self' has a kind of apparent stability in that we feel we are the same from day to day, the self also has a capacity to reflect, make different choices and change over time (O'Sullivan 2006). In this book I will therefore assume that, as part of recovering from depression, people can and do make choices, and so are able to make different choices and so very gradually change over time. Indeed, as the lay accounts told to me testify, the suffering of depression can be a great motivator to make personal changes.

Third, Frank (1995, p.4) has noted that our present-day illnesses now 'feel different' from days gone by, there is a circulation of illness stories where medicine is no longer enough, and the label of 'postmodernity' captures this change. In postmodern times, as Frank outlines, stories are localised, and lay stories have their own meanings and inherent values as they resist medical colonisation. At the same time, our identities have more widely come to be considered fragmented, multiple and changeable rather than fixed and singular (Strauss 1997). As such, this book is not so concerned with finding uniformity and consistency in people's sense of self and stories. Rather, I assume that identities and stories are context-specific, changeable and even contradictory. Fourth, another theoretical perspective with a close parallel to the way people describe their experiences of the self in depression is self psychology (Kangas 2001). Self psychology has a focus on 'the self', the importance of dialogue with early caregivers, and (re)storying of the self. Kohut (1971) (the founder of self psychology) focused on the early childhood potential for 'narcissistic vulnerability' of the self as well as the potential for 'healthy narcissism'. For Kohut, a healthy sense of self/narcissism develops when: 1. others respond to the child with joy, supporting its natural creativity; 2. when the child is involved, and merges, with powerful others; and 3. when the child feels like these others. Narcissistic vulnerability can occur when this process goes wrong. In line with the many stories told to me for the present study, self psychology puts a lot of emphasis on early childhood experience, being heard and understood by an empathic other, and (re)narrating personal stories – including inner conflict – in ways that are life giving rather than life depleting (Young 1996). Participants in the current study told many stories about how life got in the way of a healthy sense of self. Thus, self psychology is the final conceptual framework that underpins the analysis in this book. Below is some more detail about the ideas that underpin the concept of 'self' in this book.

Box 1.1: Some ideas that underpin the concept of 'self' in this book

Symbolic interactionism
From this perspective humans can only be understood by looking at the meaning of their social interactions (Pilgrim 2007). Here, the self is able to reflect on itself as an entity in the world (Gecas 1982), and attribute meanings to itself. If people attribute certain meanings to themselves, then it is these meanings that have profound implications for behaviour. For example, male sex workers may understand the commercial sex they engage in as 'not real sex' (compared to personal sex), with condoms being considered 'work equipment' that protects against work injury (Browne and Minichiello 1995). Subsequently, the use of condoms may have links to the degree of the real self that sex workers decide to share with clients.

The reflexive self

It is argued by some that the 'self-concept' is a little different to the 'self' in that the self-concept is a *product* of the reflexive action of the self (Gecas 1982). In other words, the self-concept is like a 'snapshot' of a self that is actually in flux. This perspective also means that any sense that our identities and characteristics are fixed is incorrect.

Apparent contradictions in self

While we often think of fixed identities like heterosexual and homosexual, many men who have sex with other men may not identify as gay or bisexual, nor ever enter a gay community (Connell 1992). Such men may more readily identify in other ways, through their other social roles, including husband, father or labourer. Scratch the surface of identity, and others may emerge!

Self psychology

Narcissistic injury is thought to occur in children when caretakers do not empathically mirror the child, nor see the child as special or admire the child (Mann 2004). Through gradual exposure to reality and its discontents in a supportive (mirroring) environment, early and socially inappropriate 'narcissistic' states can be slowly transformed into 'healthy narcissism'.

Mental health and the self-concept

People with chronic illness in general have heightened concerns regarding 'the person they see themselves becoming', as they come to understand their vulnerability in the face of disease (Charmaz 1983, p.190). In the area of mental health, a range of influential thinkers have traced people's concerns about the self as emerging very early in life, as far back as infancy. For instance, the work of the British paediatrician and psychoanalyst Donald Winnicott with disturbed children and their mothers articulated a model of the true and false self (Winnicott 1992). A false self develops when the mother–child relationship goes wrong, and the child moves disturbingly far away from true feelings in the direction of putting on a mask to satisfy the agendas of others, beginning with the mother. For Winnicott it was not that a 'true self' is there waiting to be discovered within us, but more that we have the capacity to construct a true self that *feels* grounded, creative and real. This true self/false self tension resonates with the false selves and stories of authenticity that participants in the present study revealed to me.

Researchers Laing and Esterson (1964) used detailed case studies of families to show how it was possible for the distortions in the individual self in severe mental illness to originate in the family, rather than the individual. For these researchers the interior world and the behaviour of the individual became intelligible only once family dynamics were taken into account. Rather than mirroring back an authentic self, in extreme cases, the person was only affirmed if they adopted distorted understandings of themselves and what was happening in the world around them. The authentic self could then remain hidden into early adulthood and beyond. Likewise, participants in the present study reflect on the distortions in their families that they absorbed and carried over into adult life. Thus, in this book, the notion that there can be distorted, false and 'true' selves, and the powerful human need for mirroring of the 'authentic' self by significant others, is assumed.

Narrative and mental health

What is narrative? Although the concept of 'narrative' is used in diverse ways in different academic disciplines, generally narrative refers to stories that order events in time (with a beginning, middle and ending), where these events involve changes over time (Hyden 1997). Rather than being drawn to rational, objective and scientific forms of thinking, people prefer to understand their health conditions (and lives for that matter) as stories, involving characters, events, motivations and meaning (Gold and Ridge 2001; Hyden 1997). People commonly select and tell stories to themselves and to other people in an attempt to better understand the world and their place in it (Elwyn and Gwyn 1999; Frank 1995). Additionally, people grasp their sense of who they are as the 'unfolding story' of their lives (Whitty 2002). As outlined in this book, narrative is an overarching framework for the way people retrieve, attribute and transmit meanings about the self and their lives (White 1987). It has been argued that medical training thwarts doctors' abilities to elicit and appreciate patient stories, replacing these skills instead with cold, hard 'scientific' abilities to elicit a factual history or account (Greenhalgh and Hurwitz 1999). In doing so, an enormous amount of meaning is thought to be lost, including:

• the ability to approach patient problems holistically

• key interior qualities such as the ability to feel pain, sadness, hope

• understanding between professional and patient

• useful analytical clues and therapeutic options

- the therapeutic value of story telling in itself
- abilities to reflect and generate critical thinking.

From the 1990s, narratives came to be much more central to our understanding of illness and wellbeing, with a number of consequences (Hyden 1997):

- Patient suffering is put more squarely on the agenda.
- Life stories are more central to everyday people.
- Patients are given more of a voice to articulate the illness experience and challenge medical 'colonisation' of their narratives (Frank 1995).
- We are compelled to face the difficult existential and moral issues entailed in stories.
- We can better explore different ways of relating to illness through stories.
- It has enabled people to tell powerful collective stories about illnesses like AIDS.

While illness narratives have ambiguity born from their lack of clear endings (Hyden 1997), telling a personal illness story is very much part of patient illness and healing in any health-related condition (Frank 1995; Kangas 2001). In the telling and retelling of stories, the patient's narrative ends up having considerable influence on his or her subjective wellbeing (Young 1996). Here, if there is any such thing as truth, it is about telling stories that allow the person to be heard and to construct their experiences and selves in life-enhancing or perhaps even authentic ways (Kangas 2001). There is now considerable patient narrative research evidence that finding a way of telling a life-giving story about the self supports wellbeing, and is indeed a key element of healing (Bochner 1997; Frank 1995; Holmes 1992; Jackson 1998; Pennebaker and Seagal 1999; Ridge and Ziebland 2006).

There are calls now to develop collective narratives of illness and recovery as a way of challenging dominant medical and community discourses that might stigmatise or limit the potential of patients (Frank 1991; Rappaport 2000). The present book contributes to this collective project in the area of recovery from depression. Collecting patient stories is important because these accounts bring to life rich experiences and insights not currently available in professional discourses. Essentially, the collective story of this book is about telling depression and recovery stories that feel right and make sense to people's lives, 'finding multiple useful treatments and approaches that enhance patient stories of recovery', and finding ways to live more authentically to reinvigorate lives (Ridge and Ziebland 2006). From the 'patient as expert' perspective assumed in this book, (re)storying the self for recovering is never straightforward. The complexities – and rewards – involved in trying to tell a better and more useful story about the self are a key focus of discussion in this book.

Methods used in this book

If recovery from depression is a unique narrative journey for each patient then the research approach used to understand it must take into account this 'real world' complexity (Robson 1993). Qualitative research is the best approach to explore complexity. In-depth interviews in particular were chosen for this study because they allow personal stories to be told and can get to the heart of patient meanings (Patton 2002). For the current study I interviewed 38 people in the UK between September 2003 and May 2004 (Ridge and Ziebland 2006). I personally met with and talked to people who were previously diagnosed – or self-identified – with depression. People were encouraged to tell their stories in their own words and in their own time, from their life before depression through to present-day experiences. Open-ended interviews allowed people to provide rich life, illness and recovery narratives. One of the aims of the study was to explore a broad range of different patient perspectives on and experiences of depression. Thus, participants were recruited to include men and women; different age groups, ethnicities and social classes; people from a wide variety of locations in the UK; people with different kinds of depression and treatment experiences; and those who had been diagnosed recently and those diagnosed many years ago.

The audio-recordings from the interviews were transcribed verbatim, corrected and returned to the participant for checking. Software (MAXqda2) was used to aid the coding, organisation, searching and comparison of text from each interview in order to analyse thoroughly the interviews for this book (Richards and Richards 1994). An earlier analysis was also scrutinised and added to by Sue Ziebland at Oxford University in order to write the *Health Talk Online* website and academic papers. None of the participants in this study reported suffering from mild depression, and all reported that their depression was moderate to severe. Most (34) had experienced multiple or prolonged episodes of depression, 18 had been hospitalised and ten reported experiencing mania as well as depression. Names used in this book are pseudonyms.

Conclusion

Depression is a common experience in the community and yet much depression goes undiagnosed. Classification systems used to diagnose depression rely on an uneasy consensus of various stakeholders. This apparent consensus may cover over the complexities associated with depression, such as substantial variations in the way depression is understood, expressed and remedied. One particular issue in depression that is often overlooked in the literature is the rich interior experiences of depression, and the way that people give meaning to – and self-manage – their recoveries. A recovery perspective on depression, as advocated in this book, tends to elevate patients to being the natural experts on their condition. Government health departments themselves are now adopting the discourses of recovery and expert patients. However, there is still much to learn about how people with depression understand their condition and go about recovering, and this is a focus of the present book.

This book assumes that 'the self' is central to depression and recovery for the people who were interviewed. This self is active in the world, able to make choices and think about itself as an entity. With ailments like depression the self can come to be seen as vulnerable and problematic. Nevertheless, the telling and re-telling of stories to others is a key way for people who have suffered from depression to make sense of and re-work the self to go on living. This book initially emphasises the problems that can develop in the way that people view themselves from early on in life. Additionally, like other researchers (Strauss 1997, p.362), I emphasise the importance of identifying 'authentically' felt and 'emotionally salient' experiences of self in recovery. Here, the connection to a better story about the self provides people with a particularly helpful foothold on the road to recovery. As argued in this book, recovery from depression from the patient perspective is not usually about achieving complete recovery. Rather, recovery recognises that, despite limitations, people can seek effective help, self-manage their conditions, tell more useful stories about the self, assemble helpful and multiple approaches or 'tools' to facilitate recovery, and understand themselves better in order to provide better foundations – and even joy – in life beyond depression.

Chapter 2

Life Prior to a Diagnosis

Before moving on to discuss depression and recovery in detail I will briefly outline a range of early life issues that patients mention as relevant to their later development of depression. Even if some believe chemical changes in their bodies play a role in the development of depression, patients are just as comfortable talking about the possible psychological and social issues underpinning their depression. As outlined in this chapter, people felt that early life problems, particularly in families, and severe life events (e.g. death, workplace problems, motherhood) could help trigger or prolong their depression. In the first part of the chapter, key issues prior to depression raised for discussion include overwhelming life demands; dysfunction in families; the development of self-defeating cognitive blueprints; feeling different from an early age; and problems with developing 'self authenticity'.

In the second half of the chapter, the early problems people had in identifying their experiences as to do with depression are outlined. These problems include finding a language to describe interior experiences related to depression; the initial externalising of interior problems; and initially attributing interior problems to more benign conditions than depression. Rather than an in-depth analysis of antecedents to depression, what follows is a broad-brush approach. The idea is to canvas a range of issues that play a role in later depression and recovery.

Precursors to depression

There are a number of interesting accounts in the literature showing how depression is often pre-dated by difficult and extraordinary life experiences. These experiences may begin in childhood or later (Kangas 2001). The patient accounts in the current study reveal narrative threads linking prior experiences, subsequent episodes of depression and recovery approaches. Precursors to depression included one or a combination of problems including deprivations in early life and the stress of life events like the death of a loved one or a relationship breakdown (Kangas 2001).

Life demands and severe life events

Some participants believed that chemical problems in the body could trigger or prolong their depression. They identified triggers like brain chemistry and hormonal changes. Anne, for instance, became convinced that hormones played a role in her post-natal depression.

> So my psychiatrist and my GP agreed to put me on a contraceptive pill which had the same hormonal ingredients, whatever they are. And I'm subsequently taking that and I would say that was the one thing that's worked... This had all happened since I'd had my son, and that's obviously... The hormones are all over the place. I said, 'Is it hormonal?' I'd read books where they'd said proges- terone treatment can work, and then there'd be other books that say, 'Oh no, that's rubbish, it doesn't work.' And I said, 'Well, can we try it?' And it was, 'Well there's no point, there's no point in trying that.' So it's a bit ironic, really, that five and a half years later I stumble on it [the contraceptive pill], and I am feeling better. (Anne)

Belief in biochemical problems triggering depression did not necessarily exclude psychosocial explanations. Some believed that a combination of chemical changes in the body and life events led to their depression (see the second quotation from Anne, below). For other patients, difficult life events were considered enough on their own to cause depression. While chemical hypotheses of depression causality may be favoured in our culture, longitu- dinal research also backs up what the latter group of patients said. A recent study (that has tracked participants from birth) found that work stress on its own seemed to precipitate depression in previously healthy young adults (Melchior et al. 2007). Consistent with such findings, some people in the current study believed that it was experiencing overwhelming demands and severely difficult events that triggered their depression. Examples of demands included death of loved ones, relationship breakdown, work stress and bullying, and the gap between idealised motherhood and the reality of being a mother.

Patients' narratives describe events where they became psychologically 'overloaded' in the lead-up to depression. Many, like Peter below, described multiple and severe events leading to a 'breaking point':

> In 1995 my wife and myself, we had the death of a parent on each side of the family... I worked in an office at that time, and it was a time of great change. A

lot of people [that] left the company weren't replaced, and the rest left behind really had to take up the slack and try and do their duties as well. During the course of 1995 we had my father-in-law move in, we both felt, my wife and me, that it was…it was right he should come and live with us… And that meant we had to move house to accommodate him, to have a downstairs bedroom and a downstairs toilet. So that all came about within five months of [the two] parents dying. And then soon after, I think it was possibly early October, my daughter and her son who was a babe in arms suddenly turned up on the doorstep, and she said, 'Our marriage is over, please can I come and stay with you?' (Peter)

As well as coping with a traumatic birth and suspected hormonal changes as described above, Anne was overwhelmed by the death of her own mother as well as her mother-in-law's passing, and subsequently became severely depressed:

When I first became depressed I was 34, which was after the birth of my son. I think now, with hindsight, 34's too old to have your first child and have a big upheaval to your life. Whilst I was pregnant I was doing a very busy job. Didn't really have a lot time for me, didn't rest very much… Also…towards the end of my pregnancy my mother-in-law died. I had an emergency caesarean after a very difficult labour, and my son didn't breathe for about ten minutes. So I had a real trauma, basically. And then…six weeks after my son was born, my Mum died. And, basically, everything just fell apart. Everything that I felt was in my control had just completely gone out of my control… I became very depressed… (Anne)

Loss of loved ones in particular was interwoven throughout a number of people's stories as they described what underpinned their depression.

When I was about five my grandmother lived in our house and evidently she died one night… Then the next day when I asked where she was my mother told me she had gone away on holiday and…that's all she told me. And it was around the time I was starting school. So what happened when I went to school was that when my mother left me, I became very anxious, and every morning I used to throw up in the playground and this seemed to be like a daily event. And I ended up being taken, I can remember being taken to see this man. My mother told me afterwards it was a child psychologist. And he interviewed me and then he saw my mother and apparently he said to her, 'His grandmother's died hasn't she?' And she said, 'Yes, but we've kept it from him.' And he said, 'Well, he knows and now he's anxious that you're going to, going to disappear.' (Lee)

Motherhood issues were identified by a number of participants as leading up to their depression. The demands of motherhood identified included hormonal changes, sleep deprivation, lack of social support for mothering, lack of acceptable ways of talking about the problems of motherhood and unrealistic expectations of motherhood (Lafrance and Stoppard 2006; O'Hara 1986).

> But after [my son] was born, I was very rigid about how to look after him. I mean, I'd had no experience of looking after babies or really small children. I had no family to support me. It was really quite terrifying… But possibly, the necessity of looking after him prevented me from becoming depressed again. I was in a very strange state after the birth though… I couldn't remember how to boil an egg, for example. I suppose it could have been a form of depression. But it was a strange mental state which maybe most people would put down to post-natal blues, not real post-natal depression… (Elizabeth)

The qualitative research literature in particular identifies internal conflicts between reality and social expectations of being a good mother as being significant in the onset of depression (Beck 2002). Women who feel unable to live up to social expectations of motherhood can feel like failures, they may fear being morally condemned as not 'good mothers' and they may believe that no other women experience what they are going through (Lewis and Ridge 2005).

Early life problems

There are two key points to be made about early life problems and depression. First, rather than early life problems precipitating later depression, it is worth pointing out that, in hindsight, a group of participants believed that they had diagnosable mental health problems – including depression – even as children. Some people like Patricia could barely (if at all) recall life without depression:

> I've suffered from depression since I was very young. I've never really known my life to be any different. And so there's not really a point when I can turn round and say, 'I started suffering from depression at this time.' I've more or less been unhappy a lot of my life. That's I think mainly down to family life… So probably, early stages around sort of six or seven… (Patricia)

> Whilst I always believed that my depression started in my teens, I've more recently come to the understanding that, in fact, it started around the age of seven. (Pamela)

> It was a kind of gradual slide from about the age of ten, I think, into something that was depression… I was standing in a dinner queue at school once, on my own. And somebody comes up behind me and he said, 'You know, you radiate depression.' Which was at the age of 13. (Paul)

People who identified their depression as beginning in childhood felt that it could be difficult for adults to recognise internal problems in children. There was a sense that adults might not be looking for hidden problems:

> Hopefully there is more recognition there, that children do have mental health problems. But I think when I was a kid, it just wasn't the case… I was perfectly average at school. I didn't get noticed for being bad or good, which suited me fine. But nobody ever looked beyond that. I guess the system doesn't look for anything that appears to be going right. I think I probably could have benefited greatly from some help. (Rosey)

Second, distinct mental health problems were thought to arise out of childhood mental distress that might not necessarily be diagnosable. Even though only eight people in the current study had a diagnosis of depression by the age of 20, 28 out of the 38 participants made a link between their earlier life problems and depression. Early life problems that were raised as connected to later depression were wide ranging and included feeling different and out of step with others, feeling cut off from others, loss of significant relations and being neglected, bullied or abused.

> And even as a young child, seven, eight, nine, I would sit with other people, other children, and it was as if I was on the edge. And I wasn't part of it, and there wasn't a lot of joy or happiness. I had friends, but even that, it never seemed to be enough. (Pamela)

> Some of the other children [at school] I saw were at that time…I've been thinking quite a lot about this of late, were quite unpleasant people… I used to be called queer and gay for no particular reason… And it really hurt. And the upshot was that in about 1982 I was punched in the…in the eye, or in the face by one of these nasty boys and I thought, I can't take this any more. So the following year when I was about 15 in about 1983, I transferred to a hospital school… It was a sort of a unit for those who had slight mental health problems. (Adam)

In line with previous research there were many narratives connecting earlier dysfunctional family circumstances and later experiences of depression (Karp 1994). As discussed in more detail in Chapter 8, as people reflected on their early lives, dysfunction within families was a common story told. The problems identified were broad, yet could have enormous impact on participants at the time they were children and thus utterly dependent on caregivers. Early family problems included perceptions of confusing messages being given by parents; unpredictable parents (e.g. parents who argued a lot or became angry without warning); uncaring or harsh parenting; feeling like scapegoats for family problems; feeling pressured to succeed; emotional and physical neglect; as well as the lack of mirroring of authentic selves by parents. Sometimes the problem described was that family dysfunction, like depression, was hidden and not highly visible.

> It's very difficult for me to think back as to when it started because my childhood was quite unstable and not... People around me probably didn't think it was. But my parents had a lot of problems and there were a lot of problems within the family that were kept kind of secret if you like... I know when certain key things happened in my life at quite a young age which must have had an effect on me and... But as to when the depression really kicked in, probably after I lost my grandparents. It was quite traumatic for me. (Belinda)

In some more extreme family circumstances instances of emotional and physical abuse were described by participants, some of which were visible to outsiders. For Patricia, a complicit mother made her father's violence towards her possible:

> My dad was very abusive with us, as children as well. And she [my mother] would actually stand back and let it happen. Simply because, I think she was too afraid to actually intervene, because if she did intervene, then she would end up taking the rap for it as well. (Patricia)

Dysfunction in families was also described in terms of parents providing support that could get in the way of healthy emotional development, as Michelle explains:

> Just as parents can be abusive in terms of, hitting you over the head with a brick, equally some parents, and probably my parents, were just too, support-ive, too kind of... They didn't allow me to get out and get a couple of knocks... I don't think until you're better you can really explain to them [parents]... I organise my life and they don't necessarily ask me about things. It's a bit of a Mexican stand-off I think because I don't tell them, and they don't ask, so nobody knows. (Michelle)

In trying to cope with the aftermath of family problems in later life, people talked about how they initially grappled with their families in ways that were ultimately detrimental to themselves. For instance, Julie came to realise she developed a conflict avoidance and 'being a good girl' approach to life as a way to survive her family. Her survival strategy was carried over into adulthood, contributing to her anxiety and depression.

> It [childhood] was an anxious time. It wasn't… It wasn't awful, but there was a lot of anxiety. [It] felt like you were walking on egg shells and not… Just being very careful not to upset the apple cart, not to say things out of place. To be quiet, to be a good girl. Just to keep the peace really. And there was…there were a lot of arguments and a lot of noise. So it was a very anxious… I lived on my nerves which I can reflect on now having had counselling and…I can recognise where the depression sort of stems from. And the anxiety. (Julie)

While it may be necessary for children to deny their parents are not caring or trustworthy for survival, participants in recovery came to see such parents as having limitations that contributed to their later depression. The ways in which parents were thought limited included lack of imagination in understanding their children and their inner worlds; inability to demonstrate care; and the denial of reality, including significant problems within families. These limitations were described as very difficult for participants to cope with. As children, they did not have the abilities of adults to adequately interpret what was happening in families, nor reframe these problems in ways that could be helpful to their development. So as children, participants' narratives were about struggling to read the signals, make sense of what is happening in their families, and then cope with the problems they perceived they were facing. Only as an adult could Sue understand more about what was happening in her family:

> I think most of my childhood I spent trying to prove to my parents that I loved them, and that I was a good daughter. And that I was worthy of their love. But I never seemed to have got any [love] back… Because my Mum had had such a bad time having to run me…twice a week to…for radiotherapy or radio treatment, whatever it was. It was cancer…I had. And I now believe that it was a heck of a trek. Then [as a child], I used to think 'Why doesn't she love me? Is it because I'm sick? Is it because I'm causing too much trouble?'… I had to grow up very quickly. And therefore I had a confused mind. (Sue)

Sometimes family dysfunction could be so mystifying that participants felt especially disturbed by their families. For Carol, the demands placed on her as a child – including unacknowledged family secrets – framed her severe depression in later life:

> I've been telling my Mum actually that something happened when I was a wee girl like and she said, 'Oh get out my road'… I had just, there was an awful lot happened to me when I [was young]. Dad took a nervous breakdown and he

was in [hospital]. But apart from me trying to cope with my Mum's money [problems], and the house and everything, you know, and the four children, you know. I realise now, I didn't at the time but this is all... I keep going back [to] this. It was far, far too much for me... It's [family] secrets, right. And I was just left when I asked... I'd have felt better if she'd [my mother] of said 'Oh yes that's right...', you know, but no it was always swept under the carpet. (Carol)

Laying down blueprints for distorted cognition

As a number of people undertook their recovery from depression they discovered that they had developed unhelpful and persistent patterns of thinking in childhood. These distorted cognitions could be traced back to specific events. For Richard as a child, not only did his father not mirror back his authentic self, his interpretation was that his childhood joy actually caused his father's pain:

> My father was a very melancholy character, and he had a very strong influence on me because I...I was aware very early on that if I was cheerful around him he didn't like it, in fact he really couldn't bear it. And so I got into the...into the way of sort of feeling sort of slightly sad when I was in his company. So I wouldn't show any signs of exuberance, because I knew that then the atmosphere would get so painful. And also I thought he would blame Mother for my bad behaviour, you know if I shouted or ran around or anything like that... (Richard)

The quote from Richard points to the way that participants as children were especially prone to blaming themselves for events happening around them. And blaming oneself for outside events, particularly the failings of parents, is a common pattern among children (Rowe 2003). The alternative – that parents are not loving, adequate carers, or even interested in their children's wellbeing – can be too much for a child to contemplate. But automatically blaming oneself for the ills of the world, beginning with parental inadequacy, is also a path to unhappiness and depression.

> That's taken me a long time to understand, that you can still be a good person and have bad things happen to you. But as a child when bad things happened to me the only way you could make any sense of it whatsoever is that you're a bad person. Because people who love you don't do things that hurt you. The only way it makes sense is that you've done something wrong, and from there it's only a short step to carrying that through your complete adult life...that anything that goes wrong, happens because you are bad... [Without therapy] I would have known the end result which was that I feel lousy, but I wouldn't have known the process that my mind goes through... But now through

therapy, I can actually look at situations and think well how could I possibly affect the outcome of that? How can I take away from this that I've hurt that person? (Rosey)

So blueprints for thinking about how we relate to others are laid down early on in life as a kind of survival mechanism. Many participants came to see that these early blueprints created distortions in the way they interpreted the world. Such distorted cognitions lead to falsities. For instance, Dorothy Rowe (2003) talks about how it is common for children to feel they had one good and one bad parent, such as in circumstances where one was abusive and the other comforting. As Rowe points out, in reality both parents were inadequate as neither protected the child. Not only do misleading accounts of parents and the social world develop from early maladaptive cognitive blueprints, but so too do false selves:

> I can remember just having an inkling that there was something not quite right about being Black... And I didn't work it out until decades later that I had a way of surviving that by making myself if you like as 'untouchable' as possible... So to avoid the possibility that I might excite any kind of hostility of the kind I'd experienced in one single but very ugly incident at school, I made sure I was as clever as anybody, as good at sports, as nice to know as...to know the rules. Now that became my way of relating to the world. Now it kind of worked in a kind of childlike adolescent way because I mean I achieved a lot, did a lot... There were lots of people that really liked me, but it kind of killed 'me' off as well. (Derek)

Unhelpful blueprints for thinking are carried over from childhood into adult life unless challenged by participants. It is as if a 'childlike' cognitive and emotional part of the self persists into adulthood to powerful effect, as some participants articulated:

> I had a child's mind and a grown-up's mind. And it's taken years to separate the two. (Sue)

> We [in therapy] talked a lot about childhood experiences and we, I definitely, it sounds clichéd but I did reconnect the pain that I felt as a child, and that I hadn't properly processed or hadn't been told it was OK. That was incredibly powerful and it hurt a hell of a lot. (Matthew)

The important point about unhelpful cognitive blueprints from a narrative perspective is that somewhere along the line the person has made a choice to adopt their way of thinking and storyline about themselves. Even if the choice was made in early life, the fact that a choice has been made is actually very useful. This is because different choices can be made as adults. Many participants described attempting to change their problematic thinking and stories about themselves, such as through talking therapies (see Chapter 8). However, like real children, childlike aspects of the self do not respond well to harsh methods of trying to change self narratives and feelings. Instead, participants who described success in changing their narratives talked about needing to find kind and respectful ways to acknowledge and accept the childlike part of self first.

> But say to yourself, 'OK, if you were trying to comfort someone, let's say a child who's crying or a friend who's crying, what would you say to make them feel better because you'd want to?' And I found that sometimes quite helpful to say, you know, even something as trite as 'It's going to be all right and you're OK,' and this sort of thing. (Matthew)

> I think that one of the big lessons for me [from depression] has been to reappraise the expectations I have of myself, as a mother, wife, at work and generally. And – I – it's that actually I was the one setting these high standards. There wasn't anybody else externally doing that, albeit it may have been a legacy of childhood. But now I've practised speaking to myself in a much nicer, softer way, much more encouraging... I don't use words like I should do this, I should do that, now. And paradoxically that has really improved my relationship with my son. And I now enjoy that relationship so much more... Because I've taken the pressure off, I can enjoy it. (Jenny)

Feeling different

While participants varied greatly in their descriptions of their early personalities, a thread weaving through many of the narratives was of 'difference' – of somehow feeling out of step with others from early on in life. Difference was described in various ways, including being especially bright, feeling emotionally sensitive, coming from a non-white cultural background, feeling anxious in general, being non-heterosexual, feeling like an outsider, or even sensing there was something wrong without necessarily knowing what it was. These kinds of felt differences were considered important in contributing to social isolation:

> I was an only child. I didn't feel my parents understood me, even as quite a small child. I didn't get on with my fellow classmates at the primary school. This was an ordinary state primary. I didn't make much attempt after that to get on with my classmates... So I was a loner and I liked that to some extent, and didn't relate to others. So there was a conflict from the beginning. (Elizabeth)

...if you've been one of those people who simply doesn't fit in, and that's something that's a problem I've encountered not only during my school days but at college, at work... Where you're not part of the social infrastructure. Yes, I do find that it's a part of why you become so depressed, and why you become introverted and reclusive. (Shiad)

The shared quality in stories told by participants was about how they initially struggled with their feelings of 'difference' with the limited resources of a child. Confirming insights from self psychology and the qualitative literature (Jackson 1998), these participants who felt out of step with the world around them found it hard to communicate with others and gain acknowledgement for their authentically felt selves. The resulting lack of mirroring of authenticity of self was universally described as painful:

But I mean I always felt under quite a lot of pressure as a child to kind of be cheerful and to be happy. And I'm not getting at my parents at all, but I think I felt they didn't want... What they wanted was to see me happy, and I don't think they would've been very good at me being able to say 'Look, sometimes I don't feel great.' (Matthew)

I was so different from them [parents] that they didn't understand me. They had somehow produced this bright kid. They'd both left school when they were 14, which is what people did in those days. And they weren't particularly into reading or studying, or didn't particularly have enquiring minds. So they really didn't understand me at all, and I was often very frustrated with them... (Veronica)

In circumstances of difference and lack of authentic mirroring, interactions with others were recalled as moments of unmet need that – along with distorted cognitive blueprints – contributed to difficulties in participants understanding themselves. For Lee, feeling like he had to be the man of the family (even as a child) pulled him away from his authenticity, including his unacknowledged fear and grief around death:

...and I think I was quite an anxious child looking back. When I was eight my father died... Although nobody told me he was dying, I knew he was dying, so it wasn't a surprise to me. And then I felt that I had to be very responsible, I had to be very brave, very strong. I was the only child and I think half of me was trying to be mummy's little man. You know, I can remember trying to cut the grass with the hand mower and it was nearly as big as me, and I was trying to push this mower and I was trying to do everything I could to support her... But at other times, I had terrible bouts of crying, I just cried and cried and cried. (Lee)

Naming the problem

Having briefly discussed key themes preceding depression, I now turn to a discussion of the problems participants had in identifying their experiences as depression. There was usually a lengthy period of time described from childhood through to adulthood when people did not have an adequate vocabulary to identify and name their suffering (Karp 1994). With all the barriers to the recognition of depression and help seeking as outlined below, people can struggle on alone not realising they have depression for decades.

> I sort of like worked out that since my teens, really, I've, I've suffered from depression. So I would say, I don't remember a time before depression. I suppose when I hit puberty I sort of like...you know, realised that there's something strange about me, but nothing was ever... Nothing was ever diagnosed until only about three years ago. (Sophia)

There are a range of reasons why the path to a diagnosis can be such a long one, including a lack of language to describe interior experiences in our culture; initial externalising of problems; and difficulties in thinking about the self because of the cognitive distortions associated with depression. A range of issues in arriving at an understanding of depression are described in more detail below.

Language

One particular problem involves trying to find the words to express and then communicate interior feelings. Interior experience is not something we have a readily available language for (Jackson 1998), and so people go through long phases of struggling to make sense of their internal lives.

> I just put everything down, left the house myself, and found myself standing at the top of a tower block thinking this doesn't work, I've had enough, I want to stop you know. And there was no language to describe it... It was just really clear. Enough. It was very extreme. I don't know why I didn't actually jump off, I just didn't. (Derek)

Unfortunately, depression itself can contribute to difficulties in articulating internal life. For instance, people may not be able to concentrate or think well, and they may lack confidence in their interpretations and abilities to speak up for themselves. These kinds of issues are taken up in more detail in the next chapter.

Initial externalising and denial

It is possible for people to be unaware that they have internal problems. Karp (1994, p.13) notes in his research that in the initial phase of depression recognition (which he calls the 'inchoate feeling' phase), many people focus their attention on problems in their external circumstances, rather than problems within themselves. This may encourage the thinking that changing external circumstances might result in personal discomfort disappearing. The present study confirmed that, in retrospect, people could initially project their inner problems onto the outside world, and this could be a barrier to recognising that the interior self was the problem. A real possibility for recovery from depression arises when people discover that their problems are internal. This is when people move into the next phase: identifying that 'something is really wrong with me' (Karp 1994, p.15). As described in more detail in Chapter 8, it can be very painful for people to recognise that there is something wrong internally.

> Psychotherapy has certainly been good as well…it goes right back through your childhood…to see what, what the precursors might be to make you vulnerable… I got an awful lot out of it but the eight months I was doing the work was quite distressing, and I was seeing my therapist once or twice a week… I mean I would go home and cry and go to bed…to go to these two appointments…that was about all I could manage because it was so exhausting. But the end result of that has been really good… (Ruth)

There is a process involved in people overcoming denial and coming to accept they have deeper emotional problems that extend back into early life.

> I think he [the psychiatrist] did ask a couple of questions. 'What was your earliest childhood experience?' And it was just like oh, very textbook stuff to me and it put a barrier up. I instantly thought, 'Fuck you, you know, you're not getting any where near me, there is nothing wrong with me, and actually I even said it a few times: 'Nothing traumatic has ever happened to me. I have, I had a very nice childhood thank you.' I said it loads of times and that was so untrue. I said it and…and it was untrue. (Belinda)

People resisted acknowledging depression for a range of reasons, including stigma and fear. As one woman came to see it, depression was a double-edged sword: her medical records showed she needed the help of a psychiatrist, but she was also grateful she could finally get recognition for her depression, as well as access to potentially effective treatments. Interestingly, even people who were well aware that they get depression can deny or initially miss looming bouts of depression. Diego was aware of what depression felt like because he had had it before. Nevertheless, he feared depression, and it took him time to acknowledge his new episode:

> I decided to go to the doctor and talk about the problem of losing interest in sex, and I was quite embarrassed about going to a doctor and saying, 'Well, you know...'. And funnily enough he asked me, 'Is this anything to do with...', he didn't say depression, I don't remember what he said, but he asked me if this was related to stress. And I said, 'No', almost as if I didn't want to accept the fact that, you know... So I said, 'No, no, no,' I said, 'it's actually very embarrassing.'... But I realised that I felt horrible because in fact it was not even the fact of performing sex, or not, it is not even wanting to have sex at all... And so it was like six months, almost for myself to accept that I was...or something was utterly wrong with me...to go to the doctor and ask for help, you know. Because in previous depressions I had managed not to go to the GP. I never took medication for depression before. (Diego)

Manifestations of depression can also be very complex, and this complexity can throw people off track. This was the case for Jenny, who initially focused on physical problems with her gut and tiredness, rather than her miserable feelings:

> And then I became physically unwell, and I had a very debilitating stomach bug. It took me a long time to work out what was happening, and I lost a lot of weight and had to take quite a lot of time off work. And...I didn't realise it, but gradually the depression was coming back. But I didn't recognise it, even though I had been so depressed before. I didn't recognise it because it wasn't my mood that dipped initially, I...I became very fatigued, very lethargic, very tired. I noticed that I wasn't sleeping, so although I was very tired I couldn't rest. I was seeing a GP for my stomach, and I was having various tests, and she didn't pick up that I was depressed, although I was telling her that I was spending most of my time just sitting in a chair. (Jenny)

It can be easier for people to attribute their problems to less serious and less stigmatised conditions including stress, overwork, insomnia or fatigue.

> But a lot of times with depression nobody else will recognise it. And that you sometimes have to make that first move, and I think that's what holds a lot of people back. Either perhaps when they don't recognise that, you know, it is depression that they have. They just think it's a down period in their lives or that it's related to being stressed or overworked. (Liza)

> It did cross my mind when ME (chronic fatigue) was in vogue that that might be what I had because yes, if you don't have any energy to get out and do stuff, then that's another part of the problem that tends to cycle round to things. But no, I use the word fatigue, I felt... Actually a lot of it was probably because I

wasn't sleeping very well. I actually tended to stay up very late for a strange reason, just because I was bored, and I wanted...I don't know quite what I wanted... (Paul)

So for a range of reasons participants often needed to develop an understanding of their emotional problems over time (Ridge and Ziebland 2006). It was common for people to talk about their struggle to gain insight into their depression over many years, as discussed in more detail in subsequent chapters. However, as Sophia notes, accepting there is something wrong internally means giving up a part of the story about the 'false self', and this can provide some immediate relief.

When I accepted [a depression diagnosis], although it was difficult, it made it easier... Because it relieves the pressure that you're trying to, this pretence that you're not ill and, you know, you keep a happy face and a happy-clappy... And oh, everything's wonderful. And basically underneath you're dying. (Sophia)

Role of others

Recognition of depression can also be difficult for friends and relatives for a range of reasons including the hidden and interior nature of depression; lack of information about depression available to the general public; and the ease with which signs of depression can be attributed to other problems, like laziness. Paul relates a childhood memory where his father did not understand the nature of depression:

I think I said [to my teacher], well actually I think I said, 'Well I'm really depressed, and I don't see the point.' And so I suppose the teacher realised it's not just a simple problem of laziness, which my Dad didn't actually, as far as he was concerned, I was just lazy. And I got a lot of criticism from my father actually, for all kinds of things, and it actually did... It probably did hurt actually, but I just ignored it. (Paul)

As discussed in Chapter 1, people can present a false self to the outside world to manage themselves and cope with others. People with depression can find it particularly difficult to relinquish this façade of the self coping, acknowledge their difficulties and reach out for help, even when they are very unwell (see Chapter 3). In terms of what depression feels like, people may feel like a burden to others anyway, and so they may not be able to imagine that they can reach out for help.

> The worst thing for me was being alone in the house during the day, not wanting to burden any of my friends, because when you're really depressed, you feel that you're a burden to everyone. You don't feel like contacting anyone. (Kate)

In the end it may only be a crisis, such as feeling suicidal or being unable to work, that forces a person's hand in seeking help for their depression. When people do recognise they have a serious problem and reach out for help, an important first step in developing a more useful life narrative has commenced.

> And, I tried to jump out of a three-storey building window. At which point I was caught and sort of taken down by somebody in the house, and it was then that I realised that I really should not be feeling like this. I had no support from the family environment. No one was picking up on how severe things had got for me, I knew it wasn't the norm to be doing things like that. So I took it upon myself to go and see my GP, and speak to her... You know, she said, 'Yeah, you've been, you've been suffering from depression for a long time, we had thought it.' (Patricia)

Conclusion

Participants in the present study described various kinds of issues beginning in early life which they linked to their experiences of depression. Early feelings of difference, lack of mirroring of their 'authentic' selves by significant others, grief and dysfunctional families were commonly reported. While participants varied greatly in their descriptions of their personalities and circumstances, a thread weaving through the narratives was of feeling different or out of step with others from early on in life. Difference was described in various ways, including being bright, feeling (or being labelled as) sensitive, anxious or sad, being non-heterosexual, as well as feeling alone and misunderstood. The shared quality in stories told by participants was about how they grappled with their early difficulties with limited resources and not a great deal of initial success. Even for people who described chemical changes in their bodies or being overwhelmed by life events leading up to their depression, there was acknowledgement that earlier life problems could play a role in depression.

In feeling out of step with others, social interactions were recalled as moments of disappointment. Such moments contributed to participants' problematic constructions of self. Under these circumstances, there were particular outcomes. First, participants variously learned to construct a distorted self – one not well connected to their authentic experience. The false self seemed to be constructed to cope with the tensions between how participants felt and social realities as they experienced them. Second, habitual cognitive distortions could easily develop in conditions where the authentic self was not being mirrored. Distortions in cognition translate into unhelpful 'blueprints' for later adult thinking. While these blueprints were developed as a means of *surviving* from early life, they were ultimately maladaptive, undermining the authentically felt self. Yet, as adults, many participants later realised they could make choices to challenge these unhelpful blueprints for thinking (see Chapter 8).

Initially, participants really struggled to find a language to name their problems, let alone understand their depression. Identifying personal experiences of depression was frequently a long-term project for a range of reasons including a lack of language for interior experiences; stigma attached to mental health problems; denial of emotional problems; participants hiding their true selves and so not really knowing themselves from an early age; as well as others not necessarily being attuned to the outward signs of depression. Key life narratives emerge early on in life and have implications for depression and recovery. These threads include cognitive distortion, feelings of difference, lack of mirroring of authenticity and the construction of false selves. Some of these threads are picked up in the next chapter where the existential experience of depression is outlined in considerable detail.

Chapter 3

The Experience of Depression

While only those who have had depression can fully appreciate the interior landscape of the condition, the current chapter attempts to convey something of the experience of depression to readers in general. The hope is to familiarise readers with depression to aid understanding about what the experience is like from the patient perspective. I will discuss the more gradual slide as well as dramatic transitions into depression, and cover elements involved in the interiority of depression, including the impact on people's thinking, feelings and bodily sensations. I will then turn to behaviour and, more specifically, spend some time discussing suicide, since depression is a significant risk factor here. Finally, I discuss the potential for the self to crash and effectively disintegrate in depression.

Depressive interlock

Depression is frequently episodic, and here people must make a 'transition' into and out of depression. The transition into depression is experienced as a kind of downward spiral of distressing emotions, thoughts and bodily sensations (Beck 2002; Karp 1994; Segal, Williams and Teasdale 2002). Ultimately, an onslaught of negative thinking, emotions, distortions in the way people view themselves, apparent chemical changes in the body and physical manifestations were described by people as they descended into depression. For Michelle it was an onslaught of emotions triggered by events at work that led to what she described as a kind of 'shutdown':

> And I can still remember, the whole sort of thing unravelling. Going... I was at work and I think a colleague was having a baby and somebody else was getting married. And I can still remember coming home from work on the bus, and slowly I could just feel all the emotion was just sort of taking over me. And I think I just went into some sort of shutdown. As if it was too much to cope with, so that was the actual, that was the event that precipitated it... (Michelle)

For some, the transition into depression could happen so gradually that people were unaware they were going into depression.

> ...so it had been sort of very much a slow approach with depression. It had been a slow increase in the amount of frustration and pain and all that alienation, I would say, I felt over the course of my teens... Because the depression had approached slowly I'd become used to it. I'd not really had a focus for it; I'd not known what it's about. (Paul)

Depression could be so gradual that even patients well versed in depression could become depressed before they were aware of what was happening. Marcus resorted to regularly using a depression inventory on himself to work out if he was going into depression.

> Even after 15 years I find it difficult to know when I'm getting depressed. Being tired can be a symptom, but there are many shades of grey: one book warns that there will be 'no flashing lights as the depression descends'... I find doing the *Beck Depression Inventory* at regular [like weekly] intervals useful, to monitor how I am progressing. (Marcus)

At other times, the onset of depression could be very dramatic indeed, as Michelle described above. Participant descriptions suggested that a rapid descent had the feeling of a 'runaway train'. Some researchers use the term 'depressive interlock' to describe this phenomenon of uncontrollable negative thinking, feelings and sensations (Mason and Hargreaves 2001). Depressive interlock could be so dramatic that people were able to describe vividly the exact circumstances – even time – of their descent into depression.

> It was on 5th December 1994, seven o'clock in the evening, actually I know exactly. But of course it must have – I must have been leading up to it for months or years, in fact... And well, I was quite some weeks ill before I got taken to hospital. (Elizabeth)

In situations of dramatic interlock, people painted vivid pictures about the suddenness of overwhelming thoughts, feelings and bodily sensations. Being overwhelmed in this way was said to involve a reaction whereby people felt debilitated (see the quotation from Michelle above). Veronica described interlock as very much happening through the body, as if some kind of chemical reaction had swept through her. In keeping with this embodied theme, Peter described it as if a 'fuse' had blown in his brain:

> I was very busy at work, and on 5th November, I can remember it quite well because it was Fireworks Day, a fuse blew in my brain I felt...that's the best

thing I can describe it as. And I could not, I just could not cope… I'd reached, I suppose brain overload with all that was going on. (Peter)

And I suddenly became aware that I didn't think I could stand up out of my seat on the bus. I was just aware. It was like I felt this massive chemical change take place in me and completely debilitate me. And I kind of thought 'I'm having a breakdown.' (Veronica)

Depressive interlock could appear at the time to come out of the blue. However, as described in the previous chapter, narratives frequently linked prior life circumstances to experiences of depression. For instance, difficult family circumstances, overwork, coming to terms with sexuality issues, and abuse were some of the precursors to interlock. (See Chapter 2 on life prior to depression for more detail.)

I didn't really have a name for depression, I didn't know what it was. I was 14. And it was an extreme experience of kind of teenage angst/parent stuff, but it sort of it…just suddenly without any real warning I realised that you know, something was out of control. Having had a difficult relationship with my, my father which, you know was managed at a certain level of discomfort… He was violent towards me, and I think I was also coming to terms with first intimations to being gay, but there again, I didn't know what gay was, and I certainly didn't have a consciousness of it. (Derek)

The depression episode

The kinds of symptoms involved in depression were outlined in Chapter 1. Certainly, depression can involve symptoms like a low mood and loss of enjoyment in life, as is the popular perception.

…you just generally feel that life isn't the same anymore. Life isn't sort of as colourful…and I know it's been described to me as a…like if your…if your life before was in colour, depression is like black and white and very plain and very… Everything is very muted. You don't get any enjoyment out of things that perhaps you would have got enjoyment out of. I became very sort of insular…didn't want to go out. (Anne)

However, the people I spoke to also wanted to make it clear that depression – particularly severe depression – was much more distressing on an existential level than just having a 'low mood'. People painted vivid and disturbing pictures of the interior world of depression, with some likening the experience to a living hell:

> You know, there you are faced with, with you know, depression is terrible, it, it's a torment, it's a real torment. Actually subsequently, somebody asked me what it was like when you're depressed and the best definition I can come up with, 'It is like rotting in the depths of hell.' That's it, that's absolutely... You just feel so utterly, utterly wretched and you can see no way out... (Craig)

I was told about a very wide range of experiences that people associated with the misery of depression. These experienced can be roughly grouped into categories of thoughts, feelings, bodily changes and behaviour.

Thoughts

Thoughts were qualitatively different when people were depressed. People reported an onslaught of negative thinking that could not be dismissed, confusion, racing thoughts and having obsessive thoughts. At the same time, people described how the mind and body could come to a standstill, so that people could only concentrate on their thoughts.

> And on the one hand, it's like your mind's racing because I had so much to think of, you know...I've got to [do] this or that for, for the baby or I've got to get to see my Mum in the hospital, or I've got to do this or I've got to do that. But on the other hand, it's almost as if you're going in slow motion. If you've seen these films where you're standing still and everyone's going around you, it was almost like that. (Anne)

For Veronica, the suffering involved a paralysis of negative thoughts that was managed by looking at a bad day as having lots of smaller chunks:

> I can remember particularly bad days, I would take the day in ten-minute chunks because...I couldn't bear to think I've got all day at home here feeling like I can't do anything... Everything in my head was negative. (Veronica)

Not being able to concentrate or think was also commonly reported, e.g. 'I really couldn't string two sentences together', or 'I remember putting my eldest daughter to bed and trying to read her a child's story, and I actually found I could no longer read. I no longer had the concentration...'.

Problems with thinking were described in vivid ways, such as like having a 'million bees buzzing' in your head, or 'things go around in your head so you don't sleep anymore', or your mind 'zoom[s] into miserable places', and as a 'sheer onslaught of negative thoughts'. The result of these kinds of distortions in thinking was that wrong conclusions were easy to arrive at. Anne described how she jumped to negative conclusions during depression, even to the point of paranoia:

And…your brain sort of leaps to conclusions about things and you think, well all my friends haven't phoned me, it's because they don't like me anymore. Rather than my friends haven't phoned me because they're busy, or because their baby's sick, or they're busy at work or what have you. You just think, you… You leap to the wrong conclusion almost every time. And I think that just sort of makes you become even…a little bit paranoid, certainly I was. I'd think, 'Oh why aren't they ringing me? Why are people looking at me like that?' I'd take my baby to be weighed at the doctors and I'd think, 'Everyone's talking about me', that's not … That's very…sort of a strange feeling. (Anne)

What was clear in the accounts was the way that people's cognitive abilities can break down in depression. One man (John, who had both cancer and depression) described how depression attacks the mind, making it supremely difficult to think clearly about your condition or about yourself. He described the experience as like 'running in blinkers':

With cancer you can say, 'Oh, I've got to have a treatment, let's see if that does any good.' And there is a sort of progression. But being involved inside the depression, you can't see the wood for the trees, and you depend on people close to you to point the things out that you are unaware of. So you are sort of running in blinkers with depression, which isn't the case with cancer. (John)

When depression affects thoughts significantly, people are unlikely to be able to use their mind effectively to deal with their depression. Indeed, Shiad felt that depression was more dangerous than a physical illness because depression is invisible to others and the mind is actually 'broken':

…if you can imagine someone who's going through a physical illness that's serious and you can imagine the physical pain that the person has to endure and deal with, you can actually provide support for them because it's all very visible and tangible and you can see it. However, with depression, because it is a mental anguish, very often the full brunt of what that person may be going through may not come out in the way that you would see in a physical way… I feel having a mental illness is far more serious than a physical one… Because I feel a strong mind, a sound, focused, stable mind can deal and cope much better with any kind of physical disability, trouble, illness than a mind that's diseased with mental trauma. (Shiad)

Feelings

As with thoughts, there was a wide range of feelings associated with depression. Feeling very cut off from other people and isolated in distress was a common thread that connected participants' accounts. Physical metaphors were used to describe isolation; for example, one man described it as 'I just felt I was locked within myself somehow.' Marie and Veronica described the experience as akin to being locked inside an impervious bubble that keeps the person in, and others out:

> Another way I can describe what you feel when your depressed, is that you have a sort of bubble round you. It's a thick, Perspex bubble that you cannot break and nothing from outside gets through to this… Even if the Queen came here, I…you wouldn't snap out of it. (Marie)

> It was like being inside a very, very thick balloon and no matter how hard I pushed out, the momentum of the skin of the balloon would just push me back in… So I couldn't touch anybody, I couldn't touch anything… I didn't know where it was going to go. (Veronica)

Within this sphere of isolation, feelings of anxiety, fear and even terror arise. As one person said, it was 'terrifying because I could not get across to people how I was feeling'.

Other feelings associated with terror included sensations of drowning or falling; being in a 'black pit'; irritability (e.g. 'I'd sort of snap at people, whereas normally I'm a very patient person'); feeling bad, guilty and worthless (e.g. 'I felt I was such a horrible person that I would contaminate anybody somehow by even sitting beside them'); lack of confidence; emotional numbness or, conversely, being overwhelmed by feelings; feeling a burden to other people; and not being able to eat.

Bodily changes

Along with feelings being described using physical metaphors, bodily changes were commonly associated with the experience of depression. In his account of cancer, Arthur Frank shows how illnesses are experienced by people through their bodies (Frank 1991). He suggests an approach of 'wondering at the body', by trying to trust the body and what is emerging within the body (p.59). In depression, difficult feelings may well be expressed somatically in some people, rather than necessarily felt emotionally (Jadhav, Weiss and Littlewood 2001). Many interesting bodily sensations, changes and conditions were commonly linked to depression by participants. These links were complex. For example, one man said that when he is very depressed, 'I have this sort of pressure around my brain, you know, I feel that someone's got their hands inside there.' A few people even noted that depression was directly expressed through their body, with some saying that their posture and even voice changed during depression:

I spoke in a low monotone. My posture…I tended to stoop and just looked generally dishevelled and not at all, not really able to cope, actually, quite despairing. Despairing of being able to do something for myself, despairing of ever being anything myself, despairing of being normal which, you know partly, I would like… (Paul)

And this last time I became, I could feel my body becoming ill, I could feel the physical changes… My voice changes, I stop, and I can't sing any more, I love singing to music in the car or in the kitchen. My…you can hear from my voice, it completely changes. I think my, also my posture changes I think, I suspect. And I can't describe the physical changes. They, they, it's as if, you know, there's a whole sweeping change inside my body. It's very difficult to describe what it is. The most noticeable is my voice. (Kate)

People also described a spectrum of problems with their levels of energy that really affected their abilities to do things when depressed. Some people felt a lack of energy, while others described complete exhaustion. Some even believed they also had chronic fatigue syndrome:

And then there's just a sense of, you know, quite often it could manifest as just waking up and for no apparent reason just not feeling equipped, not feeling up to [getting up]. And even, you know, life may be going quite well but you can't…you can't work out why there is no energy, why you're feeling quite miserable in a way… You know what to do but you can't actually connect with the normal energy levels that get it all to happen. (Derek)

I've had kind of like chronic fatigue symptoms. It's a feeling of mine that it's kind of a…[in] that depression naturally makes you sort of do less. And maybe it's like you kind of feel better when really you're not depressed so you're doing more or whatever. But basically you have this total like breakdown in terms of headaches, aching, can't do anything, can't move. Not feeling depressed really, just feeling like I can't do anything. Feeling, you know, just proper chronic fatigue. Then I have a rest for a while and I'm, you know, get all right again. That's not something that I'd ever had until I started taking antidepressants. (Heather)

As discussed in Chapter 2, some kinds of physical symptoms like gut problems can be confusing for patients and health professionals. These physical symptoms can add to the difficulties in arriving at a diagnosis of depression.

Behaviour

There are a range of behaviours that people associated with depression, which are briefly outlined here before a more in-depth examination of suicide. Behaviours reported including withdrawing from others, uncontrollable crying (e.g. 'I remember sitting in front of the FA cup final in floods of tears, just uncontrollable misery'); inability to cry; being sensitive to light (e.g. 'I just wanted to sit in a dark cupboard'); inability to sleep (e.g. 'things tend to start going round in your head, so you don't sleep more'); lack of interest in personal appearance; and even an aversion to hearing sounds, including music:

> You've…you've nowhere to go. So your back's to the wall, so the only way to get better is to…let the medical people help. I mean I can judge situations in retrospect, but at the time, I was almost immobilised, inert really. Yeah it was… I would sit in a darkened room with my arms over my head for hours, feeling so wretched I didn't want to eat or drink. So I was totally…almost totally withdrawn, so you're not really able to make any judgements and that's it… (John)

> …when I'm depressed, I can't listen to music… It drives me crazy, it just does. Because…I think it brings you memories of places, of people or whatever or sensations that I cannot experience or I cannot even allow myself to enjoy. (Diego)

The special issue of suicide

Depression is generally accepted as a significant risk factor in suicide-related behaviours, underpinning up to around half of all actual suicides (Anne Maria 2003; Dumais *et al.* 2005). Not surprisingly, suicidal thinking and serious suicide attempts were discussed by the participants I spoke to for this research.

> Well it was like standing outside of myself, I could suddenly see this person I was becoming, I'd seen it happen to other people in my family before. And I found that pretty terrifying, and I'd always promised myself that it wouldn't happen to me… Once I was very depressed I had absolutely no belief that I would ever come out of that state…and I had seen people take antidepressants before, and then be ill again, and I thought well I don't want to do that, I don't want to take loads of drugs and just not get better, so what's the point… And the suicidal ideation was already very developed, and I had no self worth, and I didn't want to live, so it was…it was not hard to, to follow that whole suicidal thought pattern. So I made an attempt in November of 1982 when I was 18, in the first year at [university]. (Ruth)

Participant narratives drew direct links between experiences of depression and thoughts of suicide and actual attempts. People said that the suffering in depression – and the seemingly unending nature of this suffering with no apparent way out – contributed to suicide thinking and attempts. Suffering that seemed inescapable made suicide seem like a viable option at various times for a number of participants.

> It doesn't mean I've never thought of suicide in the real pits…in the 1960s I suppose, there were times when [I thought] 'I just don't want to be here any more, this is so incredibly painful, my life is such a mess… I feel a wreck, I am so unhappy, I am so miserable… What else can there be?' This is a particular period of depression that just went on and on and on. I didn't have faith then, I didn't even attempt to… I didn't attempt suicide, it doesn't mean to say I didn't think about it. (Pamela)

> …when you're seriously depressed, and you're feeling suicidal you just want an end to the depression and, and that's what the suicide feels like. It's a positive step. You know I hear people talking about suicide, it was a cry for help, it was, you know, it was cowardice or whatever. No it was a positive step. It's the best thing that you feel that you can possibly do at the time. I felt it was, it was the best option, no doubt at all. It was the best thing I could possibly do. (Craig)

SUICIDE MEANINGS

People think about the suicide option when it seems like a meaningful choice at the time of depression. Importantly, along with apparently compelling reasons for suicide are a whole range of reasons why people do not actually commit suicide. Apart from not feeling 'courageous' enough at the time, one key reason that people find not to commit suicide is feeling that it is more meaningful to stay alive than die. That is, people do find ways to retrieve life-sustaining meanings when suicide is also a possibility:

> And the fact that finding out why you are actually on this earth is part of a healing process I think because you are trying to get the answers to take away the thoughts, the suicidal thoughts saying, 'Well, I don't know why I am here.' And, 'What's the point of being here?'… Yes you are discovering about yourself… The reasons why you are on this Earth. (Jane)

> If I commit suicide, I'm just gonna be a statistic, I'm gonna be a fading memory. I'm not gonna have left my mark. Like, you know, why was I born? What, you know, what am I here for? I've got a purpose in life. I just…'cos I haven't found it yet, just because I've had a bad start doesn't mean things can't be different. So I sort of came round to the idea [of living] myself. (Patricia)

A sense of emotional connection and having responsibilities towards other people can play key roles in people deciding not to commit suicide. It is worth outlining here a number of quotations to show that, despite the isolating nature of depression, meaningful connection with others is still a compelling motivating factor for people with depression (Box 3.1).

Box 3.1: Responsibilities and connections to others as reasons to avoid suicide

Well if I jump, well probably the best and perhaps the quickest and painless way is to jump from a multi-storey car park. But then my parents would probably have to view my body and it would probably be a right mess. And they will have to identify me or somebody will have to identify me and I…I didn't want them to see me like that. And I thought well I can't do that then. (Belinda)

So, sitting there deciding whether or not I should commit suicide, I was thinking, if I do this he's [a friend who died from cancer] gonna meet me in heaven and he's really gonna kick my arse [laughing]. He's gonna be so disappointed in me. But if I have to do it for anyone other than myself, I owe it to him. So, if it wasn't for that I suppose I probably would not have gone to see my GP. (Patricia)

When I'm like this [depressed] I avoid getting on trains or tubes because it's like sometimes you're waiting for the train and you're in a state of despair and after the train goes, these thoughts came to my mind lots of times: 'If I had jumped all this would be gone by now.' But the reason why you don't do it is many-fold you know. I know how my relatives, like the wives or my cousins of these people who committed suicide, how horrendous it is for the whole family. It's a very kind of… It's not a very easy death to digest for a relative. (Diego)

I never really felt suicidal, I felt pretty darn bad but never quite suicidal. I suppose as I've got, I'm sort of a bit of a high moral person, I think, and I'd got children, I'd got a wife and whatnot. And so even in the really worst times, I would still be conscious that I owed them, you know, something so… I realise my responsibilities, and I being, consider myself an honourable person that I try and stick to my obligations. I hate letting people down. (David)

THINKING ABOUT SUICIDE

Suicidality was on a spectrum of severity from thinking about being dead right through to planning and actual attempts at suicide. At one end of the spectrum, people talked about passive thoughts of being dead and suicide fantasies. Thinking about being dead or not existing was not necessarily the same thing as thinking about suicide.

> I mean I've never felt properly suicidal in my life but…certainly [I] wanted to be dead but hadn't felt suicidal. (Matthew)

> …it's the whole reason why you live, why you have energy, why you're bothered. And if that's empty, then there's an impulse not to exist… And for some that dramatises into a suicidal tendency, for others it's just a bleakness that is very hard to, to sort of describe or tolerate. (Jenny)

To an extent, actual thoughts of being dead or committing suicide could be comforting. Depression is a condition where people's misery seems uncontrollable, and the suicide option is a choice which can give a sense of control and hope.

> Well, since I was very little I occasionally had suicide fantasies. When I was little I used to imagine creeping out of the house at night and going on the nearby railway tracks, and that was…that was in a way a comfort for me, because, you know, sometimes I would feel like my life was completely out of my control, and I didn't have any options. (Nicola)

Such was the feeling of control it could create, merely thinking about suicide was enough to comfort some people. People here were at pains to point out the validity of such thoughts. Craig talked about feeling 'over the moon' when he realised that suicide was an option, while Sophia saw the comfort in suicidal thinking actually acting as a deterrent to suicide:

> You know, there you are, faced with, with you know, depression is terrible… And then all of a sudden I was confronted with, 'This [suicide] is it, the answer to my problems, you know, why didn't I think of this before, it's so simple.' And for the first time in a long, long, long, long time I felt great. I felt over the moon because I was actually doing something. I was taking back control of my life… I don't want my life anymore, had enough, taken control, conscious decision, this is what I am going to do. (Craig)

> And the way I look at suicide or attempted suicide is that it acts as a deterrent, and I don't know if anybody else will understand this. But the fact that I can do it and I have done it, it acts as a deterrent for me. But it's, it's the comfort, I don't know why. It acts as a comfort for me because I know I can take my own

> life, if I want to I can do it. So that deters me from doing it because I think…
> 'Well, I can't do this to my son. Sod everybody else, I can't do it to him because
> he doesn't deserve that.' But if I feel that way, I'll sit about, I'll sit and I'll think
> about it, like many people do when they're like that, 'What can I do to get rid
> of myself?' But it acts as a deterrent, it stops me. (Sophia)

While suicidal thinking can be more 'passive,' it can also move on to the point where suicide appears a realistic option, or it at least appears difficult to avoid as an option.

> But sort of the voices, the little voice in your head that we all have when we
> speak to ourselves. And it was basically saying, 'You know, why don't you just
> finish yourself off, you're just…, you're just never going to pull out of this. And
> you know, nobody likes you and… You know, just finish it off, why don't you
> just do it.' (Patrick)

At the active end of the spectrum, suicide thoughts could be so intrusive that they were described as overwhelming. When thoughts became very intrusive, they could even be cast as 'voices' that people found themselves arguing with. Here, suicidal thinking can be such that people were literally arguing to stay alive.

> And this dialogue was running in my head at the time. I had this raging suicidal
> ideation, 'You're worthless and you've got to die and just get it over and done
> with.' And the other bit thinking, my parents are going to be so distressed and
> what about my friends, what am I doing, I might get better. 'No, no you won't
> get better, look how many times this has happened. Look how worthless you
> are and you are so in debt.' 'Oh but I might…', you know… And the life force
> just won. (Ruth)

People can find active suicidal thinking so disturbing that they feel compelled to seek professional help.

> But I went through a period where in one of my very low periods, that I began
> to contemplate suicide, contemplate, actually that life wasn't worth going on.
> There was no point wading through this shit, I suppose any longer, it was just
> becoming more and more difficult. And it was at that point that…that I
> realised that if I was going to get through this, that I had to seek some help. And
> that's when I went to see my GP. (Liza)

However, people who are suicidal do not necessarily tell others, even when their suffering is considerable. Like depression, suicidal thinking is an internal thought process which others may not notice. Understandably, people do worry about the kinds of responses that others might have if they were to reveal their thoughts about suicide. While participants did talk about hiding their suicidal thoughts from others to avoid unhelpful reactions, a number of people pointed out the real value of talking about thoughts of suicide to people whom they saw as non-judgemental and understanding.

> It is extremely upsetting to find yourself with, you know, deep, deep fundamental suicidal thoughts which you are incapable of dismissing... And to find that in fact you weren't the only person to feel like that was actually a great relief. It was also a great relief to find that (on the Internet)...to find people who were non-judgemental, who were going through it themselves. That it wasn't patronising or sort of people trying to do good, or people trying to talk you out of this... You know, the last thing that you really feel, really want is people telling you not to do things, because it is something, that, that is, you know, so, so strong that, you know, you just want people to say, 'Well, yeah, I understand. I was there, or I am there. I understand what you are going through...' And it's a great source of strength that you're not alone, that there are other people out there being, feeling like that.' (Craig)

> I have one friend, who was actually, I actually went to university with, and was there when I was first unwell, so she knows me quite well, and has seen me very low before, so she's, you know, stood by me, quite well... And it's got to the situation now when I can actually acknowledge to her that I do get periods of feeling suicidal and she will actually have that conversation with me, whereas previously that was far too scary...the thought of actually mentioning it. But now that's out in the open it's made our relationship a lot stronger, that has. (Rosey)

MOVING TOWARDS PLANNING AND ATTEMPTING SUICIDE

In situations where people are not immobilised by depression, suicidal thinking can reach a point where people actively start planning for suicide. Here, a kind of suicide logic can kick in where suicide can appear more meaningful than staying alive. People also talk about 'triggers' that can result in suicide seeming logical. For example, relationship break-ups can contribute to living seeming implausible.

> I was in a state of having failed my second-year exams, and appealing on medical grounds. I went back in the following term but it was...that was obviously a disappointment. But it was not, it wasn't to be unexpected, especially considering the fact I didn't do any work and I couldn't actually do any work, I don't think. So that, and rejection from my [girl] friend were, basically it tipped me into doing something that I'd resisted doing for a long time... I was preoccupied with suicide anyway... And I think, this sort of kind of underlined,

well, you know, there really doesn't look like there's any way out of it, it's my last chance gone and in a sense... And I don't think my life's going to be any better, and I've felt like this for so long, and there's no prospect of it getting better. (Paul)

In planning for suicide, 'suicide logic' can set in where the case for suicide seems absolutely compelling, alternatives seem unworkable, and people have the energy and resources to actively plan for suicide.

I found on about three occasions with depression...that I was convinced that my family, my wife and sons would be far, far happier without me. I remember writing notes to each of them saying that it was... And it was perfectly lucid in my mind... That I was doing the best thing [by committing suicide], and I put these notes in the boot of the car with the intention of hooking up a pipe from the exhaust into the car. And I was utterly convinced I was doing them a favour. I don't think I ever told anybody... I did take an overdose on one occasion, when things were quite desperate... (John)

And I started feeling suicidal and, you know, initially it starts, sort of what I describe as being passively suicidal. You just sort of get sort of passive thoughts that, well actually you know if it was all over, if I wasn't here, you know, it would be OK. And sort of getting slowly over time, a period of about a couple of months, it started becoming more and more frequent thoughts of suicide and also of no longer being sort of passive thoughts of suicide that...but active thoughts of suicide, that in fact, you know, the reason why, you know, I was unhappy was that my family was unhappy. And the reason they were unhappy was me. And if I wasn't there they would be happy. (Craig)

However, suicide logic can be interrupted, even during active preparation for suicide, as was the case for Craig. In the quote below, Craig suggests that although 'suicide logic' seemed compelling at the time, it was as if the 'spell' of suicide logic could be broken by an event that did not fit with the interior logic of suicide:

Although I'd thought this through in such great detail I hadn't considered that the Victorian banisters might not actually be strong enough to take the weight of a, you know, 90-kilo man. And so suddenly, you know, you're faced with this problem, you know, damn, I hadn't thought of this. And it was clear, you can tie it right round the banisters, give it a tug. Hmmm, this isn't, this isn't going to hold my weight. And I was thinking, 'Well you know, goodness, what do you do?' So then I thought about, 'Well actually I could tie the rope around a door handle, you know, I could get the cupboard and door handle that would rest against the banisters and that might actually give me enough strength and I was... And the door handle was slippery and I was unsure how to tie the rope to the door handle and I was, I was sitting there trying to figure out this problem when the phone rang. And my wife phoned to check how I was getting on. And the spell broke. And I just sobbed and I sobbed and I sobbed and I cried and it struck me…you know, what I was trying to do. (Craig)

Self distortion and crash

As discussed in the previous chapter, distortions in thinking as well as the self can develop when authentic experience is not adequately acknowledged by the patient or their significant others. People talked about adopting various strategies early in their lives, to manage the emotional and cognitive conflict within themselves as they tried to relate to the outside world. Strategies for coping included trying to 'pass' as doing OK despite feeling miserable inside; overachievement and overwork; social withdrawal; and restricting life to a narrow zone of comfort.

> …and you try not to think about the fact that you limit your life in all sorts of ways. And that was what I'd always had to do. So I'd always felt I'd had jobs which were beneath me intellectually but were as much as I could emotionally cope with. (Veronica)

Despite being able to find ways of compensating for inner conflict, a self that is constructed on foundations which do not resonate as particularly meaningful or authentic does not function well. This kind of self can also contribute to depression under the right circumstances. For instance, Jane was a self-confessed perfectionist and workaholic in a job that became more demanding following workplace restructuring. She suffered a severe depression, eventually requiring hospitalisation when she could no longer cope with life stresses using her 'perfect self' persona which she had adopted to survive:

> I'd always loved my job, but it was then becoming that I was away five, six days a week, getting home and I couldn't get away from work basically, because I would get back here and there would be faxes and messages and goodness knows what and… A lot of my job was travelling a lot. I was covering a huge area, not just the UK. And one day I just sort of came home after I had been away for a week, parked my car outside, sat on the pavement and just broke down, basically. And my…[I] just cried. I couldn't, I don't even remember how I drove home… (Jane)

All of us have 'different' selves in that we juggle multiple identities (e.g. parent, wife, student, professional, gay, Black) to suit different circumstances, and present ourselves in different ways to suit those circumstances.

We present ourselves to the outside world in a manner that helps us to navigate the complex social situations we encounter in everyday life, while trying to avoid social problems like finding ourselves discredited by other people (Goffman 1963). Homeless people, for instance, are highly stigmatised and in order to manage this stigma they may avoid negative identities attributed to other homeless people, such as by considering themselves as better off than other homeless persons (e.g. such as those with drug addictions) (Boydell, Goering and Morrell-Bellai 2000). In this way, people tend to present themselves in the best possible light in relation to other people like them. Similarly, some of the problems identified by participants prone to depression were also about how to present themselves in a way to the outside world that ensured survival.

However, there were particular problems in presenting a self to the outside world for the people I spoke to. In particular, presenting the self in such a way as to get through life and survive could potentially contribute to disorganisation within the self. Participants raised concerns about: 1. the type of public persona they adopted which many saw as a 'false self'; 2. the ways in which this 'façade' of self could be very disengaged from meaningful experience; and 3. the confusions that could emerge in trying to cope with presenting a self to the rest of the world while dealing with distortions in thinking and the self-concept that were part of the depression experience.

What is clear from the literature is that at a minimum the concept of self undergoes a shake-up during an episode of depression. In more severe depression, it could be said that the self actually undergoes a kind of annihilation. Thus, loss of self is a pervasive theme in the qualitative literature on depression. Jago (2002, p.742) has described it as 'a kind of death' of the self, while Beck (2002) describes a disintegration of the self. This loss of self also involves loss in terms of what the former abilities of the self were (e.g. being able to concentrate on issues), and the identities this self was attached to (e.g. work identities, valued relationships) (Beck 2002). This experience of loss of self could be extremely frightening.

> And I know in my head I loved my husband and kids but I couldn't feel anything at all. My emotions were completely dead. And I was just very frightened. It was the most frightening, terribly frightening experience, and it looked like it was an unending one. (Veronica)

Additionally, as Beck points out, along with the loss of self and associated anxiety can be a sense of feeling 'alarmingly unreal' (p.466). Add to this the growing sense that people get that they are entering into a deep personal crisis and the picture painted of depression is disconcerting, even terrorising

(Karp 1994). And so when the crisis in the self runs very deep, people will require help to manage their depression. The greater the loss of self, the greater the loss of the foundation from which people could ordinarily respond to a crisis. Also, when there is terror and the mind fails, as is the case with severe depression, then the ongoing day-to-day construction of the narrative about the self – that is, people's stories about who they are – is doubly disrupted. Thus, people can have particular trouble knowing anything solid about themselves when depressed. One man described the experience vividly as 'your whole self gets put into the mixer and could come out in any old form'.

One of the risks of constructing and presenting a self to the rest of the world that is very distant from actual experience (as was common in the stories I heard) was ultimately losing sight of a selfhood grounded in any meaningful, embodied sense of authenticity. When lack of self understanding is paired with the onslaught of depression (with all the turmoil in thinking, feeling and bodily sensations) the result is more than confusing, it can be terrifying. In this situation, thoughts and feelings appear to come out of the blue, and can become confused with the self. Derek talks succinctly about the problem of not knowing 'how I am':

> ...you really can't put your finger on anything but you...you know bloody well you're down in that hole and there's no light and there's no energy. And – and that's, that's actually more frightening because I mean it's one thing to have something terrible happening like you have a major bereavement and you can be, you know, absolutely down there but you, at least you have some connection [with] why. And it gives you somewhere to look to, to deal with it and go and get help. But if you're just actually not functioning properly and you don't understand why, that's frightening. Well I, well I find it frightening because I like the connection with solution. What I think I'm saying is the more understanding I can have of how I am, the better it is. (Derek)

It is thus easy to see how depression is self-perpetuating, and how it is not possible for people to just step out from the downward spiral of depression. Cognitive distortions have fertile ground to multiply within the territory of the self in turmoil and the mind in confusion. Since emotion, cognition and the self in turmoil can easily become mixed up in depression, the negative thinking of depression can easily become conflated with the self. The self can effortlessly come to be seen as the same thing as the destructive thoughts and negative feelings that pertain to depression. For instance, people who experience depression can easily feel that they themselves are bad or worthless, rather than view the thoughts as an episode of depression that will pass eventually.

> I wouldn't sit beside anyone to talk to them [in hospital], I can remember that. And that may have been part of the manic thing, I don't know. But it was partly because I felt I was such a horrible person that I would contaminate anybody somehow by sitting, even sitting beside them. They would somehow be able to tell how awful I was if I sat beside them. So it was something to do with that sort of feeling of self-hatred and it was so painful. I had a feeling if they did talk to me, they'd only be doing it because they were sorry for me. I was absolutely convinced. So that period in hospital was, it was like being in hell. (Richard)

Despite the inner turmoil and disorganisation they experienced, many participants said they learnt to be good actors to hide their true selves, including their inner difficulties. Indeed, some people claimed particular talent in presenting a functioning self to the outside world that could mask immense interior turmoil.

> And socially I could rise. You know, I could wake up and feel shit, I could drag myself through the day feeling shit. But somehow I had to get out there and spark. I could get out there and sparkle! (Liza)

> I carried this 'face' around for as far as I'm concerned, 24 years. This false pretence of being somebody that I actually am not. Because I believed it to be what other people expected. That's wh– I was a character that everybody, that I thought everybody wanted me to be. I was a bubbly, lively person. I was probably one of the people you would never have thought suffered from depression. And, mainly because I hid it. And I hid it so well that it came natural to me. (Patricia)

Although divorced from any meaningful reality, acting out the façade could seem so important to people to get through life that it carried over into hiding the most severe forms of depression. Along with difficulties in finding a language to describe the depression experience, the deployment of a façade could add to difficulties people had in seeking help and getting their depression recognised by others.

> I couldn't cope with, with other people at all. And also I developed coping mechanisms. I had managed quite well to, to hide it. And if someone sort of, you know, at work sort of said, 'Well how's everything going?' I could snap out. 'Everything's fine thanks. It's great. We're doing this, this, this and this and we're doing that.' 'That's good.' And they would go. And boom. I'd go back at staring at my feet. (Craig)

Conclusion

In depression the mind is 'broken' and the concept of self is shaky and perhaps at risk of being obliterated entirely. Emotions are in turmoil and the person feels more or less cut off from the world. If there is any concept of self left, it is that the self has qualities such as being 'bad', 'worthless' and 'guilty'. The depressed mind cannot be relied upon to do what healthy people can take for granted – that is, to think about the self constructively and to tell stories about the self that allow the person to go on living. As such, people are stopped in their tracks by depression, with few remaining abilities other than to focus on their distress. Severe depression in particular compels people to come to a standstill, to disengage from their everyday life and to focus on their moment-to-moment distress. And to stop narrating their self beyond such life-depleting messages such as 'I am bad'.

Severe depression can be viewed as the self – a self carefully constructed to survive in the social world – imploding, sometimes quite quickly and dramatically, in a depressive interlock. The downward spiral of depressive interlock is ultimately about the self unravelling. Severe depression has been described as both a birth and a death by Andrew Solomon (2002, p.17): 'both the new presence of something and the total disappearance of something'. Needless to say, the inner emotional turmoil and disintegration of a viable story about the self – along with the usual roles of the self – can be extremely distressing, and most participants had experienced anxiety – if not terror – along with depression. This state is closest to the chaos narrative described by Frank (1995), where people are overwhelmed by illness and unable to narrate their experiences coherently and others find it hard to listen. As will be discussed in Chapter 4, some people come to believe that the self that is built for survival – rather than living life to the full – does actually need to fall apart before people can pick up the pieces and recover in a longer-term sense. The disorganised self is thought to be missing some of the things that more functional and enlivened selves seem to have. And so the implosion of the depressed self creates what Frank (1991) refers to as a 'dangerous opportunity'. This is an opportunity to construct a more functional and authentically meaningful story about the self. But the road map for this kind of personal journey is not straightforward, and is taken up in the chapters to follow.

Chapter 4

Recovering from Depression

Having looked at depression from an existential perspective, I will now turn to a discussion of how people minimise the impact – and attempt to prevent episodes – of depression occurring. In addition, I will discuss how people undertake their recovery from depression both in the shorter and longer term. This chapter was developed from an initial analysis that appeared in the journal *Qualitative Health Research* (Ridge and Ziebland 2006).

While episodes of depression are usually limited rather than ongoing, and antidepressants can result in seemingly miraculous recoveries from depression, there are limits to these short-term recoveries. Some people do not respond to antidepressants, or they may have subsequent episodes of depression, or report only partial recoveries where they still have some symptoms of depression or anxiety. Like the restitution narratives described by Frank (1995), where ill people just want their health restored, some participants just want to get back to life before depression. Others come to view their former selves as dysfunctional and in need of repair. Many are so fearful of another episode of depression that they want to ensure it does not happen again, or if it does, that the trauma is minimised as much as possible. For all kinds of reasons, many participants take a longer-term view (beyond individual episodes of depression) when thinking about self-management and recovery. The analysis in the current study shows that it is helpful to consider recovery as involving four phases. These phases are not set in stone, or mutually exclusive. Rather, they serve as a typology to better identify some of the elements involved in recovery:

1. preventing depression from occurring in the first place

2. limiting the impact of actual episodes of depression

3. recovering from the effects of depression in the short and long term

4. re-working the self so that it is more functional or authentically felt.

Qualitative researchers Sarah Russell and Jan Browne working in Melbourne, Australia noticed that positive personal accounts of coping with bipolar disorder were virtually absent from the academic literature (Russell and Browne 2005). They decided to investigate the expertise that people with bipolar disorder themselves had to prevent mania and depression. Their findings are pertinent to the present study in that they found it was important for people to develop awareness about their condition, as well as organise individual 'stay well plans' to prevent or limit future episodes (p.189). People in their study developed their plans and adapted them as they went along, and this is where health professionals could be very helpful in assisting patients. Here, people tried to identify 'trigger factors' for episodes and the early warning signs that indicated an episode was imminent. Strategies could then be enacted to maximise the chances of staying well, including:

- getting more sleep

- reducing levels of activity and stress

- consulting with a professional about using medication (including using sleeping tablets to get more sleep)

- increasing social support levels.

This research is valuable because it challenges pessimism about people's abilities to prevent bipolar disorder. The concept of 'trigger factors', 'stay well plans' and looking out for warning signs are just as relevant to those with unipolar depression as bipolar disorder. (The *Health Talk Online* research completed for the current book included some people with bipolar disorder, but mainly focused on people with unipolar depression.) The people I spoke to were very motivated to prevent or at least limit the impact of further episodes of depression, due to the suffering involved. In the *Health Talk Online* study people tried to 'stay well' in a number of ways, including by:

- better looking after the self (especially in between episodes of depression), such as by using therapy and self-help books

- identifying trigger factors, especially the negative thoughts that lead to depression (e.g. see discussion on cognitive behavioural therapy (CBT) in Chapter 8)

- noticing the warning signs that an episode of depression might be on the cards

- noticing the cyclical pattern of depression, especially during the actual episode
- considering short- and longer-term issues in recovery.

Most of these points will now be briefly discussed before moving on to discuss issues in short-term and longer-term recovery. The issue about identifying trigger factors is taken up in Chapter 8 under the section on cognitive behavioural therapy (CBT), and is not discussed in any detail in the current chapter.

Looking after the self

As well as using 'tools' like medication to alleviate actual depression, people used a range of preventative approaches to stay well in between episodes. We found that many different kinds of tools were considered effective within people's narratives of recovery. Indeed, assembling multiple tools went hand in hand with people's abilities to tell recovery stories (Ridge and Ziebland 2006). Tools that people described in the narratives as effective included talking therapies, medication, fish oils, meditation, yoga, light therapy and getting enough exercise. Using a variety of approaches to increase the chances of staying well in the short term – and recovering in the long term – was very important to many of the people I spoke to. Those people who identified few effective tools also struggled more to tell a long-term recovery story. The use of various medical and non-medical tools in recovery narratives is taken up in considerable detail in Chapters 5 and 6.

Noticing the warning signs

As discussed previously, the trouble is that it can be difficult for people to know when they are at risk of going into an episode of depression. And people's experiences of depression differ so greatly that it is not possible to identify common warning signs for everyone. Nevertheless, through experience, some people had become skilled at identifying their own personal signs that they might be going into a depression. For instance, some took tiredness and lack of sleep as a warning sign of a looming depression.

> I have to say it's not often now that I get…an experience which indicates to me that I'm going to lapse back into it [depression]. I'd no history of depression before this came along. If I find myself getting very tired, I take that as a warning… Well I think you see, if your brain has had a battering, it needs time and rest to recover, you know. If you're awake you're not resting it, and I think that's what happened, I think, you know, this detachment, the brain was saying

'I've got too much overload. I want to chill out', as it were. 'I want, I want "out" of this', you know. (Peter)

A few people had worked out very detailed lists of warning signs. For Belinda, her signals included intolerance of noise and music, wanting to be alone, having a feeling that things were not quite right, not feeling at ease within herself and wanting to self-medicate her emotional pain:

> The warning signs for me are I don't listen to, I can't listen to music or television. I can't bear noise. I'm very intolerant of noise. Any kind of noise actually, and I take to my bed. Or I isolate myself. I stop answering the phone and before that something must happen before that. Just generally feeling things aren't right. Something is wrong somewhere… I don't feel at ease with myself. I don't really want to be with myself. If I could get drunk… I haven't turned to drink. I have drugs, I have used my medication to get myself off my head sometimes, sleeping tablets. I've taken four or five of them a few times to just release myself. And it's the same thing as getting drunk. You kind of need to lose yourself because you can't bear to be with yourself any more. (Belinda)

Matthew experiences his warning signs as partly emerging through his body, with increased heart beats, panic, fear of being alone and a volley of negative thinking.

> The signs [of depression] are panic, yeah you just think 'I'm panicking'. And that's physical, you know your heart rate goes up, the old classics of waking up early in the morning, that happens. The fear of being on your own, that you recognise. And just the sheer onslaught of negative thoughts that you cannot push out. And then you know, you know when it's coming, you know this is a bit different from just feeling shit. You know I have crap days, you can come home from work, and you think 'Oh shit, that was awful, I feel crap'… But you know it's very different from [that]. (Matthew)

Even though people can become aware of early warning signs, some pointed out it can be easy to miss these signals. One man said that his friends and family were the best people to know he was becoming depressed, not him.

Once warning signs were detected, people said they needed to have a strategy to respond to their warning signs. Some people took their warning signs as a signal they should get more rest and/or get help. Other people had developed prior arrangements with their doctors so that they could start taking (or increase) their medication to prevent or limit a possible depression. Those people who had learnt about CBT were able to look at their thinking as a possible trigger for depression, and so challenge their thinking (see discussion about CBT in Chapter 8). For Craig, making a conscious decision to try to stick to normal everyday routines was important when he felt at risk of mania and the subsequent crash of depression:

> You know in, in the best of moments, I can do more than somebody who hasn't been brushed with the madness stick. But I do feel that every good day has to be paid for by a bad day, and yeah, sooner or later it catches up with you. And that's when you get depressed, and you have to be aware of that and sometimes I have to make a conscious decision. Why get engrossed in a project and stop going to bed at bedtime? Making sure I don't miss meals, you know, make sure that I don't get up at three o'clock in the morning because I've got this idea that won't go away. You know, stay in bed, get up at a sensible time and yeah, I have to look after myself like that or…I believe when I'm on a high, I'll lose it, and I will lose my grounding in reality. (Craig)

Noticing the pattern of depression

The stories told to me made it clear that limiting the impact of an episode of depression was possible even after depression had set in. For instance, people talked about adopting a recovery attitude to control the impact of their current depression (see discussion below for more detail). The trouble is that it can be very difficult for depressed people with runaway negative thinking to hold onto the idea that they will recover. This was especially true for people who had prolonged depression. It is very much easier for people to think that their current episode is the one they will never recover from:

> You still really kind of believe that this [episode] is it, and it's really bad… But at the back of your mind, at least you know that it's going to get better at some point. (Heather)

> In the midst of it you feel like, 'God I've felt this forever, and I will feel like it forever.' (Matthew)

So this approach of trying to find some way of holding onto the idea of depression as self-limiting is quite a subtle and tricky shift in thinking. Yet this shift could be very powerful. To accomplish this narrative shift, people kept hold of the idea of depression as being temporary somewhere at the back of their mind, even if it was difficult for people to really believe it. Therefore it could be a huge relief for people to hear from a trusted professional that there was hope for recovery when they themselves were unable to feel that hope.

One of the things that I thought was very important to me in this process was the fact that the doctor said to me, 'I'm going to get you out of this depression, but don't expect a miracle. Don't expect to be OK tomorrow. It's a long process but I'll sort you out.' Those were his words. That to me was very important... He gave me hope because if I hadn't gone there... I don't know where it could lead to, you know, so it gave me hope. (Diego)

Gaining the knowledge through past experience that depression is a temporary affliction helped some people to move towards greater acceptance – and thus better self-management – of their depression. This accumulated knowledge of episodes having limited duration helped people better endure their suffering, and at the same time could reduce the personal impact of depressive episodes. One older man, John, had so much experience of depression and recovering that he was able to apply his own way of managing his thoughts, even though he had never heard of CBT (see Chapter 8 for a discussion on CBT). This approach of trying to challenge his thoughts in a more helpful way enabled him to feel hopeful about recovery during the very worst phase of his depression:

I always try to think that there's a sort of beneficial flip side to these problems. And I tell myself that if you don't hit the bottom, you don't really know what the good things are. So when I felt absolutely as if I'd hit the rock bottom, it was starting then to feel quite joyful because I knew it was going to get better, and gradually it did. (John)

David said that noticing the limited pattern of depression, and better accepting his cycles of depression and recovery, meant that the depression was more manageable:

Well with some sort of experience of it [depression], when you've had about six goes, depressed for two years, [then] OK, [then depressed again], at least by then [I knew] I did get better. Whilst I was depressed the thought of ever getting better was the last thing on earth, desperation of just living through a day was... It was that desperate, you know, at times. And that's how I bumped along, with recurring bouts [of] about two years' depression, three years OK... It's just my life has been bouts of depression and fairly good, and then another bout of depression. And I was warned that my particular sort of depression would follow that kind of path. So you can't be forearmed against it, if it's down to you, you'll get it. What you've got to be able to do is accept it, and accepting it seems to able to make it manageable. (David)

However, while it may be useful knowing what is going to happen in depression for self-management purposes, there can still be a real dread of the suffering to come. It is important that the enormous fears that can be associated with depression be acknowledged somehow.

> And you can see it coming, and some people say to you that you recognise it coming, and they're probably right. I felt this. It makes it a bit easier because at least you think 'OK, well I've been here before, and I've got over it.' But there's also a feeling of 'Oh fuck, you know, I know just how shit this gets'... It's hard, it's really hard to think 'Oh Jesus, here we go again'... You can say, 'OK, yeah, I've been here before.' But that don't make it a lot easier... Now if it [depression] happened to me again, which I dare say it will, I'll never think, 'Oh God, I thought I was out of that,' because I think I've kind of accepted that it is something that's there now. And people will say oh how sad that is, and I don't think it is really, without saying yeah it's something that's there, but I know the signs, and I know what to do, and I know you get better. (Matthew)

> When you come out of a depression [there] is the fear of having another one. You know, because again, I keep asking myself whether this is a cycle thing, you know like there is a cycle that you are getting again and again and another one. And when you come out of one...you're terrified of getting another one. And when you have another one, having had one before, the only consolation is that you know you're going to come out. But this doesn't make the pain any easier, you know it's still very painful... (Diego)

Short-term recovery

I have already touched upon the distinction between an emergence from a particular episode of depression in the short term and the longer-term recovery project. I will now briefly talk about the shorter-term issues in recovery before turning to the longer-term issues. Consistent with research into mental health and recovery in general (Borg and Kristiansen 2004), participants described key 'turning points' in their depression. They talked about how their thinking changed, something happened, or they did something differently, and their depression began to lose its hold on them. Turning points are frequently narrative events where a new, more hopeful meaning can suddenly be retrieved. For Elizabeth, the simple words of a friend within a ritual dance created a powerful turning point, but it was short lived.

> ...one of the things I do is circle dancing now, which is a kind of world dance. It's a kind of folk dancing. But we usually do it in a circle and we do dances from all over the world. And one of the dances is a choreography of a dance about Julian of Norwich, *The Bells of Norwich*. And we were doing that, and you know she [a friend] sort of said... 'All shall be well, all manner of things shall be

well, all will be well'… That really shook [me], and for the few minutes that we just sat down, I was lifted right up out of my depression… And then I slumped down again. (Elizabeth)

Turning points can involve a wide range of meaningful narrative turns such as a patient discovering through doing voluntary work that they are capable rather than useless. Whatever the meaning of the turning point, important changes in behaviour can then arise from the shift in narrative. For Patrick, the turning point started as a series of realisations where he began to treat his depression as a kind of person he could get mad at. He also imagined the effect on others if he were to commit suicide. These shifts in thinking were then linked to a decision to get help:

I got really angry at the depression…like it was a person… I also couldn't function, I couldn't get out of bed and then got to the stage where I was having suicidal thoughts…thankfully…I actually had this image of my best friend and of my folks actually at my funeral crying. And I just thought, you know, 'I can't do it because of them'… And that was definitely the turning point and it's at that point that I reached out. And that's when I sort of got the…the extra counselling. And I also at that point started to attend a support group, which was specifically for lesbian, gay, transgender and bisexuals who were having mental health problems. (Patrick)

After a harrowing childhood, Patricia thought that the laws of karma surely dictated that her depression must break at some point. This karmic turn in her story played a role in her seeking much-needed help:

But, I had a belief in karma, and in a sense of what goes around comes around, and there's gotta be a turning point for me somewhere. And something good has got to come out of all this, I can't let, you know, let all of this, dictate my future for me. So I went to my GP in a bit of a state, and she said, right, she said right, she said, 'I need to say to you Patricia, I know I've said it to you before,' and she had said it to me before, I needed to be in hospital. (Patricia)

Particularly vivid descriptions of turning points were especially associated with antidepressant medication for some people. As discussed in more detail in the next chapter on medical tools, descriptions of emergence from depression linked to medication frequently involved bright, uplifting visual metaphors: 'the sun seems to shine better, the colours of nature are much sharper', and 'all of a sudden you realise how much colour…there is in the world'.

There were qualities of recovery in the short term that people talked about, including being able to get back into life as it was before depression, including taking up personal interests again. Many of these stories also talked about overcoming the social isolation of depression: feeling better connected with people, being able to feel emotions again, and being better able to socialise.

> Just going back into my normal life where, you know, I see my friends, I...I'm happy with my children. I just...I take up all my interests again. I've got a lot of interests, I just start living life again properly. (Kate)

> I became more interested in my surroundings. I began, it didn't happen overnight, but I began to become engaged with life and feel I was linking up with people. Because as I said before I think in some ways I was detached really from people. It's like living in a row of detached houses and then you become a terrace where you link up with people, mentally. (Peter)

> I mean getting over depression is about discovering that, I mean discovering I could have decent relationships... Again it's about that thing of joining the rest of the human race, thinking actually I'm not different. (Craig)

As indicated earlier in the chapter, people frequently talked about how their recovery from depression was only partial in the short term. For instance, as people recovered, they could still retain some aspects of depression, e.g. lack of confidence, problems with concentration, anxiety, lack of energy.

> And you sort of start noticing colours and things like that, which was great. But the pills weren't strong enough and although I felt much better, I didn't stop feeling depressed. (Craig)

> I think I was damaged by it [depression], I think I was damaged by it, or damaged during it. But I've managed really to climb out of it, to become something near to the person I once was... I can be very fragile now. I'm not very good at confronting people, I was a lot more shall we say robust in my attitude prior to it [depression] than what I am now. (Peter)

And a successful short-term recovery can end in disappointment if people slump back down into depression or have a subsequent episode of depression (Karp 1994). Given that it is common for people to have subsequent episodes of depression, many people come to realise that it is helpful to manage the partialness of short-term recoveries. So, for example, it is better to view antidepressants as just one potential tool in recovery and the construction of a more robust post-depression self (Metzl 2001). In the present study, it was found that many people attributed their depression to a 'chemical imbalance' which needed to be fixed with medication (Ridge and Ziebland 2006). Nevertheless, this biochemical explanation did not exclude other more social explanations of depression. Hence, those who favoured a biochemical explanation also reflected on the need for personal and social changes in the long term.

> And you spend years with people saying 'Oh, cheer up love, why are you so miserable?' And you're thinking it is not my fault. But you are made to feel it is your fault. The fact that these tablets helped me, I thought there was something going on with my serotonin… I felt vindicated. But after a while, I realised it sorted out my brain chemistry, but you have learnt all these negative ways of looking at things, and doing things… You've learned this behaviour, from your parents at times. And that is why I believe I need long-term therapy as well. (Heather)

The 'chemical imbalance' narrative about depression being caused by a problem with body biochemistry was only occasionally deployed by participants in a way that worked against looking for other explanations for depression. While David raises a traumatic event in his childhood during the Second World War as a possible contributor to his depression, he finally leans toward a chemical imbalance narrative. Like others in the study, he had also responded very well to medication and cognitive behavioural therapy, both of which did not necessitate revisiting the childhood event he raised in the interview for this book.

> And we got very nearly bombed… About 200 yards from the bottom of the garden was an airfield, well the airfield that's still there, and the Germans came and dropped bombs that close. My brother and I witnessed an eighty-eight machine gunning the harvesters out in the field, the men were out, harvesting the crops with the horses and carts and a plane came along and machine gunned them… I think you get it [depression] or you don't, at some time your chemicals get mixed up and that's it. You get one, a lack of one chemical, and you get an imbalance and there it starts. And the more I read about it in later years I… I'm more convinced that's what happens, that it's chemical, chemical rather than mental as such. (David)

The longer-term recovery project

So apart from trying to emerge from particular episodes of depression, and limiting the potential for (and impact of) future episodes, many people also developed the idea that they needed to recover from depression in the longer term (Ridge and Ziebland 2006). This longer-term approach to recovery involved people examining their interior life more deeply. It also involved finding long-term strategies to reduce or even prevent depressive episodes. Here, people were additionally interested in building a more robust self and not simply returning to 'normal' or how they were functioning before depression. Our research here uncovered some of the key tasks and strategies involved in patients aiming for a long-term recovery, more functional self and better enjoyment of life. These tasks include adopting the language of recovery, finding allies in recovery, gaining different types of insight and taking greater responsibility for recovery. These aspects of recovery are outlined below.

Adopting the language of recovery

As discussed previously, depressed people can feel so dire – and in an apparently unending way – that it is possible for them to be unaware that they will recover. This can be true even if people have been depressed and recovered many times before. It is all the more difficult for patients to adopt a hopeful story about recovery when professionals and the health care system do not use the language of recovery. In this situation the idea of recovery may not even occur to people at all. Interestingly, people often need to be introduced to the hopeful language of recovery before they can entertain ideas about their own longer-term recovery.

> I feel as if I have been in…in recovery for a few months now, or perhaps longer… But I hadn't actually realised I'd been in recovery. I had to go to a recovery conference to kind of realise I was in recovery [laughs]. (Belinda)

Finding allies in recovery

A key issue in longer-term recovery for patients was having an ally in recovery. Being an ally in someone's recovery is not a straightforward task, as it involves adopting particular kinds of approaches that may need to be learned (a detailed account of the qualities of recovery allies is outlined in Chapter 7). In summary, highly regarded allies in recovery shared qualities like demonstrating humanity in their care; acknowledging the seriousness of depression; applying listening skills; demonstrating a positive belief in the patient; making themselves available to patients; and promoting hope in recovery.

Gaining different types of insight

Five key insights were identified in participants' stories as important in recovering from depression in the longer term (Ridge and Ziebland 2006). These insights involved becoming aware of:

- the dysfunctional self
- the way distorted thinking is not the same as the self
- an 'authentically' felt self
- the potential for a new self
- the need to 'rewrite' the depression experience into the self.

I will now discuss each type of insight in turn.

BECOMING AWARE OF THE DYSFUNCTIONAL SELF

As previously discussed, depression forces people to slow down (or come to a standstill) and focus more on their own distress. The self is disoriented and thinking is distorted. Despite this, depression does allow people a window of opportunity to develop insights into how they are functioning in the world. This is because, paradoxically, depression not only involves distortion but also a 'heightened reflexive awareness' (Jago 2002, p.743). Within the turmoil of depression, people have an opportunity to become aware that they are not functioning well, and that their sense of self may be distorted. This process of gaining personal insight has been called 'cluing in' (Schreiber 1996, p.484). Talking therapies were considered by participants to be the most helpful approach to gaining insights into dysfunctional selves, and these therapies are discussed in detail in Chapter 8.

BECOMING AWARE THAT DISTORTED THINKING IS NOT A TRUE REFLECTION OF SELF

As discussed previously, it is easy for people to equate the self with the distorted thinking and difficult feelings that can lead to and become a hellish reality in depression. So if they feel bad and guilty, it is because they are bad and guilty. Consistent with the mindfulness approach to depression (see Chapter 6), some people were learning to see their difficult thoughts and feelings as mental events that pass, rather than getting drawn into stories that attack the self. For Jenny, separating distorted messages out from the reality of how she understood herself involved standing back and seeing her difficult thoughts as 'clouds passing by', rather than true reflections of herself. This allowed her to better deal with her fears:

> I also learned to see my thoughts as like clouds that were just passing by, and perhaps to not get involved in them, and let them float by. They are just thoughts, they're just my way of seeing things, they're not necessarily the real way. Just let it go… Just float past, rather than getting tied up in them. And that

has helped, socially. But it has also helped with the other fear that I have, and that's that the depression will come back... I still think about depression most days, it's still there in my thoughts. But I – I'm more able now to – to see that I do have moods, perhaps slightly more than other people. But because there's a dip that doesn't mean the depression is going to come back. And I'm able just to go, go with it, and through experience I know that I do come out the other side. (Jenny)

BECOMING AWARE OF AN 'AUTHENTICALLY' FELT SELF

The idea that there can be a subjectively experienced 'truer self' – i.e. involving feelings that seem authentic – has been mentioned throughout this book. A number of participant narratives discussed the discovery of authentic feelings and self as central to their recovery. While some researchers talk about '(re)finding an authentic sense of self' in depression (Stevenson and Knudsen 2008), the present study suggests that the task may well be about finding a yet to be discovered self. The thing about people establishing a distorted or false self to get by in life (as discussed in Chapters 2 and 3) is that this self does not feel particularly authentic. And lack of connection to authentic feeling makes it harder for people to function well. There was much talk among people who suffer from depression about living out false selves to get by in life and pass as normal. Here, the highly disruptive experience of depression can be viewed as creating a space for people to re-evaluate their lives, understand themselves better, and work out what is most important. For those who chose to embark on this longer-term recovery project, the repeated story told was about needing to work on the self in order to 'know yourself', 'be yourself' and live life more authentically. There was acknowledgement here that living more authentically and outside other people's agendas means giving up pleasing other people: 'You can only be yourself, doing what you have to do... If other people don't like it, that's too bad.'

I create room to be authentic. It's not that it means life is easy because there are times when, you know, in the space I create to be authentic I generate stuff that really pisses me off. But I'd rather have that and be with that... I'm aware that I'm responsible now for creating more discord around me at times... And there's a part of me that's sort of amused and there's a part of me that's well 'fuck you', you know, which was never my way of being, I used to be Mr Calm, Mr Everything's Fine. (Derek)

Consistent with feelings of authenticity, what people were saying was that it was important to accept who they were – warts and all – rather than trying to force change on themselves.

> I see myself as this is me, take it or leave it, warts and all. I'm not going to be someone for somebody else, it's not a case of right…being defined in terms of 'I will be what you want me to be'. It's 'I am me, this is me, and you know, you accept me or take me, or leave me and this is the person that you get…' I'm actually finding a more positive response from that than the one where I used to be attempting to conform to satisfy what I thought people wanted, and they were never happy, regardless of what changes you made…the solution is just be yourself. (Andrew)

There was even a sense of militant defiance in some narratives on the topic of authenticity. One man said 'You've got to be yourself…if you are gay, if you are an argumentative person, no matter what you are, if you are a bit of…a snob, just be it. And sod anybody and everybody…else!'

The thing about feeling authentic is that it is not just any narrative turn. Instead, this group of people were saying that finding out about who you are, being yourself and living authentically was critical to reinvigorating life post-depression, and developing a more functional self. Towards this end, some people advised others with depression to better accept their depression and disclose their depression, at least to trusted others, as a way to begin to live more authentically.

> And depression, albeit it is still stigmatised I think…is less stigmatised among young people than it was… You should tell someone now, it doesn't have to be the doctor or a therapist, it can be a friend you know. The older I've got, the more I've found that it's acceptable to say to people, 'I'm depressed at the moment', and they know what it means. (Craig)

BECOMING AWARE OF THE POTENTIAL FOR A NEW SELF

If there is an authentically felt self beyond depression, then it was also constructed as a self that might need discovering. This insight about there being a mysterious but truer self that lay beyond depression was particularly associated with the kind of awareness associated with talking therapies. Veronica was clear that her new, more authentic self was more robust than her old self. As taken up in detail in the following chapters, Veronica (like others) had assembled a range of recovery tools including talking therapy, medication, prayer and getting back into the workforce via voluntary work. Following five years of debilitating depression, Veronica was clear that her 'new' self was more authentic and functional than the old one, despite continuing to take antidepressants:

> To me I still get a kick out of, you know, I've been doing this job now for over five years… I represent people at tribunals. I've represented people in court a couple of times. And, you know, if you had said to me ten years ago that this is what you will be doing…I would have just said you are out of your tree… The old me as I think of it, the person pre this big breakdown, could never have done that. And if I hadn't have had a big breakdown and got to see a good doctor…got on the right medication…I would have carried on as I was, living the anxious life. Whereas I've got it sorted now. You know, I mean I have anxiety but I have what I'd call normal anxiety. And if something gives me a kick, I bounce back fairly quickly. I'm not crippled by it for weeks, you know. (Veronica)

One woman, Rosey, who was midway through a course of therapy, began to realise that she was on the verge of discovering a new, more robust self. However, by moving away from a life of dysthymia (i.e. low-level chronic depression) and recurrent episodes of depression to find this new self, Rosey was aware that she was giving up something, and moving into uncharted territory:

> When I started therapy I just wanted everything to go away. I wanted the despair to stop, but I didn't see anything beyond that. Then probably about halfway through I thought well, I just want to be able to cope with life and not want to kill myself. And now I'm probably at a point where I want to understand more about myself and actually start getting more out of life, actually start enjoying life, rather than spending all my energy on fighting depression or being depressed… But it's scary, if you're used to living in a very constrained band in your life, then the actual idea that you can take charge of your life…that's really scary… To actually live life without worrying every minute about what's going to happen next, about what people think of me, about what, am I doing a good enough job, you know, to actually take life as it is, and to take knocks on the chin, and you know, dust myself off, and not worry about it, it's just a completely different way of living. (Rosey)

REWRITING THE DEPRESSION EXPERIENCE INTO THE SELF

Once people start to challenge the idea that they are the same thing as their depression – or the self they constructed to survive – another task is for the person to find a way to 'rewrite the experience of depression into the self' more constructively. What is meant here is that people can find a way to better accept depression and integrate their depression. Here, people narrate the depression as a particular experience of the self (i.e. as a part of the self), but not the same thing as the self. In practice, people have to find their own way to do this, and there were many different descriptions given. I have already talked about how people came to accept that they would have future episodes of depression, and recover, and that this could assist people to manage their depression. Rewriting depression as a temporary, rather than apparently endless experience was helpful to a number of people. Other people, for example, tried to rewrite depression into their lives as ultimately beneficial, rather than damaging to the self:

> I definitely learned a lot from it [depression]. I think, I think it was almost like, what's, what's the thing when, you know, like a fuse going, like a fuse going when, when there's overload or whatever. It's like a fuse going, it's for a reason, it's like you're body is telling you, stop, hang on, maybe you need to go, turn around, go in another direction. (Jill)

> It's not helpful to think of it [depression] as an enemy. And it's not helpful for me to think badly of myself because I'm depressed. It seems to me it's OK, in the sense, I am OK, not the whole of me is depressed, [only] a part of me. This depression is a manifestation of a malaise, of a need to become more whole... It's [depression] rather like having a dream which is telling me something. I take no notice, so it recurs and recurs until I do. (Elizabeth)

Still others were able to rewrite their depression as a useful spiritual journey that they needed to undergo to become the person they are today, and this narrative is taken up in more detail in Chapter 6.

Taking greater responsibility for recovery

The narratives showed that wrestling with the issue of 'taking personal responsibility' in depression and recovery was fraught with difficulties. Contributing to the anxiety and depression cycle, people can take on too much responsibility in their lives, and a number of people like Lee and Rosey linked taking on too much responsibility with depression:

> When I was eight my father died ... He was dying of cancer so it was obvious to me. Although nobody told me he was dying, I knew he was dying, so it wasn't a surprise to me. And then I felt that I had to be very responsible, I had to be very brave, very strong. I was the only child and I think half of me was trying to be mummy's little man. (Lee)

> I think for me it's about blaming myself for most things, thinking that I'm a bad person, and I can expend huge amounts of energy on the mental processes that go into making me responsible for everything that goes wrong in the

world. And that's really very tiring, but I'm really very good at it. I can be responsible for things when I wasn't even in the room...in the building! (Rosey)

Certainly being able to let go of 'over responsibility' was important in some people's recoveries.

And the way she [the counsellor] put it made me think, 'Oh, perhaps I wasn't as much at fault, perhaps only partly, perhaps somebody else had a...was responsible for part, at least part of this situation.' And that was tremendous, it really was. I mean, and this, when did I last see her, possibly a year ago and I've not gone backwards. Yes, she really has resolved one or two issues with me. (Marie)

It was also inappropriate for people to try to assume responsibility for recovery while very depressed, when their thought processes were not functioning well enough. Certainly, given the nature of depression, it is easy for the issue of responsibility in recovery to translate into feelings of self-blame and guilt.

Nevertheless, while people can take on unhelpful responsibilities in depression, people also talked about helpful responsibilities that they found empowering. Taking on responsibilities for long-term recovery in a manner that is kind to the self was discussed, particularly by those with a lifetime of experience of the depression/recovery cycle. This subset of people was convinced that it was ultimately the responsibility of the person with depression to find their own path to recovery. Nevertheless, working out exactly *what* to take responsibility for was a challenge, even for those with considerable experience.

You make your own luck, you are responsible for your own beliefs and feelings, like the cognitive behavioural stuff, I've done that, and that's very good. And it does work; you have to be brutally hard with yourself, though. It is difficult... Because I want to blame [my workplace] for the fact that I'm out of work now, and to a certain extent, yes I can blame them. But then I think, well, okay Sophia, perhaps it wasn't the right place for [me]... (Sophia)

The notion of taking responsibility for depression is worth highlighting here because it represents a possible shift in the role of professionals, who are relegated to the status of 'allies' in recovery, as taken up in more detail in Chapter 7. From this perspective, only the person with depression can be the expert on themselves, and professionals can only provide help along the way. 'Responsibility' used in this way is consistent with a narrative approach to mental health: The only person who can be an expert in the interior life of an individual, and tell a personal story, is the person in question. In the end, it is the person who wants to develop a longer-term recovery story who has to retrieve meaning to develop a more life-giving story about themselves. A number of people stated the case in a 'tough love' sort of fashion:

> I guess at the end of the day that you have got total responsibility here and it's up to you. No one else is going to fix this for you. No one else is going to get you out of that prison. Only you can do it. (Julie)

> It is a case of not allowing yourself to forget that you can do something for yourself. You can get yourself out of it. In fact the only person who can get yourself out of it is yourself, and no one else. It doesn't mean to say other people can't help you. (Pamela)

Patient expertise

People who wanted to take greater responsibility for their own recovery were also clear that they had developed expertise in self-managing their depression. Patient expertise meant different things to participants, including doing library-based or Internet-based research, challenging the care they were getting, adopting appropriate tools to manage depression, and taking greater control of their depression management.

> I went to a GP not long ago and he said, 'Have you thought if you need sleeping tablets or do you need…' And I thought 'Well no I don't'… I had to be really sort of firm with him and say 'Well actually, I've been off medication for nearly two years…' [sigh] The thing is I suppose it's about the control as well, being in control of your own… I mean [sigh], bless them… I do bless them. But at the end of the day…you've got a ten-minute slot and God knows how many patients a day. Another patient, this one's got depression. Right OK. What's going to help? Let's give them some medication, whatever… But you can't stay on medication forever. And it does serve a purpose. It is helpful. It can get you through like a really rough period but it doesn't enable you to actually address what's going on, and to self-manage your illness. (Julie)

Professionals who were highly valued by patients gently encouraged them in the project of becoming more expert and responsible in their own depression management.

> I happened to have an extremely good GP in the 1980s, who, when I went to consult her, because I was going…spiralling down again, said to me 'You don't have to come to me to ask permission to start medication again, you know.' And in a way that was a turning point. I mean I must have been in my 30s then.

> Because she could give me the responsibility... By this time in my 30s I was actually managing my own medication. (Pamela)

The word 'gently' is used as a reminder that it is important to encourage responsibilities that are commensurate with where patients are currently.

> I think being your own expert is learning as much as you can about depression... Get some good counselling, there are lots of good counsellors available... But looking back when I was profoundly depressed I wouldn't have asked [for counselling]. Why? Because [whispers] 'I don't deserve it'... Because of the hopelessness and the helplessness and the lack of confidence and low self-esteem, the pit... (Pamela)

> And you need to take help from wherever you can get it but equally it's... Really, the bottom line is the person who's got it is the best person to overcome it. The only person to overcome it... They are the experts... Yes, but... The trouble is they are not in a position to feel that when they're so deeply depressed... (John)

Living life as a challenge

The narratives suggested that regardless of the success of people's long-term recovery, life does not cease to be a challenge, and life will always be uncertain. Part of that challenge is that all people suffer from time to time, regardless of whether or not they have depression. People prone to depression continue to fear uncertainty and future episodes, and so it can be surprisingly helpful to make a clear distinction between everyday suffering (i.e. bad days) and actual episodes of depression. The task for professionals here involves inspiring realistic hope in difficult circumstances (Repper and Perkins 2003), including by helping patients to:

- know that you as a professional have faith and hope in them
- consider 'everyday' suffering as not necessarily the same thing as depression
- accept they will have bad days, because suffering happens to all people sometimes
- accept failures and going backwards as part of learning and recovery
- better accept that life is always going to be uncertain, while promoting hope rather than despair.

These kinds of clarifications can be surprisingly helpful for patients in managing depression and the anxieties that living with depression entails.

I did have a bad time last week, but hey join the human race. Things looked black. Autumn is drawing on. It was a particularly foul week here last week, and one or two other things had upset me, but everybody has that. There are good weeks and bad weeks. This is going to be a good one. Last week was a bad one. (Carl)

And it's also about acknowledging that it isn't, they are not all down days. You know, in fact when you look at it in a wider picture the majority of time you are OK. It's just that when you do get down…it does affect you. But it's knowing that you've been through it before. You've got out of it and you can do it again. (Julie)

Conclusion

Being an ally in patient recovery involves professionals recognising that they themselves and patients can adopt a 'recovery attitude' at every point in the depression–recovery spectrum. Between episodes, patients can be encouraged to have 'stay well plans'. Patients can learn to notice the warning signs that a depression is imminent, and begin to do something about it (e.g. talk to others, see a professional, rest, start or increase medication). With experience, patients can also begin to notice the patterns of depression, such as the cyclical nature of depression. Some patients find that greater acceptance of depression cycles can make depression more manageable.

A distinction was made in this chapter between short-term and longer-term recovery from depression. While short-term recovery could be dramatic, and involve key 'turning point' moments in personal narratives when depression lifts, there were also narratives about the partial and unsatisfactory nature of short-term recoveries. Here, many people also talked about having longer-term recovery strategies. In these longer-term strategies, people were often interested in building more robust and authentically felt selves, rather than necessarily returning to how they were before depression. Various strategies were used in longer-term recoveries (e.g. finding useful treatments; adopting a more hopeful language of recovery; finding professional allies to support recovery; becoming more aware of the dysfunctional self and what needed to be done to develop a more viable self). If professionals can better understand the kinds of tasks involved in recovery, then they can find opportunities to better support recoveries all the way along the depression–recovery spectrum. We now turn to a discussion of some of the key medical and non-medical tools available to patients that may assist them to tell stories of recovery from depression.

Chapter 5

Medical Tools

As already highlighted, patient interiority, self-management and telling better narratives about the self are key issues in recovery from depression. Thus, professionals and the treatments they offer are allies and recovery tools respectively. The main medical tools available to professionals and patients to tackle depression are Selective Serotonin Reuptake Inhibitor (SSRI) antidepressants, electroconvulsive therapy (ECT) and hospitalisation, all of which are discussed in turn in this chapter. I will first contextualise SSRIs historically and in terms of recent controversies. Patient SSRI decision-making, effectiveness, changing medication, side-effects, length of time on medication and withdrawal will then be covered. The discussion of ECT will particularly focus on how professional and patient narratives are similar and divergent. Finally, the brief section on hospitalisation will flag patient fears and the potential benefits and difficulties with hospitalisation.

SSRI antidepressants

The most widely used antidepressant medications used today are SSRIs. Older antidepressants which include tricyclic antidepressants (TCAs) and monoamine oxidase inhibitors (MAOIs) are still in use. But these older antidepressants are not the first line of treatment for depression because their toxicity and side-effects are more severe than the SSRIs. In more recent years even newer classes of drugs have come into use including 'SNRIs' (Serotonin and Noradrenaline Reuptake Inhibitors) and 'NARIs' (Noradrenaline Reuptake Inhibitors); their effects are similar to SSRIs. SSRIs are still the most popular antidepressants and will be the focus of discussion in this chapter. Additionally, please note that all the interviews for this book were completed by mid-2004. And so, while the commentary takes into account new developments up until 2008, patients themselves do not discuss developments beyond 2004.

In the UK the National Institute for Clinical Excellence (NICE) guidance is to prescribe SSRI antidepressants in routine care for moderate to severe depression (National Collaborating Centre for Mental Health 2004). NICE does not recommend an antidepressant as a first-line treatment for mild depression (unless the person has a history of moderate to severe depression) because the benefit is too slight to be of value. Introduced in 1987, fluoxetine (Prozac) was the first of this new class of SSRI antidepressants. Prozac received enormous media publicity and became somewhat of a Western cultural phenomenon (Moore 2007). As some people in our study acknowledged, Prozac helped to shift the treatment of depression from the realm of the feared and publicly shunned into the arena of the fashionable.

> And I think I see it wasn't one of those nasty early depressants or heavy ones like…it's quite fashionable. Prozac is quite a fashionable antidepressant. And it was OK to say you were on Prozac. It's like a happy pill isn't it? I'm OK I'm taking Prozac. And then of course I knew quite a few people who were taking it as well, so it was like 'OK like join the club.' So it wasn't… I didn't feel too bad on that. (Julie)

But, alas, new drugs have a marketing life cycle that runs from optimism about the benefits to a gradual realisation of their limitations, and Prozac is no different here. After first being touted as a wonder drug in the way it could lift people out of depression, it eventually became clear that there were some limitations in the stories about Prozac recoveries (Metzl 2001). Prozac narratives subsequently became more complex, and soon included media stories of mediocrity, numbing and, even more sensationally, Prozac was linked to stories of suicide and violence among patients (Moore 2007).

A recent review of the evidence in *The Lancet* suggested that while media stories linking SSRIs to suicidality and dependency meant that the public are now more sceptical about antidepressants, the efficacy and ease of use of SSRIs have been quite difficult to dispute (Ebmeier *et al.* 2006). Nevertheless, some experts do dispute SSRI efficacy. When it comes to interpreting meta-analyses of clinical trials (a scientific method for summarising previous studies by examining and collating results) that compares placebos to SSRIs, the science turns out to be a controversial area. An editorial in *The Lancet* in 2004 bemoaned the way that selective reporting of favourable randomised controlled trial (RCT) research in the literature (and the way unfavourable research tends to not see the light of day in scientific journals) manipulates the available evidence base in the interests of those who benefit financially from SSRIs (Editorial 2004). By studying a full range of studies (including unpublished studies held by drug companies), one group of researchers caused a sensation in early 2008 when they concluded that SSRIs 'compared with placebo...do not produce clinically significant improvements in depression in patients who initially have moderate or even very severe depression' (Kirsch *et al.* 2008, p.268). In an earlier study, the same research group found a significant difference between placebo and certain SSRI antidepressants, but the difference was relatively small (Kirsch *et al.* 2002). In both studies, the researchers obtained and analysed information about all RCTs reported to the US Food and Drug Administration (FDA) for approval of widely used antidepressants. Use of FDA data to assess efficacy can overcome the problem of selective reporting of trials in medical journals since the FDA requires all relevant trials to be reported.

In the area of antidepressant use in childhood, when unpublished data are added to the published evidence base, suddenly the benefit–harm profile of SSRIs shifts from favourable to unfavourable, except apparently for Prozac (fluoxetine) (Whittington *et al.* 2004).

In the grey area of clinical trials and antidepressant efficacy, qualitative patient experience data help to fill out our understanding of antidepressants. From the patient perspective, one thing that clinical trials are not designed to investigate is the wide disparity in experience of SSRIs. The patient experience in the present study is of very wide variation in the experiences of antidepressants (see discussion on effectiveness below).

Patient decision-making

Patients bring a wide range of beliefs about medical treatment, and treatment of mental illness in particular, into their decisions about whether to use SSRIs or not. Not surprisingly, the meanings they attribute to using SSRIs play a role in the way they approach medication. As a very capable career woman, Anne initially felt that she should be able to deal with depression without medication:

> I was referred to bereavement counselling and it was suggested that I take antidepressants, which I resisted for a while because I thought, I'm better than this, I can do this, I can beat this. You know... I've got everything that I wanted in respect of a child. In the respect that my Mum had just died, no, of course I hadn't got everything that I wanted. But, so I...I was offered antidepressants and I said 'no'. (Anne)

Other people resisted antidepressants (or just used them briefly) because they feared toxic or addictive effects:

I've been prescribed it [antidepressants] in the past but I've always felt reluctant and apprehensive about taking it, largely because a) I feel that the effects are probably short term, they're not going to actually resolve the depression, b) because they do have side-effects and c) I didn't feel comfortable, myself, with taking some tablets... There was one particular tablet I was prescribed, it wasn't Prozac, but it was something that was on a lower scale which I started the course... But I only took them for a few days and I feel that, looking back now, that I didn't actually take them for long enough, anyway, to have any authority to say whether they would have helped me or not. (Shiad)

So some patient beliefs about SSRIs could work against people giving antidepressants a fair hearing. Fears about SSRIs could be based on media stories or sources other than clinical trial evidence and balanced narratives about patients taking SSRIs. Even though Richard knew others who were happily taking Prozac, media stories of suicide and violence associated with the drug played a key part in his decision-making:

Richard: Prozac is a killer and I regard the company [who makes it] as being an unprincipled killing machine. Although I know a number of people who are on Prozac, and you know, perfectly you know, happy and so on. But it's killed a lot of... Prozac has killed a lot of people and I'm very lucky to be alive because I was given, I was prescribed Prozac at one time, I wasn't warned it could... There was a danger of becoming suicidal and homicidal with Prozac but it's true... It should never be given without a warning I don't believe.

Interviewer: You felt suicidal or homicidal?

Richard: No, it didn't have that effect, I just stopped taking it, it was the first anti-depressant I'd ever taken, and I just didn't like the idea. I quickly decided I wouldn't, wouldn't receive it.

Sometimes patients like Jane were fearful of the new antidepressants based on family experiences with older-style antidepressants. Other patients like Sasha had a fear of antidepressants that developed from non-medication-based treatments.

I saw in my father... Because my father was made into a vegetable through the old antidepressant drugs that they used to have. I mean they are very rare now, but he was made into a vegetable to the point where he wasn't capable in doing anything. And in the end, it was only through two of my sisters and myself, we just took the tablets and threw them all down the toilet and went to the doctor and said, 'Look, this is our father and we are not having anymore.' And you know, my Dad now lives on his own and has got, you know, everything back together again. OK, he's on one or two drugs, but not...he's not in that vegetable state. (Jane)

I went to the doctor and I, I expected some miracle cure and...but...so she put me on some tablets and I don't know what they were, but she said to me, 'see a counsellor as well'. And because I was scared going on the tablets, I took the tablets for a little while...but she never explained to me that, she said, 'they're not addictive anyway'. But I was still scared...but they're not addictive and they weren't that strong, but they did make me feel more confident. I could walk up the street with a smile on my face, yeah, they did help...but my grandmother had electro-therapy. And because of all that, that's what I was scared of, and I don't know if you can understand that... I was frightened, that's why I won't take tablets... (Sasha)

Reasons for not taking antidepressants could also be based around beliefs in the causality of depression. A number of people resisted taking antidepressants because they wanted to find a way of tackling their depression that got to the 'root' of the problem, rather than use something that appeared to address only the symptoms. Lee and Patrick both wanted to tackle the underlying causes. Both expressed some pride because they grappled with their serious personal problems and made progress without taking tablets.

I saw a locum and as I said the word depression...he grabbed...he reached for a pad and started writing out a prescription for an antidepressant and explained to me that that's what I needed. And I said, 'No, I need counselling.' And I left without a prescription. And he was, I think pretty pissed off with me that I hadn't taken the prescription. But I knew I didn't want a drug treatment, I wanted to sort out what the... I needed to sort out what the problem was. I'm not anti-drugs if people really need them... And he didn't want to know anything, he didn't even ask me what I was depressed about... (Lee)

I even came through the suicidal period without antidepressants. I just didn't want to. As I used to say to my GP, 'I don't want to cover up the symptoms, I want to get to the root of it.' And getting to the root of it for me was going to counselling and going to support groups... All the progress that I've made has actually been made while I was off the drugs, and it was all self... Sort of done by myself, really. (Patrick)

Not all participants were immediately concerned about tackling 'root causes'. An alternative construction that motivated some patients was that people should avail themselves of anything – including antidepressants – that could potentially lift them out of depression. From this perspective, life was short, and life was passing by when people endured depression unnecessarily. Here, being lifted out of depression, using any reasonable means available, was the key issue.

I don't think there's anything morally wrong with taking antidepressants, they just didn't work for me. I think if you're depressed then…you know, you really should feel able to try anything that might help you get out of it, I suppose… And so that doesn't just apply to prescribed drugs, it also applies to proscribed or illegal drugs, I think. I'm not suggesting that the people should do that by any means, but I'm just saying that in my experience I just like experimenting… My attitude to the depression was that I'm only going to be able to progress beyond it if I keep trying new things. (Paul)

I got referred to the psychiatrist. And the guy said, think about it, but I think it would help you to go on antidepressants. So I looked it up, and discussed it with some friends who were on them, and they described their experiences… And I thought…I could just see the rest of my life going ahead of me… And I thought if there is something there that might help, even though it is not in my nature to take tablets, I just thought I'm going to do it… (Heather)

There were also some mixed narratives about treating both symptoms and root causes. Since antidepressants treated symptoms, many believed, and for some it was also their experience, that SSRIs were best used together with something that could tackle the root of the problem, such as some kind of talking therapy.

The antidepressants are not supposed to be the answer… It's supposed to be in conjunction with therapy. It's more effective in conjunction with therapy than each one on its own. (Heather)

And I was very depressed last year and so I was on a very high dosage of medication, certainly a very high amount of antidepressant at one point. And I'd been able to come off the medication much more quickly and not suffer bad side-effects. And I'm sure that's because I'd been in this therapy at the same time. (Ruth)

Effectiveness

One problem with antidepressants is the time lapse between taking SSRIs and feeling better. It could take weeks or months for patients to feel any different. And this delay could be considerably longer if the first medication used had to be adjusted or changed because it was not initially effective, or its side-effects were intolerable. All the while, as Veronica points out, patients could be suffering considerably.

It takes four to six weeks to get into your system so the time is still passing. You know, you're still in this day-to-day hell waiting for…maybe this tablet will help. And then if it's not brilliant it was, you know, waiting to see her [doctor] again three months later. Tweak the dosage. Let's see you again in three months. You know, so time is just going by and you are suffering terribly. (Veronica)

At one end of the spectrum the effects of SSRIs were interpreted as very effective. Even though people usually had to wait many weeks for their SSRIs to be effective, one woman described antidepressants as having an 'amazing lifting power'. Other people talked about gaining a sense of wellbeing and, as discussed previously, still others described antidepressants vividly and as somehow miraculous in their effects.

> But I still…I was still waiting for this feeling of happiness I suppose to come in, and it didn't. And then one morning, and it was exactly seven weeks to the day that I took, you know, the first tablet. I woke up that morning and I just knew that inside myself that I felt different… It was this lifting… And, and physically more well. And, and happy again. You know, I think I began to laugh out loud again and, and that it was from inside, it wasn't just a sort of superficial laugh, it was a sort of deep inside laughing. (Liza)

At the other end of the spectrum, unwanted side-effects and lack of any discernible effect – or an effect that is difficult to distinguish from other treatments – was the experience of others, like Paul and Anne:

> …a lot of the professional interventions didn't help me, antidepressants didn't. I'm always in two minds about whether to say…give my opinion that I don't think antidepressants should be called that at all, because they don't really do very much against depression. They're more anti-anxiety, or sedating or something, possibly… Because you know, we don't know what causes the placebo response, which is nearly as strong as the response to antidepressants. (Paul)

> I think, looking back now, I probably did need antidepressants, but as to whether they worked or not, I'm probably not the best person to say. The doctors would probably say they worked slightly, or the ECT worked slightly. (Anne)

In addition, even if antidepressants were effective, some did not like the way they *felt* on antidepressants:

> I was remarkably angry, distressed, frustrated. I was very angry with the therapist for being off sick. And I thought, no, I'm not feeling anything. I thought these tablets (Lustral) are stopping me feeling things, I'm just being passive. And I'm not coping. So I thought, no, I'm going to stop taking them… (Rosey)

And even if patients judged antidepressants to be of value, their effects were not always long-lived. An antidepressant glimpse of wellbeing could just as easily be lost as it was found. This fleeting glimpse of wellbeing and robustness could be heartbreaking for patients, as Veronica explained:

> When they [Prozac] kicked in, I had two days where I was fantastic. I could have taken over in Number 10… I just had such a sense of empowerment and of thinking for the first time 'I'm a bright lady and I'm capable. I've got common sense. I've got lots of skills. I could get out there and do…' And, you know, I felt fantastic. And I thought this is…this is really how life should be. You know, I mean I wasn't manic… It was kind of a really realistic picture and I thought wow. This is fantastic. And it lasted for two days, and then I slid back down again… I had a glimpse of what life could be, and I was so heartbroken that it didn't last, you know… (Veronica)

Changing drugs

If an antidepressant did not work people found that many times the adjusting or changing of medication with the help of their health professional could make all the difference. While one type of antidepressant might not work or might have intolerable side-effects, another antidepressant might work very well. Even if patients have taken many types of antidepressants in the past with mixed results, it can still be possible to find an antidepressant with superior results. So from a patient perspective it can be worth searching for the right medication and dose.

> I've had so many different antidepressants over the years that this [Prozac] is definitely the one that makes me feel calm all day. And I don't feel docile like I used to. I used to get zombified sometimes, but I don't on these. (Sue)

> I took many different types of antidepressants before I found one that worked, and I also took lithium as well. So I guess the message is if it doesn't work initially, then maybe some other drug will work. (Jenny)

While Patricia also had a long history of taking antidepressants and failing, she found that Efexor (venlafaxine) was the best antidepressant for her. Subjectively, she could feel authentically herself (rather than unreal as she had felt on other medication) and the drug had fewer side-effects than other drugs she had tried:

> …it [Efexor] is probably the best drug I've ever taken… Because I don't feel like I'm out of control. I don't feel like I'm not being myself. I feel…[sighs] I suppose I feel a little bit more secure in myself. A little bit more in control of myself… I'm in more of a routine with it. So, you know, my sleeping patterns

are a lot better, than what they were. I did get ill on it. I've never really been physically sick, but most antidepressants I've taken have made me feel queasy for a couple of weeks. Efexor was a bit different. I felt sort of queasy a lot less... (Patricia)

Some patients said they appreciated doctors giving them choices and involving them in the decision-making around their antidepressant treatment:

And then what my doctor does, which is really good is, he will explain to me what they are, which ones are similar, the side-effects and sort of which one do you fancy trying. So, I tried one, I don't remember what it was, and that was no good, so I tried this other one and it was fine. Does the job and doesn't make me want to go to sleep all the time. And it was a more modern one. (Marie)

Side-effects

As previously discussed, the subjective qualities patients associate with medication are very important to them. If patients do not like the feelings they have while taking an SSRI (e.g. feeling numbed or unreal), then they may be disinclined to continue with it.

In the past, I've taken myself off medication, because of side-effects, because of the way I felt. All sorts of reasons. I've just thought, right OK after three months I'll take myself off. Six months later I'm back in the doctor's again and I'm on a different one. Three months later, four months later I've come off it again, and I've gone back to see my GP and I'm like, 'No, I'm not having this because of this, because of that.' So they've had to keep changing my drugs because I refused to be on something that makes me feel indifferent. (Patricia)

Equally, side-effects play an important role in SSRI acceptability to patients. While SSRIs are noted for having fewer and less severe side-effects than older-style antidepressants, side-effects do occur. From a patient perspective the side-effects of SSRIs range from barely perceptible to unacceptable. Many people said that side-effects are more noticeable at the start of medication, and then reduce or even disappear completely over time. People are more inclined to put up with side-effects (e.g. nausea, insomnia, dizziness, weight gain or loss, fatigue, dry mouth, headaches, sexual dysfunction) if the improvement in personal wellbeing is more meaningful than the side-effects. However, even when effective, the side-effects in some instances could be so severe that people felt they had to stop taking the medicine. For instance, Nicola believes that Seroxat (paroxetine) was the cause of a specific kind of suicidal thinking that did indeed result in a serious suicide attempt with injury requiring surgical repair. Nicola based this belief on her experience that the suicidal ideas, images and compulsion she experienced on Seroxat were unlike any other experiences of suicidal thinking she had ever had before.

> When I was little I used to imagine creeping out of the house at night and going on the nearby railway tracks, and that was…that was in a way a comfort for me, because, you know, sometimes I would feel like my life was completely out of my control, and I didn't have any options. But then I would always think I did have another option, I could take my life into my own hands… And then I could imagine how people would feel if I did kill myself. And you know, it would remind me that people did love me… I had certainly never thought of cutting myself, but while I was on Seroxat, I did start to get sudden images in my head of, you know, cutting long gashes in myself, and just…just seeing the blood running everywhere. And, you know, the feeling of compulsion to do it. You know, feeling a need to see that, and I did used to get images arriving in my head of lying in a blood-filled bath or jumping into a river or off a tall building. And those images would just sit in my head for a long time until they just melted away, and…sometimes they left me feeling a bit disturbed, but usually they didn't cause any emotions in me… It was like I was feeling…like my personality had been withdrawn and my rational mind had been overwhelmed… (Nicola)

While all kinds of antidepressants can increase the risk of suicide *early* on in treatment (presumably because motivation can increase with treatment despite other symptoms of depression continuing), the link between suicidal behaviour and SSRIs is controversial. At one end of the debate, experts say there is no increased risk of suicidal behaviour with SSRIs compared with other antidepressants (Ebmeier *et al.* 2006). In the other camp, experts believe that there is double the risk of suicide attempts with SSRIs compared to placebo or non-tricyclic antidepressant therapies (Fergusson *et al.* 2005). There is also some evidence from this camp that aggression and violence is possible in a small number of susceptible patients on SSRIs (Healy, Herxheimer and Menkes 2006). The differences between the two camps at least partly appear to be in the way that experts choose to interpret research. Suicides are difficult to examine in clinical trials because suicide is thankfully a relatively uncommon event, and so it is hard to get enough statistical power to study the issue adequately (Gunnell, Saperia and Ashby 2005). Additionally, any suicide risk posed by SSRI use needs to be weighed up against the effectiveness of SSRIs for reducing misery and non-suicide risks of death from depression.[1] For instance, from the early 2000s there were particular concerns about prescribing antidepressants to young people. The US Food and Drug Administration directed pharmaceutical companies to include warning labels about the risks, and in 2003 the UK Committee on Safety in Medicines 'prohibited the treatment of childhood depression with any SSRI except fluoxetine (Prozac)' (Editorial 2004, p.1335). Alternatively, a more recent study in the US found no link between higher suicide rates for young people (aged 15–19) and prescriptions of antidepressants (Markowitz and Cuellar 2007). On the other hand, the study did find a link between use of newer antidepressants and *lower* numbers of suicides in this age group.

It is in the area of unusual side-effects from medication where some patients have been able to sort out the professionals who do and do not listen to them. At the time of the study, while many professionals were denying that certain SSRIs could cause strange side-effects and withdrawal symptoms, the picture was very much clearer to the vast numbers of patients who had to live with the symptoms (Medawar *et al.* 2002).

> I also remember, I remember the sort of the side-effects [of Seroxat] I didn't like. Sometimes I'd hallucinate... I'd...I was very, very, I was very, very afraid. Sometimes I would be lying in bed and I'd close my eyes and I would be completely awake and just these images would just flash in my, in my, you know...sort of into my eyes, basically... I said [to the doctor], 'You know, I've been on Seroxat', and I said, 'I didn't like the side-effects'. And when I told him the side-effects, yet again I had this disbelief and he basically stated that, you know, all side-effects of Seroxat are gastro. And I'm like, 'Well, this is what I experienced.'... I'm just thinking, 'My God, you know, they don't believe me but that's what I felt.' And then, well, when *Panorama* came on and they had this thing about Seroxat, I was, like, 'My God, you know, that's exactly what I experienced.' And the doctors were just like... It was almost like there was this conspiracy of denial against, you know, this drug. (Anne)

Length of time on antidepressants

The NICE guidance in the UK is that for a moderate to severe depressive episode, antidepressants should be continued for at least six months after the patient has recovered (National Collaborating Centre for Mental Health

---

1   Although the mechanisms are not well understood, depression is associated with an increased risk of death from causes other than suicide. Some authors speculate that behaviours, medical problems and effects associated with depression may interact to undermine biological integrity (Schulz, Drayer and Rollman 2002).

2004). Where patients have had two or more episodes of depression close together, and where they experience significant impairments in function during depression, the advice is to continue antidepressants for two years. However, from a patient perspective, coming off antidepressants can be a very frightening prospect.

> I think you mustn't underestimate the sheer psychological effect of saying I am now coming off antidepressants. It panics you… Yeah you're terrified of what is going to happen now. If you said to me okay, stop taking Prozac tomorrow, I wouldn't be able to. That's not about being addicted, probably you know. If I am clinically dependent on it, so what? But yeah, you're scared. It's really scary when somebody says, 'Okay we're going to stop taking these now.' I mean I'm about to change doctor because I've moved, and I'm really shitting myself that he's going to say, 'Okay, so why are you still taking these?' (Matthew)

Patients thus need to be consulted about their views on coming off antidepressants. Although not outlined by NICE guidance in the UK or backed up by clinical research, in patient narratives where antidepressants were imagined to replace missing chemicals in the brain, patients and health practitioners may be inclined to see antidepressant medication as much longer term or even life-long. For Veronica, who suffered from multiple, severe and prolonged depression lasting years, her psychiatrist validated her own feeling about the nature of her depression. She felt fortunate that her psychiatrist gave her permission to remain on medication indefinitely:

> …my consultant [psychiatrist] had said 'Do you realise you've got a chemical imbalance, and you've probably had it all your life'? And that was just like 'Oh thank you God that somebody official is saying what I've always known, but thought I must be wrong about.' You know, that there has always been something wrong with me. And she said 'You know, when we find that medication that suits you, if I was you, I would stay on it for the rest of your life, and I wouldn't muck about with it.' (Veronica)

Of course not all health practitioners see antidepressant medication as being about replacing missing chemicals in the brain for all patients. If a health professional sees medication as a short-term solution then patients who believe they need ongoing medication to be well may feel anxious and as though they need to argue their case to stay on an SSRI.

> …I did sort of tail it [Prozac] off over the period of about a month. And then…everything was reasonable, OK after the first few weeks, and then very slowly it began to sort of slide again. And so when I went back [to the doctor] and suggested that perhaps I could go on to this medication again he said, 'Well

OK.' He was happy enough with that... And so, I feel well, and for the next four and a half years' from now I am quite safe. I can still continue taking that. But in five years' time, do I have to go back and sort of plead my case again? Ask as it were if I can continue taking them? Or do I have to go back through that misery of feeling that it's all going pear shaped again and maybe existing for a number of months not feeling well? (Liza)

Clearly, patient and practitioner discourses about the role of medication in depression both play a part in the length of treatment. Patient and professional beliefs may not always be aligned, as is evident in this chapter. Several patients felt they benefited from being involved in the cost-benefit analysis about long-term use of antidepressants.

And when people say to me 'Oh I'd be worried about the long-term [effects of being on antidepressants]', well alright let's say Seroxat is more likely to make me...I don't know, let's say, or even to take five years off the end of my life. I'd say well it's better than feeling fucking awful now. Which is, you know, I can honestly say antidepressants work, work well... I've taken fluoxetine, I've taken Seroxat, they both work. Fluoxetine is one of the best things that's ever happened to me [laughs]. (Matthew)

Withdrawal from antidepressants

The idea that patients can go into withdrawal after stopping certain antidepressants and have unusual symptoms was once quite controversial. Only now, after more than ten years, is there more support from the medical establishment that people can experience problems when withdrawing from antidepressants (Ebmeier *et al.* 2006). As such, patients in the present study – interviewed in 2003 to 2004 – who forgot to take their SSRIs did not always link their subsequent symptoms to the possibility they were suffering withdrawal. Withdrawal problems were not discussed with these participants routinely by professionals at the time.

I forgot for a couple of days to take my antidepressants and actually, again bizarrely enough, I woke up on Boxing Day with cold turkey withdrawal from the Efexor which was extremely unpleasant... It's like you've got stinging ants crawling around under, under your skin. Kind of like pins and needles except much...more unpleasant. Also unbalanced as if I was going to fall over. My mouth felt as if it was enormous, as if sort of, [laugh] my, my mouth and lips and chin had swollen massively except it weren't. My sense of touch on my fingers felt completely wrong and, and completely skewed. I couldn't, couldn't understand it at all. I really couldn't realise what was, what was, what was happening. (Craig)

While there is little clear evidence to suggest that antidepressants are physically addictive (and even experts seem to mix up the concept of withdrawal with addiction), there is no doubt that some patients are liable to suffer withdrawal symptoms when they stop or change doses of SSRIs. The abrupt stopping of some kinds of SSRI medication (especially venlafaxine or paroxetine) was described as causing particularly difficult problems for a number of people.

> …if I forgot to put my prescription in, and I would go about a day to two days without it, the symptoms would start. About 48 hours of…after stopping the tablet, if I missed a dose, and the…and the symptoms were so acute it was very frightening. You feel sick, nausea, the nausea was awful. And just panic, really. (Sophia)

While some SSRI withdrawal problems could be very disconcerting and even frightening, some experiences were described as bizarre by patients. Symptoms of electric shock sensations in the body, buzzing in the head and lurching sensations were included in these descriptions.

> [Withdrawing from Efexor] basically, you start getting this …sickening lurch in your head. You can't really describe it unless you have experienced it. It is horrible. It is not nice… Well, the other one that I get is, it's a kind of numb feeling, slightly like an electric shock as well. Sort of like a tingling sensation mainly in my hands but also sometimes on my nose as well. (Heather)

> …You get the fuzzy head… Yeah, I had a week of withdrawal. And when you experience those they're the strangest things ever. When you make a gross movement, a gross muscle movement, you get this incredible, uh…it's not a tingling, you get this incredible buzz in your head. (Rosey)

> The thing that really struck me was the …it just felt like electric shocks…it was just sort of through the whole body. It was just like… You'd be lying in bed, and all of a sudden you would just feel like the whole of your body would just jolt as you…as if, you know, someone had just plugged you in. (Anne)

Patients need to hear about the potential for withdrawal symptoms – including strange ones – if they miss doses or stop taking certain SSRIs. When patients come off medication like venlafaxine and paroxetine, withdrawing gradually may minimise withdrawal symptoms. Craig describes how he initially tried stopping venlafaxine and suffered very unpleasant withdrawal symptoms. He felt health professions and the manufacturer were not up to speed with withdrawal at the time, so he found a technique for withdrawing from the Internet:

> ... stopping the venlafaxine...actually turned out to be extremely, extremely difficult... So I had to go back onto 75mg and then try taking it one pill every other day, and then one pill, leaving it as long as I could until the withdrawal symptoms became unbearable and taking another pill and they would go away. And eventually I could kind of get to about one pill every two and a half days. Really terrible nausea and also motion sickness...and when the withdrawal symptoms got too bad, I broke it [the pill] open and I would take half a pill and then again leave it for as long as possible and then take another half pill and eventually I weaned myself off... That took a long time. It took about eight weeks and it was very unpleasant... I started looking on the Internet for other people who had effects of withdrawal symptoms...and actually a lot of people have had effects of withdrawal symptoms and a lot of people are quite pissed off with the makers for not really saying what the withdrawal is like. But, you know, I got through it. (Craig)

Subsequent to the interviews conducted for this book, some doctors have developed protocols for withdrawing from SSRIs. Physician David Healy, for example, believes that withdrawal can be hazardous and so it is something that patients should do in consultation with sympathetic physicians. He has written guidelines which appear on the MIND website (Healy 2008).

Electroconvulsive therapy

In clinical terms, electroconvulsive therapy (ECT) is generally thought of as useful treatment for severe depression when all other treatment options have failed (UK ECT Review Group 2003). However, treatment efficacy, individual experiences and whether or not patients find the treatment acceptable are different things. In the present study, eight participants talked about receiving ECT. Those who were given ECT were so badly depressed they usually needed to be in hospital at the same time as having the treatment. Michelle gave a particularly vivid account of recovery from depression (including psychosis) as 'almost miraculous' following the administration of ECT. Nevertheless, she admits she was not in any state to give informed consent for the procedure. Her treatment was outside of the UK in Northern Europe where a group including professionals and lay people jointly gave consent on her behalf.

> The treatment inside the hospital was [ah] was very good in terms of...I'm sure I got the best possible care. It's scary, because for the first week or so you're not really too aware of what's going on. And my depression caused a psychosis which had to be treated with ECT. And all I can recall of that,

because I was not in the… because I was not aware of my consent being sought, I remember though that, there, I was examined, or interviewed by a group of people including a social worker. I think there was a minister, religious minister, and somebody else, to see whether my condition warranted my having ECT. So I wasn't given that without their consent. So the change in me though after the ECT was almost miraculous… It all sounds very scary, but you really don't… You don't see anything because you are anaesthetised, so you are asleep. And you wake up, and I… You have a slight headache, but apart from that, I had no side-effects. And, I'm not too sure how it works, but I… My mood improved instantly, and I was talking and laughing… And to the point where the nursing staff were saying, you know, 'What's the story, you're meant to be depressed?' (Michelle)

However, other study participants reported less clear benefits from ECT, including feeling only slight improvements or being unsure if there was any benefit at all. For those who experienced small or equivocal improvements with ECT, the costs of the treatment in terms of side-effects could outweigh any benefits. This was the case for Jenny who reported losing autobiographical memories of valuable family events post ECT:

And when I came out of it I felt very sick and headachy and really quite unwell. The first time I had it my mood did lift a little bit, but I did have three or four other treatments and it made no noticeable difference… I also feel that it has affected my memory. I was told at the time it would affect my short-term memory but I feel there are certain things that it has wiped out. When I talk to my husband I just can't remember actually doing them now… Just certain events and activities that we'd shared as a family with [my son], that I just have no recollection of. And my memory generally is just not very good now, but as I said before, that may be age, it may just be that I'm quite busy. But I wonder if there is some lasting effect from the ECT? But I have been told [by health staff] that shouldn't be the case… It's very tough. It makes me feel a great sense of loss. I've lost part of [my son's] childhood. (Jenny)

Participants linked ECT with problems such as severe headaches, tearfulness and feeling confused and frightened before and after the treatment. As mentioned above by Jenny, autobiographical memory loss (temporary and more permanent) was of particular concern.

I think I had about 20 sessions. And I would come out of it with a splitting headache, and no memory. Couldn't remember where I lived, and how I was going to get home. But my wife was there, and she took me home… We went on holiday. And to this day I have no recollection of where we went or what happened or anything. So that was a bit frightening. And then I was determined to go back and do [my] job. So my memory was affected by this time so I got into the habit of carrying a notebook and putting everything down that I'd to do. And so to all intents and purposes, I was back to normal, or I felt I was. (John)

A few people developed a particular fear and loathing of ECT, and some were especially traumatised by their treatment, particularly if things went wrong, as was the case for John:

And one day it was rather a terrifying experience because in order to have the treatment, as I said I had a general anaesthetic. And they would give curare to relax the muscles and so forth. And so I was strapped onto a trolley, and up round my feet and waist and chest and my arms at the side. And then I was in that state, with two anaesthetists who stood by me talking about something, I don't remember what. And I swallowed my tongue and I couldn't move or shout, so I thought 'I'm going to die if these two don't soon notice what's happening'. So I moved my body as much as I could and hit the one of them with the trolley, and they were terribly apologetic and asked me if I wanted to go on with it. And I did, but ever since then I've had quite a lot of surgery. And I always ask the anaesthetist to be careful not to let that happen again. (John)

Some people came to associate the look, smell and experiences of the ECT theatre with their negative expectations and experiences of ECT.

[ECT] was very traumatic, and I had to go to a separate part of the hospital, so I wasn't on the main ward. And sit in a quiet room and wait for the treatment. And there had been an anaesthetic. And it was just very daunting, just being surrounded by all the equipment there, and the nursing staff. (Jenny)

People who were afraid of ECT attempted to manage their anxieties, including by finding the humour in their experiences in retrospect. Anne felt frightened and confused after ECT. When she tried to exchange her contact details with another patient who had also just had ECT, she found some humour in the exchange that cut through some of her trauma:

I just remember being so frightened going into a room with a bed laid out and they'd get you to lie down on the bed, and give you an anaesthetic in your hand, which would basically make you go unconscious. But just that two minutes when you might have gone into the room and been waiting, I was just so frightened… I remember talking to one of the women in hospital, bearing in mind I was in a mother and baby unit, and we discovered we lived quite close. And we agreed, she was leaving, so we agreed we'd swap telephone numbers, and I couldn't remember my telephone number… And she couldn't remember her address. And you think, well… She'd had ECT as well, which is hilarious, it's laughable because you can't remember some of the most basic things about yourself. [Like] you know, how old am I? (Anne)

These patient findings resonate well with the first systematic review of research looking at patient views on ECT (Rose *et al.* 2003). Significantly, this review included researchers who had experienced ECT themselves, and so the research was particularly attuned to the patient experience, finding that:

- Patient views on ECT tend to be complex, and not easily captured in short clinical questionnaires which tend to disallow complex patient narratives.

- Patient-led research rates the perceived benefits of ECT lower than clinical studies do.

- It is possible for the costs to outweigh any benefits of ECT for patients.

- Memory loss (especially the erasing of autobiographical memories) is a concern for patients, affecting three to eight out of every ten patients.

Clinical studies have tended to measure the formation of *new* memories after ECT, prompting some professionals to claim there is no research evidence that ECT has an effect on memory. While technically this may be a correct statement (partly because the research has not been done), it is misleading from a patient perspective. This situation has resulted in patients with memory loss frequently having to grapple with their losses in the absence of professional validation or support.

> It can be very embarrassing because I can't find simple words sometimes too. For example, in my new job, I'm always directing every day thousands or hundreds of patients to the Outpatients Waiting Room. And one day I couldn't think of the word 'outpatient'. I said, 'If you would like to go to the…' Maybe that's normal, I don't know, but it seems like that happens all the time. I can't think of simple words. And this didn't happen before… But nobody wants to hear it. I've tried to talk about it with the doctors at the hospital and they say, 'Give me an example.' And I give them an example and they say, 'Oh that's normal, that's just normal, that's not the ECT, that's normal.' I mean when they hear it, they don't want to hear, you know. They don't want to know, but if you look on the Internet most American psychologists or psycho-therapists, psychiatrists believe that ECT causes long-term memory problems…it can damage the brain. (Belinda)

Another problem with using ECT in severe depression which has already been flagged is related to informed consent. Being severely depressed it was difficult for participants to make decisions about simple everyday issues, let alone about whether or not ECT was the right treatment for them. One man said 'I didn't know what ECT meant,' even though he was embarking on a series of 20 sessions of ECT. A descriptive systematic review of the literature has found that around five in ten patients who were administered ECT reported that they did have enough information about the procedure and its potential side-effects (Rose *et al.* 2005). However, about three in ten felt they had been coerced or had not freely consented to ECT, even in cases where they had signed a consent form. While clinical studies give these kinds of results a more positive spin (e.g. 'patients trust doctors when it comes to ECT'), patient-centred reports are more inclined to question the trust placed in health professionals in obtaining informed consent for ECT.

Hospitalisation

Patients can get a bed in a National Health Service (NHS) psychiatric hospital voluntarily or through being 'sectioned' involuntarily. Patients usually have to be suffering from severe problems (e.g. a danger to themselves or others) to get an NHS bed. Even though the realities of modern-day NHS hospital-based mental health care may not live up to negative community perceptions, patients can still feel ashamed and fearful about being hospitalised.

> It's probably the public's view of… My Mum's always very ashamed and didn't want to tell people that I was in a psychiatric hospital. Didn't want anybody to know I was in there. Wouldn't tell anybody. Always a big secret. And that in itself didn't have a good effect on me. Because it made me feel ashamed of myself and that I was in there. (Belinda)

If a patient has private health insurance that covers mental health treatment, they may be able to go to a private psychiatric hospital. Although not all private hospital treatment rates well with patients, some described private treatment as more humane, engaging and supportive than that available in the NHS:

> The private hospital was…there was a lot of love, a lot of care in there, sincere care. And I won't knock the NHS because they are obviously very limited to money in a way, but there was no care… In the private hospital you felt like you were being treated as a human being and they were understanding and, you know, you felt they understood. You felt that yes, you could get well here because they cared. …Whereas in the NHS it was like, if you were lucky, if you went to say you wanted to speak to someone, it wouldn't necessarily be there and then because as I say they were all too busy. And you might be lucky to see

one that day, you might not, by which time you might be in a worse state… But then I can't knock all because some of the NHS nurses there, some of the nurses are generally genuinely there because they want to care for people and they were different. But there's an awful lot there who… You felt as though it was people saying to you, 'Oh, for goodness sake pull yourself out of it,' and 'Get yourself together,' which you don't want. (Jane)

However, whether the care was NHS or private, many patients came to the conclusion that there were benefits to be had from hospitalisation, including getting time away from pressures of daily life (although some participants felt it was easy to become dependent of hospital life). Expert selection and adjusting of medication; more specialised care; involvement in creative activities; and access to discussions with professionals (including counselling) were also some of the benefits of hospitalisation.

And I was also doing a lot of things like pottery and so forth, I was good at that. They gave me a few, some extra time to do that on my own because I was very keen on doing that. So I got back into painting which I hadn't done for many years, and I had a box of paints in the hospital and stuff by my bed that I could, that I could use. I mean I did drawings of other patients, even one or two people paid me for drawing their children which was very, which helped quite a bit… It was something I… Just something I loved doing, and being able to do something that I really loved doing, it made a huge difference I think. (Richard)

However, it is equally true that patients – including those with positive hospital experiences – reported difficulties with hospitals, and NHS hospitals in particular. For instance, in the NHS some people felt traumatised from mixing with seriously disturbed patients, while others simply felt a sense of not being cared for.

I was seeing a NHS psychiatrist and he was concerned about me and, ultimately, he sectioned me. They refused to transfer me to a private hospital because I was specifically under a NHS consultant… And I was furious [laughing], absolutely furious about that because it was a horrible place. I can't remember the exact event that precipitated me going into hospital, I think it basically… It had got to the point where my husband felt he couldn't cope with me. So I…I did go into hospital and I remember putting a plastic bag over my head in there, and I remember that the nurse just took it off my head, didn't say a word to me and walked away. And it just really sort of enforced the feelings that they just didn't care at all… So, and then I didn't eat for three weeks while I was in there, and they didn't seem to notice. (Anne)

Hospitals also have accident and emergency (A&E) departments which people with depression may use from time to time, such as when they self-harm or attempt suicide. Participant experiences of A&E and non-mental health staff were mixed, ranging from hostility for their attempted suicide, right through to sensitive and supportive care. For instance, Nicola was in her late teens when she attempted suicide. Her surgeon took a paternalistic yet ultimately caring approach from her perspective:

> ...the surgeon had asked me if I had told anyone the truth about what had happened [her suicide attempt], and I admitted that I hadn't. And he said that he wanted me to at least tell my parents before I left hospital. When my Dad was there the surgeon came in and asked if I'd told him yet. And then of course I had to say, no I hadn't. So he went out, and my Dad asked what all that was about, and so I told him that I'd had depression for a while and I'd been taking antidepressants, and that the reason I was there was that I had cut my wrists. And, you know, he just looked stunned for a while, and didn't say much. Like I said, I wasn't very close to him at the time. So he...he then wanted to know if I'd told my Mum yet, and I said I hadn't. So then he said he'd bring her up the next day, for me to tell her. So, then the next day they both came up, and he left me alone to tell her. And she, she just looked distraught, when I told her. She looked like a pit had just opened up in front of her. (Nicola)

Conclusion

Consistent with a perspective where it is patients themselves who must ultimately narrate their depression and recovery, it is important to involve patients as much as possible in making decisions about the medical tools used to promote recovery. Patients will come with prior assumptions about medical approaches, and so it is important to ask about – and address – patient fears and assumptions. This chapter makes a number of key points about the use of medication and ECT including:

- Patients experience the effectiveness of medical treatments very differently.

- Changes to medication can sometimes make a big difference to patients.

- For both medication and ECT, the costs may outweigh the benefits for the patient.

- It is important to respect patient narratives about memory loss associated with ECT.

- Patients can be involved in decision-making about treatments.

- Informed consent can be gained with patients who are depressed.

In circumstances where patients are severely depressed and require hospitalisation, patients are really looking to address their fears and hopes. They want to feel cared for, and they can benefit greatly from specific kinds of hospital activities, like creative pursuits and discussions with professionals and patients.

Chapter 6

Non-Medical Recovery Tools

A key finding in this study is that patients need to identify recovery tools that make sense and appear effective within their narratives of depression. Identifying multiple recovery tools seems to go hand in hand with telling a good story about recovery from depression (Ridge and Ziebland 2006). On the other hand, those with few recovery tools identified told stories of struggling. In this chapter I discuss the less conventional recovery tools that people used for depression. The approaches discussed include the St John's wort herb, meditation, books and the Internet (bibliotherapy), exercise, yoga, omega-3 fatty acids, homeopathy and spiritual approaches. The discussion here does not represent a comprehensive examination of helpful recovery tools for depression. For a broader discussion, readers can refer to reliable Internet pages such as the *Bluepages* at the *Australian National University* (Bluepages 2008). *Bluepages* lists a wide range of approaches to treating depression and has a simple rating system to show which treatments have the best scientific evidence to support their use. Rather than providing a comprehensive discussion, the current chapter outlines a small number of approaches in detail, bringing together the evidence for the approach from available quantitative research as well as qualitative patient experience. The intention is that the format will show how quantitative and qualitative data can work together to increase our depth of understanding of recovery tools. In particular, the qualitative data help us to understand the subjective ways in which recovery tools might work for patients.

One of the key findings reported in this chapter is the value of supporting patients to find relatively safe non-medical tools that they consider effective. For instance, a doctor's advice to do physical rather than intellectual things was thought to be crucial to the way Matthew recovered from his depression. More specifically, Matthew felt that gardening distracted him from his negative thoughts and helped him to get the upper hand over these 'bad thoughts':

People tell you to do things, they say, you know, in this case, work in the garden. And you do it the first few times and you just think, 'Oh fuck off, this isn't going to work.' And strangely, these sort of laborious tasks do begin to work, so you have to stick at it... And it was crap at first, but gradually it was all right, you know you start to think, 'Yeah, this is kind of distracting me a bit.' And there was one day I remember having my Walkman on [laughs] and I was trying to listen to a record, I can't even think what record it was. And of course the bad stuff comes, the bad thoughts come. And I remember the first time that I felt, 'Oh I'm winning here...' And for the first time I felt hey, this fighting is working. (Matthew)

St John's wort

St John's wort (*Hypericum perforatum L.*) is a traditional herbal remedy that has been around for centuries and is now most commonly used to treat depression. St John's wort is usually bought from health food shops, pharmacies and supermarkets. An extensive review of the research has found that extracts of St John's wort are more effective than placebo (and can be as effective as antidepressant medication) in treating mild to moderate forms of depression (Linde *et al.* 2005). However, the herb appears to be only minimally effective for more severe forms of depression, including major depression. Side-effects for St John's wort are usually less severe in comparison to antidepressants, and commonly include problems like dizziness or nausea. The herb is also well known to adversely interact with other drugs such as those used to control HIV and cancer. However, it is known that patients may be reluctant to discuss their complementary and alternative medicine (CAM) use with non-CAM health professionals (Tasaki *et al.* 2002). For this reason it may be the health professional who has to initiate discussion about St John's wort so that communication about possible side-effects and drug interactions is possible. As a further note, the potency of different brands of the herb does vary, and so choosing an effective preparation can be a problem. The other disadvantage of using St John's wort is that it can be more expensive for patients compared to obtaining antidepressant medication. Despite these drawbacks of St John's wort, from a patient perspective the herb can be considered effective.

I asked the psychiatrist if I could take St John's wort instead of his antidepressant and he said 'Well it's up to you, but only, but you'll have to pay for it if you take St John's wort.' So I did take St John's wort and that seemed to do the trick, and it was at a time of year when this thing about light doesn't, doesn't affect you because St John's wort can make you light sensitive. (Richard)

However, like other remedies, patients can also find it difficult to know if St John's wort actually worked for them: Linking improvements to any particular treatment in depression is not always possible.

> I've tried St John's wort but I have no idea if it was good or bad. I must admit I have more faith in the Prozac, but then I'm not sure of that either! (Jill)

Meditation

> For about 12 years before the latest depression I was meditating and I'm sure, that probably aided my recovery. The fact that I'd done all that must have aided my recovery I would think. (Elizabeth)

Meditation essentially involves concentration and contemplation, but has many different forms (Roberts, Ahmed and Hall 2006). Originating as a specific type of Eastern meditation practice – especially associated with Buddhism – 'mindfulness' has recently achieved some scientific legitimacy in the West due to encouraging findings coming from randomised controlled trials into the prevention of relapse for people with chronic depression (Teasdale *et al.* 2000). Unlike cognitive behavioural therapy (CBT), which asks people to identify and then challenge negative cognitions to improve mental wellbeing, mindfulness does not require people to try and change the content of their thinking (Melbourne Academic Mindfulness Interest Group 2006). Instead, mindfulness asks people to become detached observers to their thoughts, feelings and bodily sensations, rather than getting caught up in the seductive narratives of their minds (Kabat-Zinn 1990). Trying to solve personal problems by ruminating over them (including thinking about the past and the supposed future) may seem helpful to people, but according to the mindfulness approach, rumination is unhelpful in promoting mental wellbeing (Watkins and Baracaia 2002). In mindfulness, thoughts, feelings and bodily sensations become observable 'events' (unpleasant, neutral or pleasant) that continually arise and fall away, rather than dramas to feel aversion to, or pleasant experiences to feel attached to. It is this ability to stand back from such 'events' that may lead to greater self-awareness and creativity in responding to challenges in life.

Using mindfulness-related techniques (e.g. meditation, Iyengar yoga), eventually the mind is thought to be trained to be better able to identify and watch difficult 'events'. The mind can sit through these events without being triggered into habitual rumination patterns and behaviours that could trigger the downward spiralling into depression. Because rumination is in actuality very common, easily switched on and difficult to detect, mindfulness training has to be rigorous. Mindfulness trainers are also expected to practise mindfulness since by definition, mindfulness needs to be learnt experientially: it cannot be grasped by reading from a book (Teasdale *et al.* 2003). Additionally, mindfulness is not just a meditation technique or a course, but a state of being that takes a life-long commitment. The concentration required to do mindfulness and other kinds of meditation is considerable. As such, these techniques may not be useful to people who are unable to concentrate due to depression.

> Now I have to say that while I was severely depressed, and that's this, I'm only referring now to the latest depression I had, when I was aware of…when I was aware of meditation…I was too ill to feel the benefit of my own meditation… I couldn't [meditate], I was so disturbed, so agitated with it, I couldn't. (Elizabeth)

Beyond a remedy to some forms of depression, there are positive subjective outcomes for people who practise mindfulness including greater calmness, less anxiety, gaining insights into themselves, identifying the warning signs of looming depression, gaining social support and learning new social skills through participating in training groups (Finucane and Mercer 2006; Mason and Hargreaves 2001).

> …and I've learnt to just let extraneous thoughts come and go, not try to fight them, or just let…don't get caught up in inner thoughts. Or caught up in any kind of images that come… And I've found it really beneficial to do that meditation. Very health-giving… I think I'm much calmer than I used to be. (Elizabeth)

While mindfulness is a promising approach for people with recurring depression, the adverse outcomes of mindfulness are less discussed in the literature. Nevertheless, problems with mindfulness are documented and include initial negative experiences in participating in meditation, increased anxiety, depersonalisation, and even mania or psychosis in cases where people have engaged in intense practices (Finucane and Mercer 2006; Mason and Hargreaves 2001; Melbourne Academic Mindfulness Interest Group 2006). Mindfulness is about becoming aware of interior processes, many of which are going to be unpleasant, particularly in the short-term. Clearly, adverse experiences should be anticipated and explained to patients before they embark on mindfulness. Additionally, mindfulness essentially asks people to adopt and sustain a fundamentally different approach to life. As such, the mindfulness approach needs to be understood as a change strategy requiring considerable patient investment and commitment. Given the complexity of meditation techniques including mindfulness ones, there are concerns that the current enthusiasm for mindfulness may result in misinterpretations and misapplication (Melbourne Academic Mindfulness Interest Group 2006).

Yoga for depression and anxiety

Yoga originated in India, and although there are several forms which have become popular in the West (e.g. Iyengar, Hatha, Bikram, Ashtanga), generally the different kinds of yoga all incorporate postures (asanas), breathing exercises (pranayama) and meditation. Yoga is traditionally used to still the mind, promote wellbeing, increase energy, promote personal insights and develop spiritually (Collins 1998). And like meditation, yoga can be practised secularly without reference to its spiritual roots. In the West, many people take up yoga for relaxation, to reduce stress, increase body flexibility and strength and cope with injuries. There are few studies, though, looking at the effect of yoga on depression, and where they exist they are methodologically limited. Nevertheless, the initial indications are that yoga has a potential benefit in alleviating symptoms associated with depression and anxiety (Kirkwood *et al.* 2005; Pilkington *et al.* 2005b). Further, because yoga appears to have few reported adverse outcomes when expertly taught and supervised, recognised yoga schools can be safely recommended to patients who are able to participate in yoga classes.

From a patient perspective, like meditation, yoga can be helpful. Yoga can, for instance, take attention away from the mind, instead focusing attention on the body, the yoga postures and the breathing. There are obvious links here with mindfulness practices.

> Yes, and that [yoga] was very good too, because you focus on your breath and your postures. So anything that took me out of my mind for a little bit was very positive. (Jenny)

Participating in yoga is reported to have non-specific benefits (e.g. getting out of the house, socialising). The direct benefits reported from the asanas include reducing anxiety, and increasing feelings of calmness and energy.

> But I thought the yoga was very good really, hmmm…it makes me feel more, sort of, less stressed which I think is, a lot of people feel that way, you know, with it, really, with yoga. And, sort of, feeling more, as I say, sort of rested, or relaxed, really in the body, hmmm…I do yoga and it's great. (Adam)

There are also more complex subjective changes that people link with yoga, including 'accepting' things as they are: 'I love yoga. It forces you to look at yourself. You have to accept and let go, and I have to let go of a lot of things' (Ridge, Plummer and Peasley 2006, p.510).

Cognitive behavioural therapy bibliography and Internet/computer programs

It is possible to use books, computer programs or Internet sites to do struc-tured cognitive behavioural therapy independently without a therapist being present (or with a therapist providing guidance). One common book used by *Health Talk Online* participants and which has been widely studied is called *Feeling Good: The New Mood Therapy* (Burns 1980). Meta-analyses of trials have shown that bibliotherapy for depression can be as effective as seeing a therapist (Cuijpers 1997). *Health Talk Online* participants talked about how their perspectives shifted in helpful ways after reading books like *Feeling Good*. Frequently, people found a small number of useful 'take home messages' from reading such books that helped them to cope better. For instance, after reading *Feeling Good* Patricia particularly focused on the message that she no longer had to believe the bad publicity about herself that her mind was telling her:

> It [*Feeling Good*] teaches you that you don't have to let what your mind is telling you be the case. So, for example, I could say something to somebody…cast my opinion, my aspersions on what they're talking about, and receive a negative response. And I could go away from that thinking, oh no, you know, they don't like me. I shouldn't have said that, what did I say wrong? And dwelling on it. The book teaches you how to stop thinking negatively, to argue with yourself, to stop dwelling on things. It says, you know, in effect, what are you getting out of being, thinking so negatively? You know, what is going to come of that? You're only hurting yourself. You know, what proof have you got to say those people are talking badly about you? You haven't, it's just your chatterbox telling you what your worst thoughts might be. (Patricia)

In Jenny's reading of *Feeling Good* she realised that she no longer had to be perfect. More than this, she could actually enjoy doing things in an average way:

> I found a book by Dr David Burns very helpful, the *Feeling Good* book, and there's a chapter in there on perfectionism, and I did some of the exercises in that. And I kept a mood log for a while and that was helpful. I'd just look at what I'd done in a day and rank them in terms of enjoyment and how well I thought

I'd done, and I could start to see from that, that it was OK to do things that were only five out of ten in terms of achievement. That was OK, [my son] had survived the day, he'd had a good time, whatever. It didn't need to be ten out of ten. (Jenny)

People were also able to get helpful 'take home messages' from non-CBT books. These other helpful books also assisted people to think differently about themselves and their depression. For instance, Jenny talked about how Dorothy Rowe's book *Depression: The Way Out of Your Prison* had helped her to challenge unhelpful messages she had picked up as a child, as well as understand her depression as meaningfully related to her past:

So it [Dorothy Rowe's book] helped me stop and reflect upon my childhood, and lessons I'd learned in childhood that may have been still affecting me as an adult, and causing me difficulties. So certain messages I'd got as a child that had led me to think that I had to be perfect to survive, and get by and not be criticised. From reading her book it just enlightened me really and gave me a picture of perhaps why I had become vulnerable to depression... And that was quite empowering really. It wasn't just something that had struck out of the blue. There were some reasons as to why that, why I'd succumbed to the depression, and also why perhaps it had come after...becoming a mother... I'd made the decision that I didn't want to parent like my parents. But I didn't know what I wanted to put in its place, and had set these very high standards that were impossible to meet. (Jenny)

A key 'take home message' for Julie from Rowe's book was the need to take better care of herself:

And some of it [*Depression: The Way Out of Your Prison*] is relevant, some of it is not at all relevant. And some of it I read it and thought, 'How dare she criticise like parents and stuff like that.' But other bits of it... It's the sort of book you can keep going back to. And I go back to it even now. And it's really good. It's really good because it's all about... The stuff that I was talking about... Feeling guilty and not looking after myself and it's all in there. That's probably what I'm spouting it all from because it's about... It's about looking after you and... Some of the things just make me laugh. You know, because it's so like, 'Oh my God that's me. I'm in there. That's what I do!' (Julie)

As well as the clear benefits that patients identify there are problems associated with the independent use of books. For instance, people may be too depressed to manage the reading or tasks they are asked to do as part of working through the book.

Internet-based cognitive CBT programs like *Moodgym* (available for free at http://moodgym.anu.edu.au/) were relatively new at the time of researching this book, and no one I talked to had used them. Nevertheless, such programs are looking promising for treating depression. One study found that *Moodgym* reduced dysfunctional thinking and depressive symptoms (Christensen, Griffiths and Jorm 2004). Additionally, using *Moodgym* has been associated with doing other things that could be helpful in depression, such as seeking further CBT and doing more exercise (Christensen *et al.* 2006). Nevertheless, there are still problems to be overcome with Internet-based CBT programs like *Moodgym*. For instance, it is not clear yet how to encourage people to complete computer programs in their entirety so that people can gain the most benefit (O'Kearney *et al.* 2006).

Exercise

Frank (1991) highlights the importance of the body in illness, and it is interesting how body work can be so important in recovery from depression. The evidence is that moderate exercise may be particularly effective in reducing the symptoms of depression and anxiety (Larun *et al.* 2006; Lawlor and Hopker 2001). In the UK, NICE guidance is that 'patients of all ages with mild depression should be advised of the benefits of following a structured and supervised exercise programme of typically up to 3 sessions per week of moderate duration (45 minutes to 1 hour) for between 10 to 12 weeks' (National Collaborating Centre for Mental Health 2004, pp.15–16).

Exercise can involve aerobic activity (involving working the heart and lungs) or weight training to strengthen the legs, arms and body. Whatever the type of exercise, participants in the present study generally said they felt better after exercise. As Anne pointed out, physical exercise involves specific elements like repetition that can play a role in transforming subjective feelings:

> I found that swimming really, really helps me… It's very therapeutic. I think it's the repetitiveness of movement and also it helps your breathing, and also it's a different element. It sort of takes you, being in the water or submerged…or just… It's just a completely different element, it takes you away from your usual surroundings…releases the endorphins, obviously the good, the feel-good hormones etc. And after I found I now use it [as] my main tool for stress relief, I can often… And which was very, very common during depression I'd go to the swimming pool and I'd go in, in the foulest of moods, and I'd come out feeling light, happy, relaxed. And it's absolutely brilliant. (Anne)

Exercise usually has other less direct benefits, such as socialising and increasing people's sense of achievement.

> So every morning, usually in the morning – whether I feel like it or not, whether I'm in the mood, whatever, I'm down there in the pool swimming my lengths. And sometimes I really love it and sometimes [not], but I always feel better afterwards... Well it's partly [the bodily chemicals released], but its become more than that now because I actually, you know I've been swimming for God, eight years. I couldn't swim at all before then, so I enjoy the achievement of it... I actually... It's quite an interesting social setting... You know, it's a social arena to an extent. (Derek)

> Exercise in a place where you feel comfortable in... Oh, I used to go to the [recreation centre] and I just love it in there... It's just that the whole atmosphere is just, you know...the sort of enforced exercise. Not, you know, in a sort of a ladies' fashion magazine sort of way but to get...and it really, really does work. And yes, swimming, the, the gym upstairs. Yeah, stuff like steam rooms, not for vain reasons but for just to get your...I feel like I can go in right now, just to get your bones thawed out [in winter]! (Jill)

Empirical evidence has accumulated since the late 1970s showing the positive effects that being outdoors can have on mental health, even when no exercise takes place. For instance, getting close to nature can help aid recovery from mental fatigue, help people cope with stress, improve concentration and promote a more positive outlook on life (Maller *et al.* 2006). While these findings do not suggest that nature can specifically help depressed people, all of these outcomes of interacting with nature tackle the kinds of problems that people prone to depression report.

Despite the obvious benefits of exercise to participants, some acknowledged that exercise is one of those activities which can be difficult to find the motivation for. It can be particularly difficult for people with more severe depression to complete the simple tasks of daily life, let alone engage in exercise.

> ...you know the doctor had said 'You need to get out. You need to exercise.' Which was laughable because I could hardly walk, never mind actually do any exercise. (Veronica)

Nevertheless, a number of participants were very motivated to engage in exercise even when they were very depressed. Diego, who reported debilitating depression, still managed to force himself to keep to a daily schedule, including gym. He found this structured approach very helpful in distracting him from his negative thoughts and so helping him to get through each day.

> My day would start 10 o'clock. I used to be having breakfast at 11 or finishing at 11. I never leave the house without a shower even if I go to the gym or even after work, I come back from work; if I go for a run I take a shower before. So by the time I left to go to the gym it was 12, so by the time I got to the gym it was half past 12. By the time I came back from the gym it was 3 or 4 o'clock so the day had almost gone by then for me. So it was almost time to think about having dinner and stuff. So that made the day go a bit quicker... One of the things that also kept me going was watching tennis on the television because we had tennis, yes, we had Wimbledon. So I was, there were days when I was in front of the TV from 12 until God knows, 8 o'clock with breaks going to the gym, watching in the gym all the while... So yes, exercise kept me going. (Diego)

It is important to acknowledge that over-exercise is a potential problem. Some people will over-exercise for reasons related to their poor mental health. Unhealthy uses of exercising are a potential for people with depression.

> I used to exercise a lot to try to overcome the stress and continued working on, and I was exercising like mad and in the end physically my body packed in... I ended up in hospital with several blood transfusions. (Jane)

Omega-3 fatty acids

> So it's worth trying it [omega-3 oils], whether it works or not but you know that's another element... I talked to the psychiatrist about this and he reckoned that possibly the science behind it would be that the cells can't...don't leak as much, whatever that means. But, you know, maybe then that affects your thought patterns and so on. (Andrew)

Because there are higher rates of depression in countries with less fish in the diet and studies suggesting that depressed people are lacking in omega-3, there is a hypothesis that fish oil might be an effective treatment for depression (Silvers, Hackett and Scott 2003). At the time of writing, there is some evidence that fish oils containing omega-3 fatty acids could potentially alleviate symptoms of depression, and the picture is even less clear for mania (Montgomery and Richardson 2008). However, there is also evidence that fish oils are well tolerated (Stoll *et al.* 1999). With no significant adverse effects related to taking recommended amounts of fish oils (although one wonders if these oils may contain toxins from pollution), some *Health Talk Online* participants were taking fish oils in the hope that it might be useful.

> I'm taking fishy oils, omega-3 [for] brain chemistry… I take the equivalent of 15 mackerel a day… But it's very good for your brain chemistry… I've been prescribed it as someone with manic depression… I imagine it's given to people with unipolar as well who have depressive cycles. Yeah it's the idea that it oils the synapses or something. God knows, but it's… You can get them at huge expense from health food shops, but you can also get them on prescription now, so it's worth knowing. Get omega-3 fish oils! (Ruth)

Some people talked about fish oils as a way of gaining some control over their brain 'chemistry', hoping to ward off further episodes of depression and mania. For Jenny the approval of her doctor was important in her being able to take fish oils with confidence. Jenny believed that while fish oils took time to work, she felt a specific benefit:

> *The Natural Way to Beat Depression* by Dr Basant Puri… He also says that once the depression has subsided, to stay on a maintenance dose [of EPA][1], to prevent the depression recurring… So, I take one a day, one of the tablets of 580mg a day…it didn't help immediately. I guess it must have taken about six weeks to build up. But I'd say there was a definite lifting of mood. It may have happened in time, but I, I think there was some link there. And the fact that the doctor says it can help with prevention of future depression is incredibly important to me. It gives me a greater feeling of confidence that I have some control over the depression coming back.

Homeopathy

Homeopathy treats patients using extremely low-dose preparations, based on the idea that 'like should be cured with like' (NHS Centre for Reviews and Dissemination 2002, p.2). Homeopathy does not conform to the biomedical model of disease and this causes a problem for many scientists (Bensoussan 1999). Yet, homeopathy is one of the most popular complementary therapies used in the UK and the US (Eisenberg *et al.* 1998). The overall evidence for the effectiveness of homeopathy is controversial. Some studies show that homeopathy may work over and above placebos in certain health conditions (Linde *et al.* 1997; Reilly *et al.* 1994). But a recent study published in *The Lancet* likened the effects of homeopathy to that of placebos (Shang *et al.* 2005). However, this meta-analysis has been criticised for the selective methods used to assess the available evidence (Frass *et*

---

1   Eicosapentaenoic acid (EPA) is a component of omega-3 fatty acids.

al. 2006). Perhaps we also need to view the controversy in a wider context of struggles for scarce resources in the NHS. The NHS provides homeo- pathic treatment, for example through the Royal London Homeopathic Hospital (Boseley 2006).

Quite apart from the current controversy over homeopathy, the scien- tific evidence to support the use of homeopathy (which focuses mainly on remedies bought over the counter) to treat depression and anxiety is very limited. This is partly due to the lack of well-designed clinical trials (Pilkington *et al.* 2005a, 2006). Nevertheless, homeopathic remedies are generally considered safe and are widely used by patients for mental health problems. Additionally, it should be kept in mind that homeopathy pre- scribed by a professional involves lengthy consultations with homeopaths and individualised prescribing. It is possible the practitioner–patient rela- tionship itself – as in talking therapies – contributes in some way to any healing that might take place. From the narratives below it is clear that patients can build positive recovery alliances with their homeopaths.

> I'd got to know a little bit about it [homeopathy] myself, I sort of again went and self prescribed. I bought stuff… And I actually found that it works… It worked for me, that was it. And whether my head was saying it or whether it was me, you know. And it can be part of it, could be psychological, and I'm taking this tablet and I'm going to feel better…and it works! And, and also I had my little book of homeopathy, and that I can't remember, but I used to go back to the homeopath and she used to prescribe different… You know, I'd tell her how I was feeling, and she would say take this or take that. (Julie)

It is a theme of this book that there is no one treatment for everyone and clearly not everyone is going to find homeopathy to be the right choice. As well as those who were positive about homeopathy, others felt they were not helped by homeopathy.

> I also tried homeopathy at one stage. I think that can be very effective, I felt that [it] wasn't very effective for me. (Lee)

> I went to a homeopathic hospital…for about a year or so… This was a few years ago now, about 1995, or 1996 I think it was… eventually the doctor there said 'Well I don't think we can really do much more for you.' (Adam)

Spirituality and religion

There is something about illness that can invoke spiritual or religious feelings in people. Illness experiences can point to the possibility that there is more to us than ourselves alone, and inspire people to start 'living as if that understanding matters' (Frank 1991, p.155). Religion is a social institution concerned with the way that spiritual beliefs, practices and communities are organised, while spirituality is about personal endeavours to create meaning out of life and the sacred (Koenig, McCullough and Larson 2001; Miller and Thoresen 2003). Religion has never ceased to be important in westernised societies (Davie 2007) and, while the issue is not clear cut, a number of studies indicate a positive link between health and spiritual or religious practices (Daaleman, Perera and Studenski 2004; Koenig *et al.* 2001; Sloan and Bagiella 2002). There are various ways in which spiritual or religious practices may support people, including by providing emotional and social support.

> ...although as a gay man the Catholic Church isn't, is not in favour of homosexuality and views it with some rancour, and views it as a sin...I have never ever had condemnation direct or implicit from a priest or any congregation in any Catholic Church I have ever worshipped in. Far from it, one priest in particular, no, in fact all of them in their very different ways from young men to, to much older men, have all of them in their ways been very loving and caring and supportive both to me and my partner through the bad times as well as the good. And yes, they've been very loving and very caring in the ways that I think our Lord would have expected. (Carl)

Nevertheless, the mechanisms by which spirituality or religion influence mental health are still not well understood in the literature, but are probably numerous, including prayer reducing negative thought rumination; spirituality increasing people's sense of hope; people feeling a sense of belonging through religion; the group identity and helpful ethics for living associated with religion; and finding a level of security within the clear rules of religion (Craig *et al.* 2006; Meraviglia 1999; Ridge *et al.* 2008; Walton and Sullivan 2004; Wink, Dillon and Larsen 2005; Woods and Ironson 1999).

Skilful spirituality
The available evidence suggests that it is the skilful ways in which spiritual and religious beliefs are selected and enacted that are the key to any benefits (Ellison and Levin 1998). Certainly, unskilful beliefs and practices can undermine health and wellbeing (King, Speck and Thomas 1999).

> ...actually being a member of any religion, I think, would give you a sense of community and a sense of direction and a sense of ethics, of morals. And I got the value system which I probably misinterpreted a little bit, I took Christianity

almost to mean 'others above yourself', which is really, which it definitely doesn't say, it doesn't say that anywhere. (Paul)

Engaging in religion can mean navigating unhelpful religious messages. For instance, Paul, quoted above, decided to turn away from Christianity because of his problems with the discourse of 'sin' in his religion:

> Well, Christianity has got some quite powerful symbols in it about redemption and death and somebody dying for your sins. And quite a strong feeling of sin, actually, of a feeling of blame…whether you can use the word 'stigma' in that context that attaches to somebody who's, who's somehow failed… I mean I had a conflict in my mind between science, which I felt I understood pretty well, and the Bible. And I was always trying to reconcile them. This is something I was doing, you know even as a kid, you know from the age of 11… And from the age of 11 and, ultimately, it went down to the side of being a heathen, and not really worrying about being damned. Because I don't even believe in things like sin any more. (Paul)

As patients understand it, the overturning of unskilful spiritual beliefs can contribute to longer-term recoveries from episodes of depression. Indeed, Elizabeth felt that the rigidity of her religious beliefs had to be broken down by the experience of depression itself before she could properly recover.

> I've learnt that a breakdown can also be a breakthrough. I'm one of these people that's obviously had to be broken down in order to grow enough. I'm not saying that everybody needs to do that, they don't, in the severe way I have, but… The rigidity had to be broken down. I mean, after the first depression, my religious binding, as it were…and I think religious, religion means that which is bound, but that had to be completely…that was completely knocked out of me. (Elizabeth)

For Pamela, overcoming her religious rigidity and realising that there were many paths in life, and that it was OK to make mistakes, was an important turning point in her recovery:

> I'm a Christian, and I have faith, strong faith. I have moved out of the fundamentalist (movement) and I'm now a Quaker. And even now I'm sort of moving a bit away from that into more, perhaps back into the more traditional realms of belief. But it's all part of my journey, and it will change, it's just because I've gone along one part, it doesn't mean to say that I have to stay on that. I had a fairly rigid upbringing. I actually believed…through childhood well into adulthood that there was only one path and that's the way you stayed. But I mean I know now that you can go down one road, and [if] I don't think that's

right, I can change. But I was fearful of change… Yes, and I have gone down a lot of…a lot of paths that weren't the right ones. But I am that much older now and can say that actually, it doesn't matter. It doesn't matter if I make mistakes, it's OK. Hopefully I will learn something from them. And all those things that used to trigger depression, well they don't any more. (Pamela)

Skilful constructions of spirituality can be a great source of support for people who suffer from depression, helping to organise their experiences in useful ways, retrieve meaning from difficult experiences, and support longer-term recovery. For instance, adopting and enacting religious-based ethics was important to some, and Sue talks about 'turning the other cheek' being linked to her self-esteem:

I believe now that…I am as good as the next person. I wouldn't deliberately go out and hurt anyone. And if I can do a good turn for somebody, I'd rather do a good turn than do a bad turn. I am a great believer also in religion. And there is a lot to be said for this turning the other cheek and not retaliating. You can make yourself a better person by not retaliating. And I think in the past that's where I've gone wrong…instead of verbally retaliating I've mentally retaliated… That's when you would start losing your self-esteem. You begin to think you are what other people think you are. And what you think other people think you are. Whereas if I'd have spoken to somebody about it, or if I had had enough guts in me to say, 'Wait, I'm as good as you', I don't think I would ever have got as bad as I did. (Sue)

In particular, the construction of unfailingly compassionate and just 'life schemes' (the heuristic cognitive framework used to interpret all life events (Daaleman, Cobb and Frey 2001)) could help some people retrieve meaning out of their suffering. Veronica explains below that even though she originally did not understand why she suffered from depression at the time, she later came to understand that her depression gave her special skills in her job helping people with personal problems:

And I know when I was really sick I was saying to God, 'Look I don't know what you are trying to teach me by this God but just tell me. Tell me the song then I'll sing it. Why have I got to go through this? What do you want me to learn because whatever it is, tell me, I'll learn it.' You know, and it was only afterwards I realised that what I felt God wanted me to learn was what it feels like to be clinically depressed for five years because that has been a very helpful thing to sometimes share with people in the right setting… You know when… We can go through horrendous periods of our life, where we look at suicide and think it looks like a good option. We look at everything and think I've got nothing and you can come through it. And I've got a job now that I could never have done before. I still get a kick when I see a new client thinking I've got to build a quick bridge to this person, and get them to tell me about their incontinence or whatever if I'm going to do something to do with their health. (Veronica)

Prayer

Prayer – which usually involves contemplation, and making requests or thanksgiving to a higher power – has a very long history in attempts to alleviate suffering (Roberts *et al.* 2006). Prayer can be said in a structured way or freely composed by the individual, and it can involve spiritual healing or include meditation. In a study of the use of prayer among people living with HIV in the UK (many of whom had experienced depression following a diagnosis of HIV), we found that prayer operated at six key levels to promote wellbeing, including setting up a dialogue with a higher power as an 'absent counsellor' which allowed people to talk through their concerns; constructing a compassionate 'life scheme' as a context for receiving benefits from prayer; interrupting destructive thought cycles (rumination) that contributed to misery; promoting mindfulness (see section in this chapter on mindfulness); promoting positive thinking that was thought to be important by many people for good health; and getting specific results like greater calmness (Ridge *et al.* 2008).

In the present study a number of people were convinced that prayer could have a healing effect on their depression. While people could say prayers in pre-structured ways, others simply talked to a higher power as if they were talking to another person or an absent therapist.

> I think because…it depends on how you look on praying. A lot of people find praying…they think you've got to do something really intelligent and you've got to have some special way of praying. But it isn't… It's all about talking to God as if you were talking to your friend, or your Mum and Dad, you know, whoever. And it's just about being you when you talk to him. He knows everything about us. He knows what we've done wrong. He knows everything before we even say. But it's about talking to God as if He was somebody sitting next to you. And I think until you actually realise that that is what praying is about, talking to your friend… Jesus is your friend. And there isn't anything you can tell him he doesn't already know, but he wants you to say it yourself. It's a bit like therapy I suppose… (Jane)

A number of people talked about the way that prayer can shift their feelings in positive ways. In particular, people said prayer helped them to reduce anxiety, gain a sense of comfort, increase strength and reduce their level of suffering.

> ...in depression, the depths of depression, you can't really do anything about [it]. But prayer does help, and believing that the holy spirit will sustain... that God will not allow us to suffer too much, and will give us the strength to cope. It is often rubbished, but there again, that's what I believe. I have been sustained. It doesn't mean I've never thought of suicide in the real pits... (Pamela)

> And I don't go to church, but you see in the last few months I've never spoken with God so much in my life... I said. 'I think this man is giving me the strength to carry on for what I am coming through.' (Carol)

One problem with faith in praying is that just as it is hard to feel connected to other people while depressed, it is difficult to feel connected to a higher power. A leap of faith is needed to pray while depressed. Certainly, spiritually inclined people did not necessarily feel there was any motivation for – or benefit to – praying at the time of depression. Nevertheless, some felt that praying was still beneficial when viewed in the long term. One woman used an iceberg metaphor to explain how she thought prayer gradually helped her depression:

> I didn't feel it [prayer] was doing me any good. And an image I did use, and I've used since to help other people, is of the iceberg in the sun. That although I wasn't aware that any melting was about to take place, or going to take place, of the iceberg of depression...an iceberg will be melting in the sun. And there will come a point when it's obvious and it's visible. And that's what I held on to, that there would come a point when I would begin to feel less depressed. (Elizabeth)

A note on spiritual 'turning points'

One way in which a spiritual approach can assist people with depression is by promoting 'turning points' in depression. As discussed in Chapter 4, 'turning points' correspond to personal narratives, and so they can be difficult for non-narrative-minded professionals to understand. Elizabeth, for example, constructed a touching moment she had with a baby as a key spiritual turning point in her narrative. But the significance of this event might be difficult for others to grasp:

> I was with [a friend]. She had her little granddaughter, only a baby, on her lap... And I was weeping. I was very distressed. Sometimes, it was so unbearable I didn't know where to put myself. And [her baby] was smiling at me. She kept

smiling. And then she caught hold of my sweater, like that [demonstrates]. And even though I was depressed, I was moved. I thought, that child is healing me. There's some healing vibration, literally, vibration of energy coming from that child. And I've always felt a tremendous bond with [the baby] ever since then. But that was one of the big healing things. I've never been interested in babies or small children. I've never been able to sort of relate to them. (Elizabeth)

Other spiritual turning points may be easier for professionals to access. For Veronica, a key turning point in her depression was being able to find trust in her God, despite the difficulties she initially had in understanding the suffering she endured. Here, she was able to find a spiritual narrative to validate her experiences of anxiety and depression, despite stigma attached to mental illness in her church:

...when Jesus was in the garden of Gethsemane which is what happened just before he went to be crucified and he knew he was going to go and be crucified... And it says that his heart was heavy unto death. Which I just thought, yeah he knew what it was like to be at the bottom there. You know. Because the Bible says that although Jesus was the son of God, he was also completely human when he came... You know, he had that sense of feeling completely at the bottom. And it says he actually, his sweat was like drops of blood, and I know that when people are... It is a recognised phenomenon isn't it when people are extremely anxious the... When they sweat the capillaries can actually burst in their skin, and they can actually sweat blood... And I just thought then, you know, if he... If he was anxious and depressed, it's OK for me to be as well. (Veronica)

Jane concluded that God had intervened to save her life because he had a reason for her to live. This more recent narrative turn was crucial in motivating her recovery:

I knew that God, that God had saved me, I knew that he didn't want me to be dead. And I had to try and find what it was, what it is, the reason that he wants me to be alive, and I prayed a lot... I don't know necessarily who I am, or where I belong. But I know, all I know is...that God will be there wherever I am, or wherever he needs me to be... Discovering the fact that God has put me on this earth for a reason and it's taken until now, 45 years of age, to find out why I'm on this earth. (Jane)

Conclusion

Many non-medical tools are quite safe and can be recommended or even 'prescribed' by professionals to patients with confidence. Such approaches are likely to do no harm, and may well benefit patients. From a patient perspective, gathering together a range of recovery tools is frequently helpful or comforting at the least. Professionals need to respect patient narratives in order to best support patients in selecting the most effective narrative 'tools'. By respecting patient narratives about non-medical tools and encouraging the discussion of such approaches, professionals can also play a role when an approach involves risk (e.g. St John's wort is risky with drugs used to treat HIV). In terms of spirituality and religion, the research shows that there can be a positive link between mental health and spiritual practices. The literature – and the narratives in this study – indicate that it is the skilful way in which spiritual and religious beliefs are deployed that determines any wellbeing benefit. Unskilful beliefs and practices may be risky for patients. Again, professionals who respect spiritual stories are most likely to be able to engage with such stories and encourage their skilful uses of such narratives.

Chapter 7

Health Professionals as Recovery Allies

This chapter picks up on the notion of the 'recovery ally', first discussed in Chapter 4, where the importance of allies in the success of coping with depression, and recovery, was introduced. The chapter will focus on how professionals can become better allies to assist patients in their depression and recoveries. Time and time again, patient narratives reveal that the ways in which professionals work with patients can make a considerable difference to the course of depression and recovery. For many people in the UK with depression, general practitioners (GPs) are their first port of call – and the gatekeepers to the rest of the health system – when they are seeking help. As such, many of the quotations from participants in this chapter pertain to GPs. However, the quotations in this chapter also refer (or may be generalised in some instances) to a wide range of professionals such as psychiatrists, social workers and community psychiatric nurses (CPNs). Additionally, the chapter is written in a general way so as to be relevant to the helping professions involved in the care of people with depression, as well as carers of people with depression. The chapter does not go into any detail about how friends and family can best be allies, as this is covered in detail on the *Health Talk Online* website (www.healthtalkonline.org/mental_health/depression, see 'Talking About – Friends and family'). The chapter following this one will specifically investigate the role of talking therapies in assisting patients, and so few quotations pertaining to counsellors or psychotherapists are used in the current chapter.

General practitioners play a pivotal role in the care of those with depression in the UK because they are accessible in the National Health Service (NHS) (free at the point of contact), they can prescribe medication, sign patients off work, refer patients to more specialist care and even provide basic counselling in some cases. In the doctor–patient consultation, the view that patients are merely passive objects of the medical gaze has been in decline for many decades (Thorne, Ternulf Nyhlin and Paterson 2000).

With substantial changes in the role of medicine in Western societies in general over previous decades, less paternalistic – and more equal – relationships between doctors and patients are now more possible than in previous times (Jones and Green 2006). In addition, the ways patients with chronic conditions like depression can develop expertise and become active consumers of health is recognised more and more (Fox, Ward and O'Rourke 2005). Nevertheless, there is an ongoing negotiation – and even struggle at times – between professional and patient agendas (May *et al.* 2004). Indeed, some authors consider the clinical relationship to be so complicated that even the notion of forming a professional–patient partnership is problematic. For instance, it is argued that, in serious illness, patient consultations with doctors are more like 'desperate encounters', and it should automatically be assumed that patients 'feel weak and vulnerable' (Salmon and Young 2005, p.228).

The negotiation of different vantage points between patients and professionals is all the more apparent in chronic and multidimensional conditions like depression where there is the need to make sense of issues like lack of confidence and feelings of dependence, and the blurred boundaries between the ordinary and the pathological (Dowrick 2004). Rather than just viewing the encounter from a professional perspective, professionals can also learn about patient experiences in order to increase the chances of supporting patient narratives that can make sense out of the 'dangerous crisis' of depression. This chapter is dedicated to looking at ways in which patient voices and perspectives can be honoured to support the potential for better patient coping and even recovery from depression.

Being an ally in someone's recovery is not always a straightforward task for a professional, as it involves adopting particular kinds of approaches that may need to be learned. Nevertheless, participants in this study agreed that highly regarded allies in recovery shared certain qualities. These qualities included being able to recognise and understand the existential depression experience; demonstrating a human approach; listening out for patient voices and narratives; and responding appropriately and in a timely manner. Here, allies can demonstrate hopeful – yet realistic – beliefs in patient abilities to recover, as well as know when to refer patients on for more specialist care. Below, these and other issues are taken up in more detail.

Recognising the existential components of depression

Patients may not disclose their emotional problems to health professionals for a range of reasons. As discussed previously, patients with depression can find it very difficult to articulate their feelings and can have severe difficulties discussing their depression with others (Gask *et al.* 2005). Patients with depression are also very likely to feel vulnerable in the company of professionals, lacking confidence and self-worth. Thus, it is hard for patients to talk to professionals on equal terms about their feelings and experiences. What is more likely is that patients will struggle to overcome the asymmetry of encounters with professionals.

> You've just got to feel confident [going to the GP]. You just have to prepare yourself that it's OK to feel like this. I'm not being a fraud. It really is that self belief. And it's really, really hard because if you are depressed anyway you have got such low self-esteem that you feel a complete fool. And then... In that case I guess it would be a good idea to take someone with you... An advocate definitely that can speak up on your behalf. Or write it down, write it down before you get there as well. Write down what is debilitating, how you feel and stuff. (Julie)

There are a range of other reasons for non-disclosure of emotional problems including the stigma attached to mental illness; viewing such feelings as a sign of weakness and as not legitimate for medical consultations; and considering such issues as a problem of living rather than suitable for a health consultation (Bolton 2003; Gask *et al.* 2005; Murray *et al.* 2006). Patients may also pick up subtle messages from previous consultations that talking about emotions is not appropriate (Wittink, Barg and Gallo 2006). People may also feel they have to present as good patients who are reasonably compliant and don't make a fuss. This kind of impression management can also work against a frank discussion of emotional difficulties (Frank 1991; Wittink *et al.* 2006). Frank calls this kind of dance between patients and professionals 'the deal', noting that patients may be highly attuned to keeping on the good side of professionals in order to get the treatments they need.

Particular problems even exist for patients if they are familiar with – or even have friendships with – their health professional. While Liza wanted her GP (who was a family friend) to notice her emotional problems, she simultaneously worried that she would end up being judged for her problems:

> I couldn't imagine being able to go along and tell him [her GP] any of the things that were really going on inside me. Because how would that affect our friendship? And our friendship was a family friendship. You know, we went out socially, his wife and himself, and myself and my husband. Our children played together, and I felt that if he knew the real me, you know, he wouldn't necessarily want to go out and spend social time. And it was like uncovering

> something in myself which at that time I saw as, as a weakness... Well I obviously...it all became too much and I felt myself sort of falling onto his desk weeping and he was quite taken aback. You know, 'What's wrong?' and I...it all just started and it came out one thing after the other, how miserable I was feeling...how low I felt. And I couldn't bear to continue living like that any longer... He wanted to know why I hadn't spoken to him before and I said, 'That I wanted, I wanted you to recognise that there was something not quite right, and you didn't.' (Liza)

The issue of familiarity and continuity of care can be complex. While some patients prefer to build relations and communication with professionals they know well, others find that existing relations – and the assumptions underpinning such relations – can get in the way of talking about the experience of depression freely and candidly (Emslie *et al.* 2007).

On the other hand, patients felt health professionals sometimes struggled to piece together their descriptions of 'depression'. Patients thought this was at least partly due to the interior and 'locked in' nature of depression. As one man pointed out, 'You can see a broken arm, you can see a broken leg, you can't necessarily see a broken mind.' It was also considered easy for professionals to explain away patient descriptions in a way that side-tracked mental health considerations.

> Basically I would go to bed early, I would go to bed late, I tried everything but I always felt tired, the whole time. I still have that and I don't know if it's like... You know it can be a symptom of depression, of just feeling, you know, tired or just not sleeping very well. And I think, like I went to the doctor and I said 'I can't, I sleep but I always feel tired. I've tried going to bed early, I've tried going to bed late, I've tried everything that I can think of.' And he just said 'Try getting more sleep.' [laughing] I was like, yes, I could have thought of that. (Heather)

A number of people interviewed retained regrets and anger that their serious mental health condition was missed by their health professionals.

> If I'd had had the support then that I've had since the 1980s things might have been a lot different. I might not have had to have gone through all that. If it had been recognised, it was, it was just not recognised that I was ill enough...if, if they'd at least have acknowledged how ill I was then it would have made a difference. (Marie)

Professionals may have good reasons for not wanting to rush to label patient suffering as to do with depression (Burroughs *et al.* 2006; Dowrick 2004). Nevertheless, when professionals fail to identify the patient crisis, and the seriousness of the suffering involved, the lack of voice of depressed patients is reinforced. An opportunity for patients to have their voice and narrative recognised as legitimate is lost.

> So I went to my GP. She arranged for me to see the CPN again, get in contact with the CPN again. We arranged an appointment. I think the CPN rang me and came and we talked but I didn't feel at the time she was taking me seriously. I, I didn't think she felt...I don't know. I just didn't think she was taking me seriously and, or perhaps I wasn't explaining myself very well? But I felt a lot worse than she thought I was. (Belinda)

However, some patients considered that their health professionals are very sensitive to depression, and are good at picking up their problems, even without them having to be explicit about how they are feeling (Wittink *et al.* 2006). Those professionals who did recognise depression were felt to be better able to put together what was not being said, and imagine what depression must be like internally. As such, they were able to ask appropriate questions, even when patients came in for apparently unrelated problems, such as the bodily symptoms described in Chapter 3.

However professionals conceptualise depression, when they suspect depression, not communicating this understanding to patients can have negative implications. For instance, participants talked about how it was possible for them to be treated for depression without them fully realising what they were actually being treated for.

> I think with depression there's a tendency for, in my experience, professionals to make that assumption, but not that diagnosis... I think perhaps sometimes it's quite a convenient diagnosis, uh, you can give someone tablets and [they] go away... And I think I could have benefited from that being recognised an awful lot earlier. I feel like I've almost lost 20 years of my life by that not being diagnosed. I was given antidepressants at one point, I think it was Prozac, and I was on those for about 18 months or so. But I was never given a particular explanation of what they were to do with, other than they might help – have a side-effect of weight loss. Well that's [laughs] I don't think that's a particularly good thing, but it helped me explain away why I was on antidepressants. (Rosey)

> I just feel so completely anxious and ill. You know I didn't know how to describe it. And we called the doctor out which was something we never did. And my GP came and he said 'Oh this is a recurrence of your depressive illness.' And I sort of said 'What depressive illness?' You know because nobody had ever said this is what you've got. He had been the same doctor who had treated me when I'd had this post-natal depression thing when [my son] was born... So he said, 'This is your depressive illness. I am going to give

you some antidepressants,' and I said 'But I don't feel depressed, I feel anxious.' And he said 'No, it's two sides of the same coin.' Which again nobody had ever really explained to me. (Veronica)

Beyond a diagnosis, it is helpful for professionals to convey (if and when appropriate) that they understand something about the existential experience of depression. As a teenager, Matthew was surprised – and comforted – that his middle-aged GP seemed caring and knew something about what his depression felt like:

> He was a nice man and he was a good sort of…just a warm and tender kind of chap. And he said, 'Well we're going to give you something just to stop your mind whizzing.' I remember him saying that… He was like, he made me feel okay my Mum was not there. This is you and me. You're an adult, this is between you and me, which I don't think I kind of understood that actually… And he was a kind of… I suppose before he'd always seemed a sort of, kind of rather you know, a figure of authority to go with all the other ones. Then when he starts to talk to you, then you sort of, you realise, God this man in his fifties knows what it's like to be 16, talks to a lot of 16-year-olds, knows what it feels like to feel shit. And lots of people have felt the way I feel, and that really helps. And it sounds trite but it's true. He was a good GP, he was a good GP. (Matthew)

As a recovery ally, it is also useful to help the person feel that their distress is entirely valid. Being the supremely isolating condition that it is, validating the distress of depression can help some people feel less alone in their suffering. There is something about validating suffering that can make it seem more manageable for patients.

> …when you're going through this process alone, you think that there is something utterly wrong with you…or it's just you on Earth going through that thing alone. And then when you meet other people you say, you know I have the same problems. In that this woman [I met] said 'My husband told me I was lazy blah, blah, blah', you know. She says, 'I just couldn't bear getting up in the morning.' And you know, and I say, 'Oh, I felt the same, you know. Not that I was labelled lazy, you know, but it's this kind of thing, that you say, 'Okay, so it's not abnormal not to want to get up, it's part of the process of depression.' (Diego)

Unfortunately, it is easy for even well-intentioned professionals to 'miss' patients, and send messages that they do not really understand the nature of a patient's experience. Again, professionals need to be attuned to existential patient experience enough to validate patient experience.

And then, when I came out of hospital I was assigned a psychiatric nurse... We didn't get on together terribly well, together, unfortunately. I didn't find him very helpful. I felt he was going a bit too quickly for me, I wasn't...he'd sort of set me tasks to do and I wasn't quite ready to do them. And particularly he wanted me to do physical tasks to use up the adrenalin that I was feeling, and I found them too much and too draining. (Jenny)

Conveying a human approach

Professionals come into consultations with patients from different vantage points. For instance, doctors working in socio-economically deprived areas may be reluctant to recognise and treat patients who are depressed in any depth because of perceived lack of resources including doctor time, patients' ability to access talking therapies, as well as intractable social problems (Chew-Graham *et al.* 2002). On the other hand, treating depression among more privileged patients can be considered rewarding work by doctors. Regardless of the way that professionals think about patients with depression, the present research strongly suggests that demonstrating a 'human' approach can be very helpful for patients. As outlined below, elements of this human approach include conveying warmth, empathy and non-judgement and attempting to connect with patients.

Warmth, empathy and non-judgement

It has long been known that conveying warmth, empathy and non-judgement towards patients is important in patient-centred health care (May *et al.* 2004; Myers 2000). More generally, participants were greatly assisted when someone – either a professional, friend or relative – became an ally in their recovery. This meant that the other person had put in the effort and time (including patience), to understand them, convey empathy, not rush to judgement and stick with them throughout their experiences of depression and recovery.

For me the most important thing was sympathetic, helpful people. (Peter)

...there was something about his [a counsellor's] personality as well that I just clicked with. He was just...a very, very warm, person... And just very non-judgemental. And I could talk about anything completely openly. (Patrick)

... I knew that I could talk to him [a psychiatrist] about anything. And everything. And he was patient, and quite a gentle man. But I would think very knowledgeable. Yeah so I had a great deal of faith in him. Yeah. So he was the most influential person... He never criticised. He never made judgements.

And he was terribly sensitive, or he made me feel that he was. And I'm sure he was, and I had great confidence in his skill. (John)

Non-judgement is a particularly important point to emphasise, given that patients with depression can feel worthless and guilty, and may well want to be judged based on these feelings.

She [a psychotherapist] doesn't push me to do things I don't want to do. She may suggest things but if I don't do them I don't feel that I'm in the wrong for not doing them. She's very accepting. She is completely non-judgemental, quite frustratingly so... Because I'm a 'bad' person and it would help me enormously if she did judge me! [laughs] (Rosey)

Connecting with patients

There is an art to reading patient narratives, selecting what is salient (said or unsaid) and finding a way to connect to patients through narrative. Professionals have varying abilities to listen to and connect with patients in a way that inspires. One sure way not to connect with patients is to demonstrate a lack of understanding. For instance, asking someone with depression to do the impossible and 'pull yourself out it' was universally disparaging for patients. Professionals could also demonstrate disconnection to patient narratives by instigating treatments and tasks that were inappropriate and set patients up for failure:

They [occupational therapists] were young. I just felt that they were very much coming from a kind of theoretical thing. And their training seemed to be, 'You've got to get your clients to progress every week.' So every week they were setting me some sort of challenge, even if it was only to go shopping or whatever. And I look back now and think they were well intentioned, but they were pushing me too hard... And of course if somebody is pushing you too hard then you feel anxious and you also feel a failure if you are not managing what they want you to do. (Veronica)

Participants also talked about the kind of disconnect involved when they struggled with health professionals to be taken seriously. These patients came to realise that it was not the case that professionals would always attempt to connect with their narrative. So participants deployed skills to increase the chances that professionals would engage with them.

I think once [they] realised I was fairly well informed everyone sort of treats you slightly differently. Maybe it's my perception of it. (Marcus)

I started to question the psychiatrist what they were doing for me, or what they… And finding that suddenly I started getting respect from psychiatrists because I was starting to think for myself and questioning 'Is this right for me, is this not right for me?' Or 'What do I think is right for me?' (Jane)

The findings reported in this book show that the onus needs to be on the professional to connect with what patients are experiencing and trying to say. Almost by definition, patients with depression will have difficulties in voicing their experience, articulating a narrative and connecting with professionals.

One of the most important things is having people there for you. I mean it's a bit of a… I can't think what the word would be for it, but it's a bit of an unfortunate thing that when you need people, is when you feel least able to ask for people's help or relate to people. (Heather)

So a lot is asked of the professional, because there is the potential to disempower the patient when listening and connecting goes wrong. However, in another way, little more is being asked of the professional than *attempting* to demonstrate certain human qualities. Participants felt more confidence in – and connection to – professionals who tried to *demonstrate* human elements.

She's [her GP] good because she is human. She listens and she responds to me as a human being, not as a professional. She gives me time, as much time as I want sometimes… You know, she is a human being, she has made mistakes and that's fine because she is a human being and I know she's a human being because she talks to me like, like I'm a human being and she's a human being. She is always fully present, always as a person. She's never standoffish or looking at her watch and thinking, you know, about the next patient. Never. (Belinda)

There is a qualification here. Even though it is important for professionals to demonstrate human qualities with patients, the nature of the depression experience means that patients may find some human qualities difficult to cope with. For instance, the perceived attention and kindness of a GP actually worked against Nicola feeling able to connect. Nevertheless, Nicola did appreciate her GP's kindness:

Well, she's [a GP] been ever so nice. She's been really, really kind and helpful but I've always felt that she focused so much concern on me every time I went to see her that I got completely nervous and flustered. And my voice would just get quieter and quieter while I talked to her and anything I'd been thinking of talking to her about would just go out of my head… It was just unnerving having that amount of attention focused on me. (Nicola)

Continuing with the human theme, being honest and clear about what can be provided to the patient, and then being trustworthy in providing this help, is useful in connecting with patients. This means professionals being aware of their own skills and limitations in helping people with depression.

She [a counsellor] is present as a human being and she's honest… If I piss her off, she'll tell me [laugh] because she has feelings too. And that's good for me to know. You know, there has been one, only one occasion I think, she said, 'What you said then actually hurt me.' And that was difficult for me to hear but in another sense good for me to hear because it let me know I'm dealing with a human here, another human being… I don't know how I think of her. I don't think of her as a friend or a sister or anything like that… But she is, she is a human being. She is absolutely honest with me and she is very challenging. [laugh] To put it in a mild form, she challenges me very much which is good for me because nobody's ever challenged me before really. (Belinda)

Listening to the patient 'voice' and narrative

As will be discussed in more detail in the chapter on talking therapies (see Chapter 8), patients with depression can suffer from 'voicelessness'. While voicelessness has been described in various health-related conditions (Happ 2000), patients with depression can be particularly affected by lack of ability to vocalise experience, as the articulation of interiority is fraught with difficulties. Thus, in depression, listening may also include watching out for the things that are not being said, or only said in coded ways.

I was hardly getting any sleep at all and I was becoming…walking around like a zombie really and I just went to her [her GP] for some sleeping tablets… I was working shift work at the time, that's probably why. And she kind of started questioning my mood, she is very good, I have a very good GP… And she was kind of asking me questions about my social life and I said, 'I haven't got one at the moment. I just don't, I can't be bothered and…' I suppose my whole body language was telling her something as well. And maybe my voice and how I was generally but something told her, I think, to question me a bit more than just hand me over some sleeping tablets… And I think she said to me, 'I think you're suffering with depression.' (Belinda)

At the other end of the spectrum from supporting the voice of patients, a patronising attitude from health professionals can greatly diminish the chances of doing good work.

But I think I've been very unlucky over the years with doctors, on the whole. And I found, particularly when I was younger, right up until I went to university, that I just got patronised the whole time. Like I'm not stupid, and I'd like to get something explained to me but nothing was ever explained to me until I was at university because then they go 'Oh, what you are doing?' I'd say 'I'm at university.' 'Really, where?' '[Elite university named].' 'Oh, right, my daughter's there,' and then they're suddenly, oh you're at [elite university], right… You might understand what I'm talking about because [you're] so clever. Before that, it was like you were some sort of total moron, that you just didn't get listened to, you didn't get… You know, it was as though what they were saying was, 'Well, it's just in your head, you know you don't really understand, I know better.' And I know that they're really busy and I know that they don't have a lot of time, but I really felt that I got no help at all most of the time. (Heather)

Consistent with the concerns people had about their false sense of selves as discussed in Chapter 2, many participants had lived much of their lives without really feeling authentically heard. In these circumstances, professional consultations can be an opportunity for patients to feel heard for the first time, or they can end up opening up old wounds around lack of voice. Unfortunately, it is apparently quite easy for practitioners to miss the patient voice.

… And I said I'd heard like the nurses talking about me, which I had because like the nurses' station was quite near. And they'd been sort of saying like I was withdrawn and a couple of other things, I think. And so when I said I'd heard some people talking about me he [the psychiatrist] interpreted it as a sort of schizophrenia type thing, and he was asking me had I ever thought of cutting off my penis, which was really a rather odd thing to be asked at that time. (Marcus)

A professional failure to listen out for what a patient is trying to say can be experienced as very disheartening for patients with a history of voicelessness. And as the quotations below show, listening to patients can be very difficult because the ways in which patients present can reinforce their lack of voice. For instance, there are things patients feel they are unable to say (Heather), and they say things which can be misleading when taken out of context (see Marcus above, and Rosey below).

I just wanted someone who knew what they were talking about to really like help me out. And I just didn't feel like it [counselling] was. I didn't feel like I could really talk about everything that I needed to talk about, and I think it really did make a difference that it was a children's psychologist… I think, you know, once people are a teenager, they don't want to be thought of as children... But she never really explained anything to me properly and I never really understood what she was getting at... (Heather)

I'm aware that over a very long period I used to have lots of, um, minor ailments, and again, I didn't think that any of the GPs I saw took seriously anything that was wrong with me. And they certainly didn't look at the bigger picture and think, 'Is this person unhappy, is that what all of these ailments are about?'... I don't think anyone was taking a proper view of my health, as a whole, and saying perhaps, 'It's actually, you know...' If I'm saying to this person, 'You know, it's all in your head,' then maybe I should be looking at your head? [laughs] And that decision didn't seem to be made... I [felt I] was being a nuisance for going to the doctor. For saying there was something wrong with me when the doctor didn't think there was something wrong with me, for time wasting. I felt like I was just being a drain on my doctor. (Rosey)

It is also interesting that patients who feel they lack voice can collude with the professionals they feel are not able to listen. Even though Marie had suicidal urges, her counsellor failed to pick up the crisis by normalising these urges. But notice how Marie colludes with her counsellor and pulls away from voicing her serious concerns:

And I, how many times did I see her [a counsellor]? Three times I saw her, and she decided that I wasn't, you know, I wasn't sort of needy, needing that [counselling]. And I felt obliged to say, well there are other people and you've got such a long waiting list, you know, I'll go away. And you know, sort of, after that I thought, you know what a waste of time... When I was telling her things that happen to me when I'm really bad... And when I'm...I'm really down it occurs to me when I see a train coming to jump in front of it. And again I get these compulsions, and I have to physically take a step backwards so as not to do it. And these are strong urges. And I was told, 'Oh, well everybody feels like that from time to time.' (Marie)

Alternatively, an attitude of deep curiosity about what patients are voicing, and the narratives they are trying to convey, can have entirely different results. It is difficult for patients to give voice to their concerns and develop an authentic narrative that gives real meaning to their experiences. Thus, supporting authentic voices through carefully listening to (and respecting) narratives, can make a big difference to people with depression. In fact, listening in order to pick up an authentic patient voice and narrative, and conveying an understanding back to patients, is enormously valuable, and is picked up in more detail in the next chapter on talking therapies.

I think I went over the course of about three terms, over a couple of academic years, seeing that counsellor... It was, it was quite good in a way, because it was the first time somebody had sat and listened to me, listened to my concerns, exclusively, and that worked quite well. (Rosey)

Responding appropriately

As discussed in the Introduction and in Chapter 4, recovery frequently involves people finding their voice and identifying what their authentic narrative is from a range of possible narratives. The authentic narrative is the one that allows things to drop into place for patients, or for a 'true story' that feels right at the time to be identified. Such a narrative allows meaning to be retrieved from the crisis of depression (Dowrick 2004). Here, practitioners demonstrate that they are listening by reflecting carefully on what is said, sifting through the fragments of patient narratives, and finding ways to respond to the information that relates to authentic voice and narrative.

> He [a psychiatrist] had an expression that every time I went to see him, he would say, 'How are you in your spirits today?' So I would feel free to say, 'I've...I've had a terrible time', or 'Feels bad'. And he would say, 'Oh, that's probably because of something that I'd [John] mentioned was happening...' So he was able to put a label on it to a certain extent, which made it drop into its place... (John)

Responding appropriately to patient narratives may involve helping to sort out which of the multiple narrative threads patients tell are actually important or even more likely to be 'authentically' felt. There may even be confusing or conflicting accounts coming from patients, their relatives or friends. Here, professionals valued by patients maximise their belief in the idea of an authentic patient narrative. Carol explains how the trust her psychiatrist placed in her authentic narrative gave her considerable sustenance to value herself and cope with her difficult family dynamics:

> And he [my psychiatrist] has backed me, the doctor is absolutely great and he said to me about three weeks ago, he said 'You owe your Mum nothing'... She's [my mother] been, you know, bad mouthing me, right. And I thought, 'How can she turn on me?' But I used to cry because when I was in the hospital, I was always with my Mum, right, like she was my mother but she was like my pal. We were always together, it was always me and her. And this is what I couldn't understand. I mean I took unwell. I could not cope with my own life, never mind looking after my mother. But my [sibling] was saying cruel things to me. And telling me if she [my mother] died not to come near the funeral and things like that. And I know I did nay deserve that and so did my [psychiatrist] know that. And that's why. I've got far, far too many honest people on my side. (Carol)

As previously noted, listening also involves monitoring what is left unsaid. In the quotation below, a health professional acquaintance picks up on the authentically felt undercurrent in Peter's narrative: that he somehow felt to blame for having had depression. By conveying a no-blame chemical imbalance narrative in a supportive way, the professional was able to get to the heart of Peter's concern. And in a way that helped him to shift his narrative and let go of guilt.

> You see somebody said something to me, and one of the things that really helped me, Damien… It was that somebody at church said 'It's not your fault Peter. It's not your fault, it's probably the serotonin in the brain has been knocked out, and therefore it was a chemical cause of your…' I think this is what she said, it's some time ago. But it was such a relief, I don't know if I was bearing a sort of a hidden guilt for getting this illness, I don't know but it was such a relief to be told that, it was marvellous… [Being told it was not my fault] was a major episode, that. I remember we were outside the Baptist church, and she got chatting to me, she was in the medical profession herself… (Peter)

Promoting a 'recovery attitude'

As introduced in Chapter 4, a key approach to being a recovery ally involves instilling hope in patients. Even when a person has trouble believing they will recover during the depression, the key difference between an ally and someone with depression is that the ally can really believe that the person will recover.

> But if you cling on to the thought that most people recover, and that you will get better… But it may take time, and I think I would just stress that you need hope, you need hope that it's not the end of the line for you. You very likely will get better but you need time. And you need not to be too hard on yourself and think that you're a failure and you've got it all wrong. (Peter)

The kinds of professional statements (used sensitively, and appropriately within patient narratives) that participants found helpful included ones like: 'I think I can help you', 'I believe you can get through this', 'You will recover in time, but not immediately', 'Depression is only part of you, not all of you', 'What does not kill you can make you stronger.'

Making time and being available

There are widespread perceptions among doctors about a general lack of time for consultations with patients in both the UK and the US (Braddock and Braddock 2005; Pollock and Grime 2003). Research in the UK involving people with depression shows that many perceived intense time pressure when seeking help from their GP (Pollock, Grime and Mechanic 2002). Patients were worried about wasting doctor time and so they tended to take on responsibility themselves to try and conserve time as a precious resource in the NHS. However, research on the GP perspective in the UK has shown that time constraints are not thought to greatly impede the care of patients with depression (Pollock and Grime 2003). While average consultation times may be less than ten minutes, GPs have some flexibility with their time, and may not feel the same sense of time urgency that patients with depression do. In addition, GPs are also able to see a depressed patient many times after the first consultation, thus adding considerably to the total length of time spent with the patient when considered over a year. Doctors who were highly valued by the current participants seemed to prioritise patients with depression, providing additional time that appeared to be unrushed.

> He's got a great way with patients, he's one of these people who makes you feel that it's you he wants to see, never mind the other people waiting, never mind the person he's had before. You're the one I've been waiting for. He has that ability. And doesn't mind a little joke in between. He's very business-like, we don't mess about, we don't waste time, but you can have a little joke and, and things… He doesn't sit with his pen poised over the prescription pad as you walk through the door. (Marie)

Professional allies who made themselves available in times of need were highly regarded. People highlighted the extra lengths some professionals appeared to go to in order to be available. Such gestures, even if symbolic, could be a considerable source of comfort and even strength for patients.

> And I'm, I'm extremely grateful for him [his GP] that he gave me his direct number and so if I, if you know, if it is a problem. I still have the number in my wallet now… This was someone specific who I know and I trust and, you know, if I am at my absolute worst I have entire faith that, that he could do something to sort me out. And to have that was very important and another great source of strength, and actually still is. (Craig)

> She [GP] cares and she's shown me she cares because she has rung me up before at home and said, 'How are you? Will you come and see me tomorrow?' Because she knows I'm not going to ring and make an appointment because I…I mean I'm in isolating mode, and things are going wrong. (Belinda)

Referring on

A survey in New Zealand found that GPs were aware of a wide range of serious issues associated with depression (Wilson and Read 2001). Nevertheless, GPs were reluctant to refer patients with depression to outside resources because of the limited availability and affordability of practical, psychological and social help. Similarly, participants in the present study felt that even when doctors were 'switched on', they could still wait too long to refer them for specialist help. Below, Rosey describes her relief when she finally got a referral to a psychiatrist, even though her GP was as helpful as he could be.

> But I had a GP that was quite interested in how I was, which was good...[but] I was very low physically and clearly very low mentally, and the GP... And I'll be forever thankful for him, actually said, 'I don't think I am helping with the right kind of medication for the right reasons, and if you agree I'd like to refer you on to somebody.' And it was like an immense relief, it really was an immense relief. Half of me was thinking, 'This was a disaster for me because I was going to see a psychiatrist.' And the other half was thinking, 'Hooray, somebody's actually going to treat me as somebody who has a problem here.' So I went along, to the assessment, and as soon as I said out, lots of things about my life and about the way I felt in my life, there was no sense of you're in the wrong place, it was, ' Fine, we think we can help you with it.' And it really was a huge relief, and they immediately put me on a proper dose of antidepressants, and saw me regularly. And I actually felt that somebody was for the first time, somebody was actually listening to me... (Rosey)

Being mindful about the delays in the referral chain is very important. Even when a GP is quick to refer a patient on for specialist help, participants still said they could wait too long for an appointment in the NHS. Craig had such a long wait to see a psychiatrist (he was severely depressed for a period of two months) that the psychiatrist's concern about his immediate wellbeing at the first appointment seemed too little, too late:

> I was referred to the psychiatric hospital for assessment. Although I think it probably took about two months I believe between the initial sort of GP's referring letter and getting an appointment. Which again in retrospect was way, way too long, way too long. I was really, really ill and barely coping... I went prepared to the meeting with the psychiatrist... So I...talked about how I felt and I cried and I sobbed and I filled out the, the mood forms and I scored in the extremely seriously mega-depressed range. And I remember he went to, to talk with a professor and was actually quite concerned about leaving me (in the consultation room) on my own. Which was [laugh] very nice but I

remember thinking, 'Well actually this is quite amusing, seeing as I have managed to struggle through these last two months and then, you know, by the time I come to see you, yeah, sure, realistically I am on my last legs.' And he said, 'Are you going to be OK? Do you want somebody to sit with you?' [It] was actually kind of ironic. (Craig)

From the patient perspective, the long wait for specialist help was unacceptable. Participants cited intense suffering, and the potential for suicide in particular, as reasons why waiting so long for help is indefensible. Jill believed that she would not be alive if she had to wait for therapy on the NHS.

…I'm fortunate enough, I have, I can…use people privately, private psychotherapists and all that. But the last time, if I'd had to wait… I wouldn't be here today if I'd had to wait that long. (Jill)

For some participants, delays in receiving help from a referral from a doctor to a specialist could even run into years.

I don't know what the criteria [is] for choosing who has it [therapy], who doesn't. I know there are very long waiting lists. I've known people to wait for three years, and three years is a big chunk out of somebody's life. It's just very sad…you know, because I do believe that whilst medication helps people keep going, it's not necessarily the answer. (Pamela)

I remember when I'd first asked to have sort [of] psychotherapy you get told it's like an 18-months waiting list and it's really over-subscribed, which is partly why I was sort of saying, you know, how many [sessions] was I entitled to and… But she said, 'Ring me to have one session and, you know, we'll see whether you need more or, you know, whether it's your medication or whether it's something else.' (Marcus)

The wait could be increased further when things went wrong in the NHS referral chain. This was the case for Heather because of lost information and receiving a specialist service at the end of the line that did not fit her needs:

That probably echoes a lot of people's experiences, that it's [NHS] just very, very patchy and ad hoc and sort of really random. So it's like you might get referred somewhere, you might not. You might get help, you probably won't. It depends, probably, what doctor you get, where you are in the country, what day it is… And you have to pay, which I couldn't afford to do. And I got, I got put on this list when I went to see the psychiatrist people, they put me on a list and what they usually do is to say 'Oh yes, I'll put you on the list.' And then you go back and…you say 'Did you put me on the list?' They go 'Oh dear, yes, I forgot, I'll do it now.' And then eventually I got this referral and I was like,

'Wow, I've got the referral, I've got an appointment.' Went in, this woman basically said, 'Yes, it seems like you've got depression and anxiety or whatever. I suggest you go and see a psychoanalyst, go for a student, you have to go three times a week and it costs you £7 a go because it's a student so it's cheap.' And I'm like, I don't have £21 a week to spend, because at that point I wasn't earning like hardly anything... (Heather)

Related to things going wrong in the referral chain was the issue of continuity of care, and how important it could be from a patient perspective to see the same professional every time (see Chapter 8 on talking therapies for further discussion of patient–professional relationships). Ruth talked about feeling like she was on 'crop rotation' because she was seeing a different psychiatric registrar each time she went to the outpatients department. She successfully argued to see the same psychiatrist every time:

Well I'm pretty chronic really, you know I will be 40 this year, so I've had this diagnosis for just under 22 years... Well I've had a recognised illness for just under 22 years. I've had this diagnosis for 21. I have a severe and enduring psychiatric disability. What I did do about eight years ago, and it was when I first started, when I asked to get referred to [a consultant psychiatrist], because I didn't have him at the time. It's because the [hospital name removed] have a whole teaching set-up in London anyway... Is that people [doctors] go there for six months on rotation and it's like bloody crop rotation. Because when I'm healthy I wasn't seeing anyone more than two or three times a year, so I could see a different, a different registrar each time I went. And I thought this was really stupid you know. I'm a long-term patient here, I don't go enough, but it would be really nice for a bit of consistency. Could I get referred to a consultant? (Ruth)

Other participants were also prepared to ask their professionals (and even put pressure on them) to get the right kind of specialist referral and service. Participants like Jane mustered up the courage to question professionals and ask for a better service:

...and it was only through constant pressuring the psychiatrist and the NHS that I got psychotherapy. You have to fight for it, you have to fight for it. It's not a thing that is automatically given... Because there is so few, there is so few therapists [in the NHS]. (Jane)

Ensuring supportive care in the community

Extending care in the community can be very important to the recovery of patients, particularly in situations of severe depression and lengthy hospitalisation. For instance, Belinda talked about feeling quickly institutionalised by the routines in an NHS hospital, and so it was hard for her to readjust to the real world outside.

> I think I became... in eight weeks, I very quickly became institutionalised myself. I was scared to come out because I was in this enclosed world where I knew what was going to happen. There were routines, mealtimes, getting up times, medication times, occupational therapy times. There were routines and I had no responsibilities. I didn't have, because I live, I'm single and I, you know, I pay a mortgage on this house. I have responsibilities, I have to work to pay the bills and things, and the bills need to be paid and the cat needs to be fed and, you know, I don't have children but I have certain responsibilities and suddenly I had no responsibility. I was being cared for, or I was in a place where I didn't have to think about anything, and nobody could touch me. (Belinda)

Many participants talked about the enormous value of getting practical help from friends and professionals in their recoveries, particularly in making the transition from hospital care back into independent living in the community. For instance, below, Jane talks about how she was having debilitating panic attacks once she was discharged from hospital. A community psychiatric nurse played a key role in helping her to cope better:

> ...I had visions of me walking out of the shop with this stuff in my bag and not paying for it. So I suddenly went into a fearful panic attack of 'Oh, I'm going to be a shoplifter!' And I can understand why people do it when they're not thinking straight. And I dropped the basket and I just ran down the road to the hospital and I was, I couldn't go out for ages. I went into a massive panic attack. And they put me on medication to cope with it... Then what happened was that they had to get a CPN, a community psychiatric nurse, to bring me home for one hour, gradually, to see how I could cope with being in my flat on my own. And then she'd come in here, she would spend an hour in here with me, we would do some cleaning or something. And she would take me back again [to the hospital]. Then the next time she would bring me in and we would stay two hours... (Jane)

Professionals who work in the community have the advantage of being able to work more broadly with patient networks. After a suicide attempt, a social worker helped Paul's father to better understand his depression, and helped Paul to consider positive actions he might consider next.

> ...she [a social worker] actually came round to the house where I was living with my father after I'd dropped out of university, after I'd made a suicide attempt. And she was helpful in a few ways in that she actually got my father to understand a bit more about my depression and that it wasn't just a case of laziness. It was a case of not being able to function, really...being completely

lost. And she also did have hour-long sessions with me at home and I think I got, you know, I was into talking about things and possibly I was talking about the way things could go. And that was probably beneficial, actually... I think I was completely isolated at that stage, and she would make positive suggestions...she would say, 'Well, maybe you could move away from home?' And she also investigated possibilities for doing that. (Paul)

Case study 7.1: Supporting men in distress

Men are frequently constructed as 'behaving badly' when it comes to looking after their mental health, including seeking appropriate professional help (Moller-Leimkuhler 2002; Smith, Braunack-Mayer and Wittert 2006). However, this 'male risk taking and resistances to health' narrative in the literature is well worn, and may overlook the ways in which men constructively engage in their own wellbeing. Jeremy (not a real participant, but a composite of many) is a 30-year-old married businessman who was not only keen on exercise as a way of staying fit, but sometimes used substances like cocaine at weekends as a kind of holiday from work stress. When his marriage began to break down after two years he found himself having to deal with rage at his partner, which he found very frightening. He began using more cocaine, and not just at weekends, and had trouble sleeping.

While Jeremy felt he had a good relationship with his GP, he felt very vulnerable expressing his level of his distress, and wondered if his GP might judge him as not strong enough. He also wondered if his GP was the best person to talk to about his problems. In the end, his GP prescribed sleeping tablets to help with his lack of sleep, but did not explore his feelings. Jeremy began feeling worse and worse inside, confused, and he wondered if life was worth it. Yet he felt like he had to keep up appearances at work. One night he broke down in tears when talking to his sister on the phone. His sister insisted that he talk to a counsellor. He realised he needed to do something, and was quite scared by his thoughts of suicide which were becoming more intrusive by then.

Jeremy hated the counselling waiting room, full of women, and no men. He said,

> I'm just thinking fuck you, you know, what am I doing here? And you get in there and there's the little box of tissues and you just think oh piss off. And 'How did you feel?' and all that stuff, that's how I felt it was just like my whole thing was completely negative about it. So you can see where I was coming from. It's not easy for blokes.

However, he felt like his career – and perhaps life – was at risk, and so he persevered with the counselling, even though it felt almost feminising, and was something he did not tell his friends about. In the end, though, he liked the counsellor. He thought she was straight talking, she never left him just to flounder (he was scared of not being able to answer questions), and she provided him with very practical solutions (e.g. increasing his exercise, monitoring and slowly reducing cocaine use, challenging his negative thoughts about himself), while not underplaying the need to get in contact with his inner feelings. And she seemed to know something about how miserable he felt.

> She [the counsellor] said, 'I'll tell you a bit more about how you feel...' Which was the most wonderful relief, because I thought this was just peculiar to me. And she took a great burden off my shoulders.

When he talked about how he felt, his counsellor – understanding that Jeremy was presenting with an atypical narrative of depression – was able to support him to articulate his story about how his escapist behaviour had failed to 'medicate' his inner rage at his father for leaving his family as a child. He also became aware of his anger at himself because he thought he had somehow caused his parents' marriage breakdown. And, connected to this, he thought he was all to blame for his current relationship breakdown.

And Jeremy liked talking about himself. He got in touch with some very painful childhood feelings of abandonment when his father left his mother when he was 12. It was strange being vulnerable in this way in front of a female counsellor, but also somehow empowering. He felt like he was somehow drawing strength from his vulnerability, and finally facing the truth about his feelings. He also got angry with his wife for leaving him, rather than angry at himself. He also got angry with his depression. He became motivated to struggle to get better because he did not want his father or wife to have this kind of power over him:

> You've...got to sort of reach down and...somehow find the strength deep down to start putting it into motion. It's really weird. I got really, really angry at the depression... It was as if I was treating it as a person now... I just thought to myself 'No, you are just not going to do this to me. You know, you are not going to have this control that you've had over me for the last year... I'm going to, you know, pull myself out of this.'

Strangely, even though counselling started off feeling feminine to Jeremy, in the end he felt quite validated in his masculinity. He felt more like he was being himself and being masculine, and his substance use reduced and he felt he did not need any more counselling after two years.

Conclusion

Being an ally in patient recoveries is a complex task. However, the narratives show that adopting some basic approaches to depression can potentially make a big difference to patients. Approaches include learning about the existential experience of depression including the anxiety, isolation and misery, and that patients cannot simply snap themselves out of depression. Professional allies can help patients to feel unrushed and to feel that their concerns are legitimate to discuss. Other approaches may be more difficult to learn, such as working out how to promote a recovery attitude among patients with depression, connecting with patients who are unable to feel connected to others themselves, and listening out for the things that patients do not say. Nevertheless, the patient narratives show that it is frequently the small and symbolic things that professionals do, like the comforting words they use; remembering things about the patient; displaying human qualities; following up patients who do not show for appointments; making efforts to support patient voices and to understand the stories patients tell (and what is most salient in those stories); and ensuring practical help is available in the community that can make all the difference in recovering.

Chapter 8

Talking Therapies

The purpose of this chapter is to look more deeply at talking therapies as a kind of recovery tool and make some general observations about the way that patients with depression approach and experience talking therapies. In particular, this chapter explores patient difficulties in engaging in therapy; how therapy can specifically help people with depression; the nature of the therapeutic relationship; as well as what is considered most helpful in terms of how therapists engage patients. As discussed in this chapter, the narrative evidence is that no particular 'brand' of therapy offers superior results for patients with depression. And so this chapter does not explore the different types of therapy available in any detail. Nevertheless, cognitive behavioural therapy (CBT) was most commonly available and used among participants in this study, and was highly regarded. A detailed discussion box on CBT is included towards the end of this chapter to provide deeper insights into how patients engage with – and benefit from – talking therapies.

Starting therapy

On top of the difficulties less well-off patients had in accessing the relatively small supply of therapists on the NHS, or affording private treatment, participants described their own initial blocks to getting any value out of therapy. People said they needed a certain level of self-awareness in order to get benefits from talking therapies. And it was common for people to have inaccurate preconceptions about what therapy might entail. Misconceptions about therapy were picked up from people's families and society more generally.

> And so it took a hell of a lot for me to go to therapy. You know, a) Nutters go to therapy, b) Therapy makes you a nutter. These were the kind of things that I grew up with. And it doesn't help, you know, [the] hostile kind of lower-middle-class sort of feeling about that sort of thing. We're not the sort of people that do it [therapy]. Do you know what I mean? It's like people who

live in Hampstead[1] go to therapy, we don't... And once I knew what therapy meant... I mean what I realised of my parents' position was just based on complete ignorance. You know, they thought it was, you know, Dr Freud and his couch, they didn't know anything more than that... (Matthew)

However, patients like Matthew who were initially hostile to therapy described getting value out of therapy if their therapist was skilled enough to deal with their initial views. Patricia, for instance, who described herself as initially very defensive, was pleasantly surprised that her therapist was effective in helping her to dismantle her barriers so that she could express herself so freely for the first time:

I went in there, very defensive, very, I'm not going to talk about anything, I'm not going to explain anything, I'm not gonna, you know, give her the answers. If she wants to get this out of me she's going to have to try bloody hard. I'm very stubborn. But the fact that she got beneath my surface in the space of an hour and got more out of me in an hour than a friend would get out of me in a year, shocked me. Because she hadn't really done it, I had... I wouldn't necessarily open up to anybody. So, although it was all bottling up inside me, I'd had this session and I found some things come out that I wouldn't talk to my best friend about. (Patricia)

Despite ultimately high levels of patient approval for skilful therapy, once commenced, therapy was mostly described as emotionally difficult. Certainly, some participants described first feeling much worse before they noticed any improvements from therapy. The initial phase of therapy could be particularly difficult for patients to cope with. This was especially true for participants who became painfully aware of their inner emotional turmoil through therapy. Additionally, as another fantasy about therapy collapses – that there is an 'instant solution' to suffering available – the prolonged pain involved in therapy could come into sharp focus for patients.

I remember being quite distressed at times because the counsellor had brought up things for me that were difficult to cope with. I was quite perturbed, I guess, about...I think there were lots of issues to do with bereavement, to do with my father, who died when I was three, and I think moving away from home... It was very difficult. And then the enormity of this long hard slog really hit me then. I knew there wasn't going to be any instant solution. I knew I had to live with the fact that I had this diagnosis, the reality that week in, week out I was going to be seeing somebody [for therapy]... (Rosey)

---

1   Hampstead is a wealthy suburb in the north of London.

And it's…it's hard work. It is hard work and there were times when I really didn't want to go… Or [wanted] to phone and say, 'I'm not coming in.' And there would be times when I'd dread going to see my counsellor because I just thought, 'Oh no.' And I hated it. (Julie)

A common theme reported by participants was the need to do considerable emotional work in order to engage in therapy and tackle issues they had hitherto not faced. But as Julie describes below, along with the emotional pain, could also come a kind of liberation in struggling with difficult issues with a therapist as a witness:

I just pushed myself because I just knew that it was going to, it was going to be OK. And I think the worst thing was actually for me was that fear of crying in front of him. And getting upset and stuff like that. But once I'd done that a couple of times it was like actually this is OK. I've even had an anxiety attack in front of him… And then like, we were doing the counselling and I'd sort of say, 'Can you just hold it there because I'm actually feeling… I'm having a bit of an anxiety attack.' And he would sort of say, 'What would you like me to do? Is there anything you would like me to do?' 'Well just open the window. And just sit with me, help me concentrate on my breathing.' So I had actually gone through… And once I had done that, I knew there was nothing to fear… (Julie)

Patients in this study described how they had to be ready to deal with difficult issues – like dysfunctional families – to get the most out of therapy. Fear and denial of deeper emotional pain associated with their issues meant that some participants were not willing to examine certain problems at the time of therapy.

At the time, I thought it [psychotherapy] was nothing. I thought this really is going nowhere, I don't know what this is about, because we spent all our time talking about my family. So… 'I have depression because I came from a dys-functional family?' Well, I suppose up to a point they were dysfunctional, but whose isn't? But several years later, as time went on, that did help. But I could have got a lot more out of it as I began to learn more… But fear I think held me back from actually working at it when I was in it. Because psychotherapy can be incredibly painful, very painful. And a lot of that pain I didn't want to face up to. (Pamela)

And having that space to talk made me feel better afterwards; that I'd come away and felt a little more confident and lighter. But on the whole, the kind of issues that were going on at the time, I didn't manage to get anywhere near resolving any of them… I think partly it was more to do with me because I felt a strong connection with family, it was always going to be a hindrance in my plans to move [out of the family home]. And I felt that was probably

> something on my part that I didn't have that courage to just go out and do what I felt was right for me at the time. (Shiad)

In particular, a number of people talked about the anger and even rage that could emerge in therapy as they examined their issues. Patients like Patrick needed to be ready – and feel in a safe place – to deal with emotions that they feared could get out of control:

> Anger came up as a big issue for me and that I felt anger as, a really, really over-whelming feeling and emotion. I found it almost like this... I describe it sometimes like this monster just bubbling up and just completely taking over... I just, I worried about where it would take me. I'd, I'd been in situations where, you know, I'd been potentially almost looking for fights... (Patrick)

Another difficulty in therapy was related to having no immediate vocabulary available to describe feelings and internal experiences related to depression. Participants grappled with what they felt were inadequate words to describe their experiences. Some participants even turned to less verbal forms of therapy to get around the problem of being unable to articulate their inner experiences.

> In my case I found art therapy, creative sort of therapy very, very helpful, because my creative side came out during my depression. But when I'm feeling all right, I have no creative side whatsoever... Drawing, I did an awful lot of drawing to start with, trying to express the way I was feeling, because I couldn't say it in words. So I found if I could sort of draw how I felt and then I'd explain to the art therapist, you know, what it was. And I kept all my drawings and I look back on them, you know, and try to relate to it. And also when I was seeing a psychotherapist, he said to me, 'If you find it easier to draw it, draw it and show it to me and try to explain it', which he found helpful because it helped him to understand more. (Jane)

Finally, specific characteristics of depression (e.g. lack of concentration, inability to feel) and its treatment, such as antidepressant medication, can provide additional blocks to therapy for patients.

> Prozac did help but...I wasn't taking it while I was counselling because it... To me it just wasn't worth counselling and doing that because I couldn't really get in touch with my feelings. So I needed to come off the medication to sort of work through the issues and stuff. (Julie)

> Yeah, but she [the therapist] wouldn't see me then. She interviewed me and said that I wasn't... at that point I wasn't suitable for therapy. And bearing in mind what I'd said about me choosing to go into, you know choosing to go and see a counsellor before, it came as something of a surprise to be told that I

wasn't well enough... And I was thrown by that. And she said no I need a proper support network, I need to be a bit more stable on the medication, and I was quite amazed. Because I thought, 'Well, I need to talk about my problems, I don't understand the delay.' I guess I do now, I think that was probably the best thing for me, that actually I did need to concentrate on – if I'm going to have therapy properly, who was going to support me? (Rosey)

While medication mitigated against engaging in therapy for some, other patients like Liza needed to be on antidepressants in order to be able to get into the right 'zone' to get the most out of therapy:

I think I feel probably stronger overall because of the cognitive therapy...that I don't allow situations...to overwhelm me quite to the same degree. Now, whether that is because the medication has helped in doing that, or whether it's because [of] those coping strategies are now a part of me... It would be I think quite difficult to define...if I had had cognitive therapy on its own and not the medication, I'm not sure if I could have coped with dealing with the issues. Whereas the combination of the two I felt fitted in really well together. (Liza)

Indeed, the research evidence indicates that, in general, combining antidepressant medication with talking therapy is more effective than either treatment alone, particularly in severe, chronic depressions (Keller *et al.* 2000; Pampallona *et al.* 2004; Thase *et al.* 1997).

The value of talking and therapy

While there are common perceptions that there is little scientific evidence to support the effectiveness of talking therapies for depression and other conditions, this is not the case. There is now enough research evidence over the decades to say confidently that patients with depression can gain substantial benefits from talking therapies, including reductions in depressive symptoms (Churchill *et al.* 2001; Cuijpers and Dekker 2005; Robinson, Berman and Neimeyer 1990). The patient narrative evidence is striking: Many participants came to prioritise – above all other approaches – talking through their feelings and experiences with skilful listeners as a means of coping with, and recovering from, depression. Participants said that talking through their problems – especially in the context of therapy – was a relief, and essential to sorting through their concerns so they could develop a narrative that supported recovery.

It was a big relief to have someone who I could tell anything I wanted [to], anything that was bothering me, and not worry about what they might think about it or how it might affect our relationship. And you know, it also helped

> to feel that I was doing something about my problems as well, so…just the impartiality and the friendliness, and I always looked forward to the weekly session, and it, you know, [it] helped me sort out my thoughts and feelings, describing them to someone else. (Nicola)

> I tended to lead it [discussion] wherever I wanted to go, you know. I found it very good, I quite like, I like talking, it makes me feel better. It was nice to be paying someone [laughs] a lot of money to talk. (Matthew)

On the other hand, staying silent was thought to contribute to confusion in thoughts and associated anxiety. And more than this, staying silent made it very difficult to develop a narrative about the self coping with and recovering from depression that felt authentic: a key issue explored in this book.

> It's good to talk, really. Don't bottle up your feelings because they just race around inside your mind and almost start playing… I think the mind's quite a powerful thing and it… It can start playing tricks on you, and you don't really realise. And I think you just need to talk and sort of say what you're feeling… And have the opportunity to sit and cry all day, if you want, because that's fine too actually… You need to go through the process. If you don't do it now, you'll do it in a year's time, or ten years' time. (Anne)

> And I don't think there's enough help [in the NHS]. You get your bad days, and you need to talk to somebody and it's… You need to talk to somebody instead of talking to the wall. And so that's how it is basically. I don't think there's enough help out there and enough understanding of it because…I don't know if it is just depression… I suppose if you was in a relationship, and you could talk to somebody, then when you go home it might help, I don't know. But sometimes you do need to talk to somebody who you don't know, who understands, instead of chatting to the brick wall. And instead of it going round in your head and trying to sort it out. Or you need somebody to talk to you and push the right buttons to help sort yourself out, basically, yeah. (Sasha)

The participants who were experienced in therapy left no doubt that therapy worked well for them provided that the therapist had the right skills, including those of a 'recovery ally', as discussed in the previous chapter. Indeed, participants more commonly prioritised therapy (31/38 participants) over medication (24/38 participants) as among the most helpful of all approaches they had tried to deal with their depression.

> …the benefits [of counselling] are absolutely… You know, from what… I mean from how I am today compared to what I was [like] a year or so ago. I am a completely different person and it's… And it's only because I've got the knowledge… (Julie)

Some of those who had benefited from therapy lamented that talking therapies are not more widely available and accessible on the NHS.

> It just saddens me that there isn't enough therapy about, because from my, almost 20 years' experience, I have seen people who are stuck in their depression... And I just feel, if only you had the right therapy, you could actually move on from this...it's just not available. It's there for the mega rich, because it is incredibly expensive. I was fortunate, I had mine under the National Health [Service]. (Pamela)

Consistent with the qualitative literature on therapy in general (Timulak 2007), those who had benefited from talking therapies were articulate about the *specific* ways in which therapy had helped them (see Box 8.1 for more detail). The benefits of therapy were multilayered and wide ranging and included:

- allowing people to unburden themselves of their suffering, and feel understood and thus relieved
- helping people to articulate and become clearer about issues they may not have adequately considered before, and so gain insights into themselves
- sorting through confusions and distortions in thinking
- helping people to explore, acknowledge, struggle with and better accept their difficult feelings
- helping to reframe people's narratives about themselves and their lives in more helpful ways
- promoting better acceptance of the self, and greater self-worth
- helping people to better get to the 'root' of their problems, including problems stemming from childhood
- assisting people to see how they had become stuck in repeating patterns in their lives
- helping people to make better choices in the way they approach life
- helping people to prioritise their issues and solutions, thus empowering themselves
- helping carers of those with depression understand their own needs and issues.

Box 8.1: Quotations illustrating the ways in which therapy can be specifically helpful for patients with depression

Clarifying confusions
Therapy in general, I think it's…whatever, initially helped me understand what's going on. Also, I'm not, I'm better now, I'm not great at communicating so to talk things out, just even to hear myself makes things a lot more clearer because I tend to be a bit confused, or I confuse things unnecessarily. (Jill)

Acknowledging difficult feelings
I used to fight things like anger, jealousy, and he [a counsellor] taught me that it's OK to be angry. It's OK to be jealous: jealousy is a natural thing. I used to completely refuse to be jealous of someone. I used to be…used to completely push it away, which used to make it even worse. 'I don't want to be jealous, I'm not the jealous type'…and it'd just well up and well up. So it's all now about, you know, which I've learned through counselling, also through meditation, sort of spiritual books that I've read that often talk about if you have a feeling, whether it be sadness, anger, then feel it and it will go: deny it, and it will just get bigger. (Patrick)

Self-acceptance and recognising the 'roots' of depression
I can't flag it [counselling] up enough, say enough how valuable it is. How important…and yes it might be expensive… But in the long term, you know, in three years' time, you may well be able to return to work or whatever. Or even if you don't return to work, it's just that whole sense of [sigh] just self… The realisation, the acceptance of yourself, your ability to move on in life, to understand it, to have the knowledge base there to accept, yes I am a depressive or I do experience depression, but this is what I know. This is how I need to move on… And looked into my childhood history. I can… I can recognise where the depression sort of stems from. (Julie)

Recognising habitual patterns of thought/behaviour
It's allowed me to see how some things have happened have started as patterns and rather than repeating those patterns, how I can move away from… Eric Berne talks about being in script so that the patterns, the scripts that were written when you were quite young, you keep repeating

unless you become aware of the script, and you move away from it. And it's allowed me to do that to quite an extent. (Ruth)

Positive reframing
Then of course when you start to talk about the intimate details of your problems, you do sort of get upset and everything. And you know it's horrific. I find myself telling her [the counsellor] things I've never put into words before. And she was coming back, 'Well, you're saying such and such, you're blaming yourself for this situation.' And the way she put it made me think, 'Oh, perhaps I wasn't as much at fault, perhaps only partly, perhaps somebody else was responsible for part, at least part of this situation'. And that was tremendous, it really was. I mean, and this...when did I last see her, possibly a year ago and I've not gone backwards. (Marie)

Empowerment
But he was balanced, objective and supportive in the ways that I felt I needed at the time... [I got] a return of self-esteem, I think [that] is the biggest thing. But that is one of the real big issues with depression anyway isn't it? He helped me and supported and encouraged me without laying down an agenda, which again I think is how it should be done. He helped me get my head around things and make my own decisions. (Carl)

Addressing the needs of carers
He [her husband] didn't have anyone to talk to, so in the end he did go and see a GP because he was concerned that he was going to get depressed as well. And he did pay for some private counselling sessions... And we also had some joint sessions, through *Relate*, to help us deal with the depression together, and the fall-out as well on our relationship... They were excellent... They gave us both a chance to talk properly to one another about our experience of the depression. I think before we'd kind of tip-toed round one another really. We were just so scared of it [depression]... It just seemed like such a big thing. And I'd also felt very abandoned by him, and very let down... But I was able to see through the sessions that... The pressure that he'd been under, and why he'd found it so difficult. And so we were able to talk through those very difficult emotions and feelings, and thoughts, in a safe environment. (Jenny)

The therapeutic relationship

Therapy is essentially a complex social interaction, and a relationship inevitably develops between the practitioner and the client (Gelso and Carter 1985). There were somewhat diverging ways of relating within the therapeutic interaction. While men and women could both develop close relationships with therapists and other professionals (Emslie *et al.* 2007), women focused their discussion more than men on the relational qualities of therapy. As Michelle said, therapy was 'one of the longest, most meaningful relationships of my life'. More specifically, women in particular emphasised the very human and personal qualities in the therapeutic relationship that they valued, as illustrated in detail in Box 8.2.

While relational issues in therapy (like trust and honesty) were also important to men, men focused their discussions more around practical issues and finding solutions than women did. Many men (and a few women) emphasised types of therapy – including CBT – that involved practical approaches and solutions.

> [The therapist] tended to use a few cognitive techniques… they did make suggestions about things I might concentrate on. And I think, by that stage, by 1995, I had put a lot of it together for myself and I really needed a bit more help getting reassurance that I was getting there, and help in putting the pieces together. In trying to develop my social skills a bit more, and maybe get out more, and just try a few things that were a bit more challenging, and I think they were quite encouraging, really. (Paul)

As kinds of relationships, therapeutic interactions also need to establish adequate boundaries and feelings of safety, in order to be effective.

> There were boundaries and it was always maintained, to ensure, you know… A good counsellor will maintain those boundaries and will say to you… 'You know, I'm going to take this back to my supervisor and blah, blah, blah'. And you know, that it is totally confidential. I knew that he was 100 per cent, nothing would… He wouldn't, he was just very, felt very safe with him probably. (Julie)

All social relationships involve the negotiation of power, and therapeutic relationships are no different (Spong and Hollanders 2003). Generally, greater power rests with the therapist to define the social interaction for a range of reasons, including patients being less sure what to expect from the therapeutic encounter than the therapist.

> I saw this gentleman [psychologist], who has since left, who didn't really do a great lot. A very kind man and he gave me a computer program on floppy disk,

but we just like spent the time talking about computers or things, life. Not having any other experience [of therapy] I wasn't quite sure what it was... (Marcus)

Box 8.2: Quotations illustrating the qualities of the therapeutic relationship that people may respond to

Trust...
If you can trust to tell them about most of the things you are ashamed about or unhappy about in your behaviour, I think that's the sort of acid test of trusting. And trusting the person to be appropriate with who they tell about you, how they write up your notes, being discreet in that respect. (Rosey)

Transparency, honesty, mutual positive regard...
I've been lucky in that I've seen three psychiatrists, and the current guy that I see I get on like a house on fire with. ...he is open, he tells you, he doesn't pussyfoot around, he tells you. You have to feel comfortable... this is dealing with your psyche, and unless you feel you can trust the person and you like the person... You have to like them, you have to like them, you may... On occasions you may not like what they tell you, but you have to like them. And you have to understand that they've got your best interests at heart and that they're interested in you... That they are worried that you do stay well, or that you don't stay well and that they like you as well... I guess it's like marriage, you've gotta kind of work with someone initially to sort of figure out whether or not you can work with them because you're gonna be seeing them for a while... (Michelle)

Chemistry...
But it [therapy] can dig up all the dirt from previously and you... It's knowing whether you can gel with a therapist. I mean when you first have your first meeting with a therapist, it's usually about for half an hour to see whether you gel with each other. And I think when you meet someone you kind of either feel relaxed or you can't... (Jane)

In the case of depression, where people can lack confidence and voice, power is an even more important consideration. Here, there are ways that professionals can work to hand back some power to patients, such as by explicitly talking about the issue of power in therapy, and making special efforts to honour patient 'voice', listening out for patient narratives, and reciting such narratives back to patients in ways that help patients to be clearer about their emerging narrative.

> It's always been a real partnership that she always insists that I'm as much in control of what happens as she is and that again has been quite liberating, you know because I can – I've never made choices but I know that if I made a choice, it would be respected. (Rosey)

> ...he [a therapist] didn't like talk down to me... He wasn't pompous, he didn't make me feel like, you know, I don't know, intimidated... And also he seemed tough enough to be able to... not that he was tough but he didn't... I could be however and he wouldn't... He sounded, it was like he was absorbing what was going in...he was just there, he was just, he was just him[self]... Whatever I said, it didn't seem to change him but then when he spurted out his things he'd digested it, it had all made sense to me and got me thinking. (Jill)

Finally, given that a relationship of sorts develops in therapy, some thinking needs to go into ending therapy. Therapy may be short term or longer term, yet the therapy relationship will come to an end eventually. In the NHS, some patients with depression may feel pressured to end therapy early, especially if they are concerned about consuming scarce NHS resources (Pollock *et al.* 2002). At the other end of the spectrum, patients may not trust private therapy that feels like it is being prolonged for reasons other than good treatment, such as making profits.

Women in particular talked about the need to consider the ending of the longer-term therapy relationship. For Julie, the ending of therapy was 'scary', but also an opportunity for independence:

> Yeah, they [the therapist] are on the journey and I think that it's safe...because they're on a journey that you are on, and they are with you every step of the way sort of thing... The downside is that once you've been seeing your counsellor for so long and you've built this wonderful relationship you're in... Then you've got to have an ending and that's quite scary... Who am I going to offload it onto? ...There can be a dependency culture where you think, 'Well, actually I don't want to be going alone', because that's what you've got to do at the end of the day. You have to take that step and you have to brave it on your own. (Julie)

When the therapeutic relationship is interrupted abruptly, patients can experience considerable distress and grief, and even trauma.

> I went to see her [counsellor] one night and I sat down and literally immediately she said to me, 'I'm very sorry but I don't feel as if there is any trust in the relationship, it's completely broken down. I'm not able to work with you

anymore.' … I hadn't seen it coming at all. There had been no warning signs to me. What was going on with her I have no idea… I've stopped trying to analyse it because I'm never going to find out unless I speak to her again, and that's very unlikely that I will ever contact her again. So I'm… I don't know, something was going on with her, it must have been. At the time I thought, my thoughts were, I mean it kind of cut me in half really. I was very upset but my thoughts were, 'God there must be something really wrong with me for a counsellor to reject me, a counsellor is rejecting me, is rejecting me! My God I must be so bad…' I must have been in a kind of shock then. I was bent over crying and I literally couldn't, couldn't walk straight to my car, I was so upset. And it took a while to get over that to be honest. (Belinda)

A better way to consider ending longer-term therapy is to consider the therapy as a relationship, where due consideration and time needs to be given to grief and negotiating an ending that contributes to a patient narrative of coping and even recovering from depression. Well-negotiated endings involve stories of empowerment for patients, where patients feel they have other options for support.

It's like you are taking that plunge yourself… It is, it's like learning to swim, taking the arm bands off or something. It just felt like, oh my gosh! You know, there are times when you are sort of paddling for air, doggy paddling like mad but it's like no, I can do this. I'm OK. I'm surviving. But I do, I do still think about, I wish I could speak to, you know… But then as a result of the counselling I've learnt to put other things in place. You know, it's about using the resources around you and friends and families. And now I'll pick up the telephone and speak to a friend as opposed to speaking to the counsellor. (Julie)

Therapy styles

In harmony with the research evidence (Robinson *et al.* 1990), overall, participant narratives did not identify any one particular type of therapy that was thought superior for treating depression. Instead, as outlined above, participant narratives were about benefiting in specific ways from having space to talk through their issues in their own way; having their narratives witnessed and recognised; forming respectful relations with another person; and learning practical ways of coping. Additionally, there were also practitioner approaches that participants really appreciated that were consistent with the therapist acting as an ally in recovery (see Chapter 7 for more detail). A key benefit of therapists acting as allies in recovery is the careful listening and honouring of patient narratives that skilled therapy involves. Although the 'essence' of therapeutic listening is difficult to capture as suggested in the previous chapter, people do come to therapy to be heard and understood at a deep level (Myers 2000). As writers like Arthur Frank point out, it can be very difficult for health professionals to really listen when patients talk about disturbing existential matters with no clear treatment solutions (Frank 1991). And this is why skilled talking therapy is so important. When therapists really hear the patient – including what is not being said, or what is being said in coded ways – all the while conveying a supportive understanding, new possibilities in patient recovery narratives may arise. At their best, therapists can help patients face frightening issues, helping to reframe them in more helpful ways.

> I like the way they're never shocked and I like the way they sort of make you question things, then put things in a different way, that you'd [not] thought of… (Marcus)

Although no one kind of therapy stands out as superior, participants had different preferences for therapy styles according to their particular circumstances. For instance, at the time of interview Diego wanted to sort through more immediate issues rather than delve into his past through psychotherapy. Similarly, Liza wanted to focus more on her immediate concerns of looking at her behaviour and how to change:

> I [could] go back you know, 40 years, and start talking about my childhood, the death of my parents, I feel everything is linked. But at the moment now [laughing] I want to sort out how I'm feeling now, and I don't feel, or I didn't feel this time going back and talking and talking because the psychoanalysis that I did have… They help me through you know, talking about my homosexuality, talking about the loss of my parents. So it was important, you know to…talk through the problem, or having this person to listen to you. But I do think it's a very long-term thing you know, and I think it is, it was useful at the time I did have it, but I don't feel I want to have it now. (Diego)

> I had read somewhere about cognitive therapy. And I just found it a really good idea. I have never really been a supporter of counselling. Largely, you know, I think you can talk about things till the cows come home and it doesn't actually make you any better. But this cognitive therapy, and the way that it looked at your behaviour, and there were reasons for the way you behaved in that way, and maybe reasons then to look, to…changing your behaviour, seemed to me, something that was worth trying. (Liza)

Paul talked about an approach that best suited him: not CBT, but a focus on the present and the 'real world'. In previous therapy, he had focused on the past – including the misery of depression – an approach which he came to understand as unhelpful to his own predicament:

> I think they focused on the real world a lot more, rather than some of the previous experiences I'd had where it was all talking about the past and my feelings and my sensation of being adrift and very miserable and talking about the depression itself. It was talking about the environment around me this time… And it wasn't dwelling on the depression itself, which I felt can go round in circles. (Paul)

Rather than focus on immediate concerns, other participants wanted to explore the deeper issues behind their depression. For example, Julie wanted to deal with her 'history' and its hidden feelings:

> I went to see my ex-counsellor and told him what I was talking about… He had gone to his supervisor, and his supervisor had said to him, oh CBT it's very good for, you know, depression and anxiety. And I actually said to him, no I don't want CBT, because at that stage I knew a little bit about CBT and I knew it wasn't for me. I said, 'I want to deal with the history. I want to deal with getting in touch with my feelings.' And now 18 months down the line I was saying to my counsellor, actually now I think it is time for me to try CBT. (Julie)

Another key theme about the style of therapeutic interaction was the way in which the therapy could involve feedback and the provision of a therapeutic 'map' from the therapist. The approach that came in for most criticism was that which left participants feeling lost, and without sufficient feedback to help them build an all-important 'road map' to indicate where their therapy and depression experiences might actually be going.

> … counsellors who can be a bit more interactive and a bit more…well they might almost be people who give you feedback, because it is important to have feedback, I think. Otherwise you are… You're sort of like struggling and sort of saying, 'You know, I'm in the sea and you know I'm looking for a piece of wood to hold on to or something.' And then somebody comes to you and they'll say, 'Well, where do you think it is? What direction do you think you ought to swim to shore?' And that's not really necessarily that helpful. (Paul)

Participants commenting on this issue of feedback and mapping the therapeutic terrain were clear that it was possible for therapists to provide 'roadmaps', without taking away their power to determine the actual content and direction of therapy themselves. For example, Rosey talked about a therapy experience where there was the right amount of 'silences' to facilitate her reflection and grappling with issues, yet the therapist was also able to discuss a non-directive road map.

...she [the counsellor] will explain things, she will ask questions for clarification. ...We have reflective silences, but we don't have awkward silences. Um, she's very good at analogies... one example is the idea of when you're climbing a mountain you have different camps, and you might go into another place, acclimatise yourself and go back down again. And you know in terms of helping to understand your journey through depression you may get to a point where you feel a bit happier, but then you might have a little relapse, but then you might go back to, you know, where you're moving upwards. She's very good at explaining things in a way that I can relate to. (Rosey)

Participants did have different preferences for interaction. For Heather, a higher level of interaction was thought beneficial so that she did not have to be 'flailing around' in a way that she experienced as unhelpful:

I find it's quite frustrating when with counselling they are basically there just listening to you. And sometimes you just want to go 'Speak to me, just say something, you know suggest something, whatever.' And when she did, it was kind of, that was what was helpful. But I can see that the idea is that you're supposed to work through it all yourself. I want someone to like, to sort of come up with ideas, and the person say stuff because I find it a bit, sort of I feel like I'm just kind of flailing around if I don't really know what's going on. (Heather)

At the other end of the spectrum, therapy that is experienced as too directive, or that appears to include the therapist's own agenda that is at odds with what is salient to the patient, is unlikely to be helpful. For instance, like Paul (below), patients may read things into therapist-introduced subjects that were not intended. For Carl, his therapist focusing on pre-determined categories, rather than his own priorities, was experienced as very frustrating as it blocked his voice and narrative:

The therapist or whoever it was, asked me, 'Do you love your brother and do you love your father?' And I was sitting there on the couch and I said 'yes' and 'yes' because I thought that was the right thing to say [laughing]. And I didn't want to bring up anything else that might complicate it... The message that I got was that I should and could absorb a lot of this kind of thing that was going on around me... Well...the conflict was between my father and my brother, and so they only... I wasn't there to be listened to, that's what I felt. (Paul)

But it [the counselling] was issue focused, and his issue focus, rather than: Hey, what's bothering me today? Am I having a bad week? Or did I have a good night sleep last night? Or what are the things bugging me just now? I don't really think he ever asked me, 'Carl, what are your needs?' You don't ask that in so many words, but one should, as a client or patient if you like, get that impression.

And I did not get that impression. It was, here is a list of things and… It's almost like handing out some whale music tapes, and some scented candles, and a relaxation manual. That's fine, that might suit some people, but it didn't me. I wanted to talk about what was making me upset and to [get] help to come to terms with… Or put to bed some of the issues that were troubling me. (Carl)

Box 8.3: Cognitive behavioural therapy (CBT)

While no one type of therapy was generally considered by participants to be superior, one popular approach to therapy was CBT. CBT basically argues that it is our tendency to think negative thoughts that creates our unhappiness and distress, and that we can challenge these thoughts and so feel better (Sheldon 1995). Clearly, CBT is not for everyone, and doing CBT is very difficult in the depths of depression. However, for patients who are ready and able to do the work, CBT involves first noticing the negative thought, and then doing something about it. For instance, on noticing a negative thought, some participants who had had CBT were able to catch it and just stay 'Stop.' And this simple technique could itself be very effective.

> I was having the cognitive therapy and got on really well with it, [and] the guy that was giving me therapy. I felt very comfortable in saying anything to him. He taught me a lot of the cognitive stuff about stopping negative thoughts. Literally saying, 'Stop' to them. [laugh] And I learnt to do that. And I still will do that if I'm having a bit of a negative day over something. I can still remember to say 'Stop!' And not do that. (Veronica)

In talking about the value of CBT, rather than discuss the CBT approach comprehensively, people tended to highlight a few techniques or 'take home messages' they personally found helpful. Such techniques included keeping a log and auditing the small achievements daily.

> …I did keep the mood log, where you challenge your thoughts, and I found that useful. And then I also kept a list of things I'd done in the day, because one of the things I was saying to myself and saying to the clinical psychologist was that I wasn't doing anything, that I was just sat… But once I started to write things down I could see that in fact, although they were small things, I was doing things. So I was getting [my son] up in the morning and getting him washed and cleaning his teeth. I was preparing food, even if it was just like a convenience meal and I shoved it in the microwave. Just very small things and it helped. I could see that in a very small way I was doing something. So that was useful to see. (Jenny)

> A particular example was [the therapist] said, when you go down to go to sleep, he said, 'You tend to look back on your day and think of all the failures.' And he said, 'Why don't you just think of everything that's been successful?' He said, 'With the proviso that for someone like you, who's

> severely depressed, they could just get out bed in the morning and that is a victory.' … And I started doing that. And every night I would just lie there I'd think well I shaved today, you know. I was down in time for breakfast. And I did a crossword puzzle and so forth. Well, you know, actually you've done quite a lot, you know. And then I…wake up in the morning with the memory of that. So just things like that, a few things like that with cognitive therapy. You know, I think they helped quite a bit. (Richard)

The basic skills that patients pick up from doing CBT can be very powerful in shifting their perspective away from negative and distorted thinking towards more realistic thinking.

> I think one of the analogies [the therapist] used first off was, if I was walking down the street and somebody came walking towards me that I knew, and I knew well. But that they looked away and walked past me, how would I feel? And I said 'Well, you know, oh my God, you know, what have I done?' Or trying to remember the last time I met them, I mean what had I said? You know, feeling guilty that it was obviously my fault. It would never have crossed my mind as he would suggest, as he suggested to think, that the person might well have had things on their mind, may not actually have seen me, may have been distracted by something else… And I, I saw for the first time, other people had other issues that were quite separate from me. … And it made me realise over a period of time that… If something happened that I felt unhappy about…I only saw it from one angle. (Liza)

Interestingly, some patients like Heather who had not had CBT developed CBT-like techniques for themselves to help them to cope better. After many episodes of depression, Heather found her own way to challenge her negative thinking that she would never recover from the latest episode of depression she was experiencing.

> But I see myself as having…through experience, experiencing it [depression] myself, having got better and able to cope with it… Even though if you get depressed you always still, you still really kind of believe that this is it, and it's really bad. But at the back of your mind at least you know that it's going to get better, at some point. (Heather)

Conclusion

As a key kind of recovery tool used in depression, there are many blocks to patients undertaking talking therapies, including shortages of such therapies in the NHS, the costs of private therapies and patients' preconceived ideas about what therapy entails. Therapy can also be experienced as emotionally painful and exhausting, particularly in the early stages. Patients may need to have supports in place in order to undertake therapy effectively. Participants frequently talked about needing to do considerable emotional work over extended periods in order to use therapy to recover from depression. Nevertheless, participants described how skilled therapy could work very well for them.

People who benefited from therapy were articulate about the specific ways in which therapy functioned. For these patients with depression, the 'brand' of therapy was much less important than the way that the therapeutic relationship worked. Helpful therapeutic approaches included focusing therapy on issues that are most salient to patients at the time of therapy; reflecting back patient narratives in new and helpful ways; allowing an authentic patient story to emerge; and providing enough feedback so that patients did not feel like they were always adrift or drowning in possibilities. A good therapeutic road map can help patients to restore meaning and direction in their narratives, without disempowering them. Due attention also needs to be paid to the relational nature of therapy, including the negotiation of an ending that takes into account the grieving work patients do when therapy ends and the supports they need post-therapy.

Chapter 9

Summing It Up

In this concluding chapter I briefly recap the key findings in this book, pointing to the implications of these findings for professional practices. The intention of the chapter is to cover issues that professionals might consider in order to best support patients during their depression and recoveries. Recall that the focus of this book was not on whether or not the accounts of patients and their preferred treatment approaches were objectively effective. Rather, I have been at pains to point out that the narrative approach to depression involves respecting and engaging with patient narratives; allowing 'authentic' stories to emerge; helping patients to select the narratives that feel most true to them; and learning about the narrative 'tools' that patients believe are effective within their narratives of managing depression. While it is not possible to know as much as the patient does about the interior experience of their depression, it is possible to think in narratives and thus better engage with patients. By engaging with patients in this way, professionals have the best chance of supporting patients in the work they need to do to cope with their depression.

Leading into depression

In this book, participants outlined diverse life narratives and yet there were a number of interesting threads running through the narratives that professionals can acquaint themselves with. One thread included early life problems, particularly dysfunction within families. Other threads included feelings of 'difference,' or being an outsider from an early age; grappling with social problems as children without sufficient cognitive or social resources; the laying down of unhelpful blueprints for thinking in childhood; feeling that the self is somehow disorganised, confused or even 'false' (e.g. feeling like one is 'acting' all the time); and having to cope with difficult and multiple life events leading up to depression that overwhelmed coping resources.

Although depression is common in the community, less than half of people with depression currently access professional help. I have argued that depression is largely experienced as an isolating interior condition, to do with difficult thoughts, feelings and bodily sensations. Partly due to a limited vocabulary to describe interior life, depression is difficult for patients to grapple with themselves, let alone explain to others. Although it is hard to know exactly what is universal to people experiencing depression, the common thread running through narratives of moderate to severe depression was an existential misery (described as hellish for some) that could be supremely isolating.

People make transitions into depression, and this transition (or depressive interlock) involves a cascade of distressing emotions, thoughts and sensations. While depressive interlock could appear to be very dramatic to participants, it is difficult for people to describe what they are going through at the time. Nevertheless, in retrospect, many participants were able to paint vivid and disturbing pictures of depression, such as involving an onslaught of negative thoughts; feelings of intense and insurmountable isolation; misery described to the point of 'hellishness'; and anxiety even to the point of terror. The way that the depressed mind tends to stop in its tracks to focus on its misery – which may seem unending at the time – is another distressing part of depression for patients. Additionally, the depressed mind has great difficulty telling any story about the self that would allow the person to go on engaging with life. Nevertheless, this slowing down of experience – to focus on misery, disrupted self and personal story – provides a 'dangerous opportunity' for something else to emerge, including a longer-term recovery and more functional self. Clearly, professionals who are able to understand something about the existential nature of depression are better able to offer even the most depressed patients hope for recovery. For example, professionals can point out that while it may not seem like it, the patient will tend towards recovery in time, there are effective treatments available, and so they can expect to get better.

People also talked about the double whammy where their unstable foundations for their sense of self could become mixed up with the destabilising onslaught of depression. In severe depression, people even talked about how the self gets 'put in the mixer and could come out in any old form', as one man put it. Nevertheless, even in severe depression, people described being good actors. As one woman said, 'I could wake up feeling shit... But somehow I had to get out there and spark. I could get out there and sparkle!' These kinds of fundamental issues in the self point to the longer-term recovery project that many patients felt they needed to engage in: to live better, feel better, and better 'know thy self'.

I also spent some time discussing the risk of suicide associated with depression. Depression is accepted as a risk factor in suicide, and many participants talked about thinking about – or attempting – suicide. People said they thought about the suicide option during depression because it seemed meaningful and even somehow logical at the time. However, it can also be meaningful to stay alive (e.g. due to responsibilities to others). Helpfully, professionals can access patient narratives to support reasons to live (e.g. to not be just another statistic, responsibilities to loved ones) and challenge 'this logic'. Also, patients in this study said suicidal thinking is on a spectrum from passive to active. In the latter case, 'suicide logic' can seem thoroughly convincing. People talked about triggers which could result in 'suicide logic' (e.g. a relationship break-up) as well as those triggers that could snap them out of 'suicide logic' (e.g. a phone call from a loved one during a suicide attempt). To an extent, thinking about suicide on its own can be reassuring in that it can give people a way of expressing themselves, and a sense of control over their depression. As such, skilled professionals would not shy away from allowing patients space to express such suicidal thinking. However, equally, suicidal thinking can become intrusive and disturbing to patients, and professionals should also be on the lookout for this kind of thinking.

Recovery

In setting the scene for this book, I argued that recovery as a discourse in the mental health field has been on the ascendancy for many decades now. While recovery itself is a complicated social construct, recovery turns out to be a deeply personal journey that each person with depression attempts. We know that patients tend to undergo various kinds of transitions in depression and recovery. For instance, as already discussed, the self appears to disintegrate to some degree in depression, and while recovery might be about getting back to life before depression for some, for others recovery can involve a longer-term project of putting the self back together, this time more 'authentically'. Here, (re)telling a 'life-giving' story about the self is an important part of any healing.

There are shorter-term aspects of recovery in that each person tends to recover from episodes of depression. As noted in other mental health research, people described key 'turning points' where something happened and their depression loosened its grip. For example, getting angry with the depression, deciding to get help, coming to see depression as a spiritual 'crisis' and even the touch of a baby or a ritual dance were described as creating space for 'turning points' to happen. Particularly dramatic turning points were associated with antidepressant medication use. Nevertheless, turning points – while very useful to patients in revealing the potential for recovery – do not always result in lasting improvement, and people could slump back into depression without additional support and recovery 'tools' at their disposal. The important point here is that notwithstanding effective tools like medication, turning points are frequently meaningful as narrative events. When the professional is aware of the narrative underpinning the turning point, they can be more effective in supporting patients to select more useful stories about the self turning a corner towards recovery.

Although people tend to recover from depression as a matter of course, recoveries may be temporary, partial or otherwise unsatisfactory. Thus, beyond the usual short-term recoveries to depression, many people felt motivated to find ways to recover more fully from depression in the longer term. This involved people working more deeply on themselves, and included goals like minimising the frequency and impacts of actual depression episodes and finding ways to feel reinvigorated in between episodes. Preventing depression in between episodes and minimising the impact of actual depression could involve keeping an eye out for warning signs of looming depression, as well as using approaches like fish oils, exercise or yoga. A number of people minimised the impact of depressive episodes by cognitively noticing that they follow a cyclical pattern and so logically they would be on an upward slope to recovery once they had hit rock bottom. However, the language of hope in depression is not always apparent to patients, and even experienced patients can forget that they will recover. Thus, professionals can be particularly helpful in assisting patients to adopt 'recovery attitudes' no matter what point on the depression–recovery spectrum they are on.

The longer-term recovery project is closest to the idea of quest narrative as outlined by Frank (1995), where the patient as hero undergoes a journey to retrieve meaning out of an illness experience that may not be altogether curable. In the long-term recovery journey, patients talk about enduring suffering and developing different types of insights, for example becoming aware that the distorted thinking of depression is not the same thing as the self; finding out that a more authentically felt self is possible beyond the confines of depression; that it is possible to rewrite the story of their depression more constructively into the story of themselves (e.g. depression as ultimately helpful in authentic living, rather than an enemy of the self); and that creativity and joy is possible beyond depression. There are also spiritual growth stories that recast depression as a beneficial experience in the long run. All of these kinds of patient narratives coincide with those psychotherapy models of self that identify the interior life of authenticity with aliveness, vitality and inner warmth (Meares 2004).

With experience, patients talked about the need to take greater responsibilities for their story of self, including their recoveries from depression. As such, ultimately, professionals are relegated to the status of 'allies in recovery' by more experienced patients. Certainly, valued professionals were able to support patient expertise by supporting 'recovery attitudes' and patient expertise that were commensurate with the place on the spectrum from depression to recovery that patients are on.

Medical and non-medical recovery tools

A key finding in this book was that recovery tools considered effective by patients go hand in hand with telling a good story about recovering from depression. Consistent with a perspective where it is patients themselves who must ultimately discover and narrate their depression and recovery, it is important to involve patients as much as possible in decision-making about the medical and non-medical approaches they use to promote recovery.

Patients will come with prior assumptions about medical approaches, and so it is important to ask about, and address, patient concerns. For example, while patients described initially having negative views of hospitalisation, their experiences did not always match their expectations. People were able to describe benefits gained through hospitalisation.

A number of key points about the use of antidepressant medication and electro-convulsive therapy (ECT) were made by patients:

- Narratives about the causality of depression play an important role in decision-making.

- The time lapse between first taking medication and the medication working can be a very difficult time.

- The effectiveness of SSRIs as judged by users varies enormously.

- Adjusting doses and/or changing medication can make a big difference if the right medication and dose can be found.

- The feelings and side-effects associated with Selective Serotonin Reuptake Inhibitors (SSRIs) and ECT will play an important role in their acceptability.

- Withdrawal symptoms from certain SSRIs are experienced as very real, and people need to be told of the potential for such problems from the outset.

- It is more helpful as a recovery ally to respect rather than deny narratives about memory loss associated with ECT.

- Due to cognitive deficits associated with depression, it may sometimes help to repeatedly explain the full information and risks of ECT to help people understand the procedure and thus better provide informed consent.

- The costs of medication or ECT may be viewed as outweighing the benefits, even when the benefits are also clear.

Many non-medical tools like yoga, omega-3 fatty acids, homeopathy, moderate exercise and getting out into nature are relatively safe narrative 'tools', and can be recommended or even 'prescribed' with confidence. These tools do little if any harm, and indeed may well be of great benefit to helping patients tell good stories about recovery. While some professionals may consider certain tools to be placebos, this is not the point. Anything that is relatively safe and can increase hope (as placebos may) and contribute to a more helpful narrative of living, is potentially valid for patients with depression. From a patient perspective, assembling a range of tools that contribute to life-giving narratives can help make a good depression recovery story. At the very least, having a range of approaches available to tackle depression can inspire confidence that recovery is possible, or even likely. By respecting and engaging with patient choices, professionals can support patients in selecting the most effective tools and narratives. By encouraging open discussions of non-medical tools, professionals can also play a role in the patient narrative when an approach involves some risk. For instance, while St John's wort may well be effective for mild to moderate depression, it can interact with other drugs (e.g. some drugs used to treat HIV) and thus have negative consequences. While mindfulness may be effective for those with three or more episodes of depression, there can be adverse outcomes that patients need to be aware of, including an initial increase in anxiety when patients face up to issues they have been previously distracted from.

In terms of spirituality and religion more widely, the research shows that there is some evidence of a positive link between mental health and spiritual practices under certain circumstances. The mechanisms by which such practices help people are probably multitude and include the social support available at places of worship, the helpful ethics for living available in religions and the way that prayer can simulate aspects of counselling and work to shift the way people are subjectively feeling. Nevertheless, the literature shows that it is the skilful way in which spiritual and religious beliefs are deployed that determines any benefit. Unskilful beliefs and practices – e.g. believing that homosexuality is sinful – can potentially undermine wellbeing. Again, professionals who respect spiritual stories are most likely to have the honour of hearing – and working with – spiritual narratives. Many patients will adopt spiritual narratives regardless of the beliefs of professionals. Engaging with these stories means it is possible to encourage skilful uses.

Recovery allies

Working as a recovery ally is complex and involves engaging effectively in patient narratives. This approach may well need to be learnt by professionals. However, the narratives investigated for this book suggest that even adopting some simple alliance approaches can make a real difference to patients. Some of these approaches are easier to master than others, such as being able to imagine the existential experience of depression, helping patients with depression to feel unrushed and being mindful of ways to reduce the impact of waiting times in referral chains. Other approaches may be more difficult to learn, such as listening out for the things that patients do not say and helping patients select the narratives that most resonate with authentic feelings out of a range of available narratives. Nevertheless, it is frequently the small and symbolic things that professionals do that really help patients to feel supported. Small gestures like the comforting words professionals use; remembering things about the patient; displaying a human side to the patient; following up patients who do not show for appointments; making efforts to give space and respect to the stories patients tell; and ensuring practical help in the community can make all the difference from the patient perspective.

Case study 9.1: Being an ally in patient strategies to resist stigma in depression

It can be very difficult for people to deal with social stigma (i.e. the actual and perceived negative labelling and discrediting of the person (Scambler 2004)), especially when mental illness is involved: 'I had very little sympathy for myself. I think the stigma started with myself.' (Ruth)

Professionals can tap into the variety of narratives patients use to challenge stigma in order to support patients. For instance, the story of depression being the consequence of a reversible chemical imbalance is a particularly effective strategy for some people in side-stepping stigma: 'I actually felt happier that it [Efexor] worked, because it proved to me that what I had been suffering was a physical thing…chemicals in my brain' (Heather).

The chemical imbalance theory of depression can help people to normalise depression as an illness beyond their control, and counter deep feelings of guilt and blame (Kangas 2001), and professionals should be aware of how this approach could be helpful within some patient narratives.

Other patient stories that can encourage a sense of self-worth and challenge social attitudes could also be helpful to people with depression. For example, some people tried to 'normalise depression', such as by pointing to the considerable number of people with mental health problems in the community, including celebrities. A few people pointed to the more fashionable aspects of depression as a way of discounting stigma, such as the use of Prozac. A number of people even encouraged people with depression to 'come out' with their diagnosis, either selectively to friends, or more publicly, including by using the media. Patricia, for instance, effectively took direct action in her workplace to address stigma:

'Why have you been off work?' And I went, 'I've been in hospital.' 'Oh, are you all right?' 'Yeah, I'm fine thanks, yes, thanks for asking.' 'Um, nothing too serious I hope?' 'Um, hmmm, yeah it was, but I'm ok, I'm dealing with it, thanks for asking.' And they went, 'Oh, oh wh- what was it then?' You know what people are like, they will try and get it out of you, and I think if you try to hide it, it gives them something to use against you. So I was just really outright, and I just said, 'OK, I was in a psychiatric hospital for a month and then outpatients for a further month and now I'm at work part-time to try and get back into the swing of things slowly.' And he just looked at me… Honestly he, his eyes were just, popping out of his head. His jaw hit the floor, and he just didn't know what to say to me. So he touched my shoulder and I said, 'It's OK though,' I said, 'I'm not loopy' and he just started laughing, because I'd just turned it into a joke. (Patricia)

Resisting stigma has been described elsewhere in relation to other illnesses (Chapple, Ziebland and McPherson 2004). Resistance in depression has a clear objective: to avoid a discredited self and real consequences, such as being considered less employable (Warner 2002).

On a wider social scale, professionals can become aware of the parallels with the stigmatisation and liberation of other marginalised groups in society. For instance, the narratives of 'guilt' and 'innocence', 'otherness' and 'difference', 'biology' versus 'environment', putting on a front to pass as 'normal' and challenging 'normality', 'low self-esteem' and assertion of 'self-respect' are apparent in the life stories told in this study. Additionally, these kinds of narratives are similar to those that emerged with the regulation and stigmatisation of homosexuality that began in earnest in the mid-nineteenth century (Foucault 1986). Since gay liberation, the political response to HIV and the emergence of gay identity politics, gradually the locale of pathology has shifted from within the homosexual individual into a society that is considered to be oddly fearful of homosexuality (homophobia) (Plummer 1999). By making this comparison, it is not suggested that people with depression would celebrate their depression as other minorities might celebrate their sexuality or ethnicity. However, patients with depression can and do celebrate their difference, such as when some participants talked about appreciating the sensitivity and intelligence of people who have had depression. Similarly, if professionals could focus on bringing out and celebrating the positive qualities of patient narratives (e.g. stories of survival, overcoming obstacles, finding joy in life post depression), then this could also help patients to overcome the limiting effects of stigma. Additionally, it may help patients to understand their experiences of depression using more life-affirming narratives.

Talking therapies

Participants pointed out that there are many blocks to undertaking talking therapies, including severe shortages of such therapies in the NHS, their own initial stereotypical understandings of what therapy was about and patient denial around personal problems. Therapy also requires patients to have a certain level of self-awareness and can be experienced as emotionally painful or exhausting by patients with depression. Participants talked about needing to do considerable emotional work in order to use therapy to recover from depression in the longer term. Nevertheless, participants described how skilled therapy could work very well for them. Therapy was thought vital by many for dealing with confusions and sorting through personal problems associated with depression. Further, people who benefited from therapy were highly articulate about the specific ways in which therapy worked. For these patients with depression, the 'brand' of therapy was much less important than a range of other issues, including:

- being given the space to express feelings and thoughts free of the therapist's own personal agenda

- the therapist respecting and trusting the patient and the process, and so allowing the patient's authentically felt story to emerge

- getting the right level of feedback from the therapist, rather than being left alone too much

- patients being allowed to focus on more immediate issues or their past, according to their preferences

- learning practical skills to overcome problems associated with depression

- developing an honest, trusting and safe relationship (with adequate boundaries)

- therapists ensuring they listen deeply and stay with the suffering and uncertainty of fragmented selves and stories, handing back as much control as possible to patients.

For those with distorted or even false selves, therapists must have considerable skill to nurture truly felt selves. Here, therapists need imagination, sensitivity and an ability to convey empathy and respect for the patients in order to help bring out inner stories that pertain to authenticity (Meares 2004). Finally, participants – particularly women – said that due attention also needs to be paid to the relationship-like nature of therapy, including the negotiation of an ending that takes into account the grieving work patients do when a therapy relationship ends.

A final word

This book has been dedicated to the narratives of those courageous people who have experienced depression and found a voice to tell their tales of struggle, disappointments and triumph. What was most moving for me as the researcher on this project was the validation of the human spirit in the narratives I heard, regardless of how much 'recovery' had occurred. People did not view recovery as an exercise in perfection. Rather, people constructed recovery variably in practice according to what was possible, available narratives (that also needed to adapt to changing circumstances including new episodes of depression), and what was available in terms of recovery 'tools'. Even though, sadly, talking therapies were not more widely available, people still managed to find ways to tell better, more useful stories about themselves. The more expert the participant in narration, the more of an ally professionals needed to become in these stories. Professionals who are able to think in narratives (and see themselves as allies), and so engage with patients at this deeper level, are at enormous advantage in assisting people with depression. The hope is that this book will be valuable as a collective snapshot of depression and recovery from the patient perspective. Perhaps this book might also be a useful companion to those who are inclined to respect human interiority and narrative as holding a key to wellbeing and a life well lived.

Participant Biographical Details

John   **Age at interview:** 75

Age at diagnosis: 35

Sex: Male

Background: John, a former brewer, feels he was probably depressed even as a child. He has had a number of bouts of depression and currently has cancer.

Brief outline: Treatments have included ECT, hospitalisation, talking therapies, lithium and medication. He was on a preventative, low dose of Zoloft (sertraline 100mg/day) due to his wife's recent death.

Heather   **Age at interview:** 27

Age at diagnosis: 16

Sex: Female

Background: A graduate of an elite university, Heather believes a chemical imbalance – as well as learned behaviours – lies behind her depression.

Brief outline: Effective approaches include medication (currently Efexor 75 mg/day), hypnotherapy and counselling. Heather was finding it difficult to find therapy in the NHS.

Peter	**Age at interview:** 66

Age at interview: 66

Age at diagnosis: 57

Sex: Male

Background: A retired married man whose depression came about in 1995 after a whole range of life stressors (e.g. increased workloads, loss, increased family demands). It took four years to overcome his depression.

Brief outline: He had sympathetic doctors who took the time to listen. With early retirement, his religious convictions and the gradual resolution of the life stressors, his depression lifted.

Matthew

Age at interview: 31

Age at diagnosis: 17

Sex: Male

Background: A married teacher living in London. Multiple episodes of depression starting in childhood, bouts tend to occur when he is doing well.

Brief outline: Has responded very well to Prozac (20mg/day) and CBT.

Craig

Age at interview: 33

Age at diagnosis: 24

Sex: Male

Background: Craig is a married man with children, a computer programmer, who has had a number of episodes of depression; the most recent was very severe.

Brief outline: Has very good care from his GP. Medication was somewhat effective. He recently stopped taking Lithium and Efexor.

Liza

Age at interview: 44

Age at diagnosis: 41

Sex: Female

Background: Married female health professional, with four children, living in Scotland. Has probably suffered since her teens. She experiences mainly depressive episodes with some euphoria in between.

Brief outline: Liza has responded very well to Prozac (currently 20mg) and cognitive behavioural therapy, and feels she should be on an antidepressant permanently to correct a chemical imbalance.

Diego

Age at interview: 45

Age at diagnosis: 45

Sex: Male

Background: An athletic man who was originally born in Brazil, now living with his partner in London. His most recent episode of depression started in late 2002 and was triggered by workplace pressure.

Brief outline: Diego used a raft of strategies to recover including time off work, attending a support group, counselling, physical exercise, interaction with nature and pets, and spiritual healing.

Belinda

Age at interview: 33

Age at diagnosis: 24

Sex: Female

Background: Works as a receptionist. She had a difficult childhood. She has been sectioned in the past, been on numerous medications and had ECT which she did not like.

Brief outline: With the ongoing care of her GP and ongoing counselling with a skilled practitioner, Belinda has been in recovery since early 2003. Not currently on medication.

Paul

Age at interview: 35

Age at diagnosis: 17

Sex: Male

Background: Paul is a computer technician, who has been depressed for most of his life. There was conflict and early death to cope with in his family, and he has not responded to medication.

Brief outline: Since 1995 Paul has undergone a recovery which has involved therapy (systemic consultation) as well as learning social skills, engaging in enjoyable activities and involvement in self-help groups.

Patrick

Age at interview: 30

Age at diagnosis: 26

Sex: Male

Background: Patrick is a male working part time in the tourism industry, living in a coastal town. Patrick suffered depression and anxiety at a time when he was in a highly confrontational customer relations job.

Brief outline: Helpful approaches include counselling (which has helped him to address past abuse as well as his being gay); removing himself from a bullying workplace; settling debts; swimming; and moving away from London.

Anne

Age at interview: 39

Age at diagnosis: 33

Sex: Female

Background: A married woman who was a customer manager until the birth of her son in 1998 and the death of her mother, at which time she had a severe post-natal depression.

Brief outline: Hospitalised, but experienced poor service in the NHS. Helpful approaches included the contraceptive pill (acts as a mood stabiliser), good GP support, private hospitalisation and Home-Start help in the home.

Marie

Age at interview: 60

Age at diagnosis: 27

Sex: Female

Background: Marie is a retired secretary with a grown son. She was first diagnosed with depression in 1970, and has had a number of episodes since and was hospitalised twice.

Brief outline: Helpful approaches include support from patients in hospital, counselling and medication (Lofepramine). She understands depression as a passing phase and feels she is well past the worst of it.

Richard

Age at interview: 69

Age at diagnosis: 39

Sex: Male

Background: Richard is a retired man who has suffered bipolar disorder since young adulthood, and has had severe bouts of depression requiring hospitalisation.

Brief outline: Has only recently seen himself as getting better, being helped by therapy (e.g. CBT, Gestalt), a clairvoyant therapist/doctor, the learning of meditation techniques and medication (Efexor 75mg, Lithium 400mg/day).

David

Age at interview: 73

Age at diagnosis: Early 20s

Sex: Male

Background: David is a retired, married man. He has two grown children and grandchildren. He has had numerous episodes of depression and has suffered from anxiety.

Brief outline: David has responded well to CBT. He has the support of his wife and has built his confidence in a local sporting club. He recognises depression as a phase that passes.

Patricia

Age at interview: 24

Age at diagnosis: 14

Sex: Female

Background: Patricia, working as a PA, survived an abusive father and complicit mother. Patricia left home at 18 and was taken in by a caring Irish family. Patricia has suffered severe bouts of depression and suicidal urges.

Brief outline: With the help of a caring GP, her counsellor, private hospital treatment, Efexor (150mg/day) and self-help books, Patricia is now feeling better and is keen to continue her healing and help others.

Carl

Age at interview: 49

Sex: Male

Age at diagnosis: 37

Background: Carl is a gay man living with his partner. He has had a number of major episodes of depression. He has experienced difficult work environments as well as homophobic violence.

Brief outline: The most helpful approaches for him have included getting rest, counselling, lifestyle changes (involving moving to a better community and living on less money), spirituality and a partner.

Adam

Age at interview: 35

Age at diagnosis: Not known

Sex: Male

Background: Currently not working, Adam is living with his father. He endured bullying at school and in the 1990s his mother died from cancer. He battles depression and anxiety (including depersonalisation).

Brief outline: Current medication includes Seroxat, Zyperxa (olanzapine), Lamactil (lamatrigine). Adam is grappling with building friendships and what he wants to do in life. He has found one kinesiologist in particular to be very helpful.

Nicola   **Age at interview:** 20

Age at diagnosis: 19

Sex: Female

Background: Nicola is a woman living and studying in a university town in the Midlands. While experiencing isolation and bullying in secondary school, she was able to make a close friend at university.

Brief outline: Nicola became depressed while looking after a friend with depression. Nicola believes Seroxat contributed to her suicide attempt. With counselling and new medication (venlafaxine 150mg/day) she is getting better.

Veronica   **Age at interview:** 50

Age at diagnosis: Unknown

Sex: Female

Background: Veronica, married with children, was anxious as a child and felt ill-fitted with her family. She left university due to anxiety and struggled for years at a bullying workplace before a debilitating five-year depression.

Brief outline: Veronica has managed to find joy in life through approaches including medication (currently venlafaxine 150mg and chlorpromazine 25mg), counselling, partner support, Christianity and voluntary work (which led to rewarding employment).

Michelle   **Age at interview:** 47

Age at diagnosis: 32

Sex: Female

Background: Originally from Northern Europe, Michelle is a health professional. In 1989 her 'emotions caught up' with her, and she became severely depressed and also had psychosis.

Brief outline: Her recovery initially came about after hospitalisation including ECT. With supportive long-term therapy and medication (Prozac and lithium) she has been in recovery ever since 1989.

Kate

Age at interview: 55

Age at diagnosis: 53

Sex: Female

Background: Kate is a female divorcee and teacher with two children (12, 15 years). She has had three episodes of depression (bipolar) each year for the past three years, but tends to recover by the end of each year.

Brief outline: Effective treatments include lithium (400mg/day), day care centre activities (e.g. creative activities), distracting herself from depression, counselling, diet changes and Internet research.

Rosey

Age at interview: 40

Age at diagnosis: 37

Sex: Female

Background: Rosey is a divorcee who is currently on Cipramil (60mg/day). She has had dysthymia and bouts of depression throughout her life, yet she has only been diagnosed recently.

Brief outline: Rosey is now managed by a skilled team in the NHS, which includes long-term therapy. Therapy is addressing her distorted thinking patterns and difficult past. She now understands she can move beyond depression.

Lee

Age at interview: 50

Age at diagnosis: Never clearly diagnosed

Sex: Male

Background: Lee is a gay male academic. He experienced early loss of family members as a child, bullying and sexual confusion. He has suffered ongoing anxiety and depression.

Brief outline: While avoiding medication, helpful approaches have included counselling, self-help books and alternative therapies (e.g. re-birthing). These approaches have helped reduce negative thinking and anxiety.

Pamela

Age at interview: 59

Age at diagnosis: 19

Sex: Female

Background: Pamela is a woman who has one son and one daughter. She was unhappy as a child. She has had post-natal depression and numerous severe bouts of depression. She has not needed medication for many years.

Brief outline: Helpful approaches have included medication, self-help books and tapes, and personal development courses. Pamela received long-term therapy on the NHS. Recently, Pamela discovered she had dyslexia, explaining many of her difficulties.

Sue

Age at interview: 63

Age at diagnosis: 30

Sex: Female

Background: Sue works in the service industry and is a married woman with four grown children. Sue had a difficult childhood family life. She has had ongoing bouts of depression.

Brief outline: In recent times, Sue has faired better with a new supportive husband, a caring GP and Prozac (20mg/day). She continues to struggle against feeling to blame for things outside of her control.

Julie

Age at interview: 36

Age at diagnosis: 34

Sex: Female

Background: Julie lives with her partner and young daughter and recently gave up full-time work in a social welfare role. Julie grew up in a difficult family and has experienced anxiety and depression since she can remember.

Brief outline: Not currently on medication, Julie has found the best approaches to include counselling, self-help books, alternative therapies and adopting a more authentic lifestyle (including enjoyable voluntary jobs).

Jane

Age at interview: 43

Age at diagnosis: 40

Sex: Female

Background: Jane is a divorced part-time carer. Before her depression and suicide attempt she was a workaholic in a job that was becoming more demanding. Her depression required hospitalisation.

Brief outline: Her main helpful approaches include hospitalisation, various therapies (including art therapy), Citalopram (40mg/day), reduction in work hours, Christian prayer and diary writing.

Elizabeth

Age at interview: 58

Age at diagnosis: 20

Sex: Female

Background: Elizabeth was initially a foster child who was adopted, but felt different and alone since childhood. Feels she has probably had depression since childhood. Now married with one grown son.

Brief outline: Multiple severe bouts of depression/ 'euphoria', most recently in 1995. Has been hospitalised and had ECT. Most helpful approaches include the drug venlafaxine (75mg/day), music, poetry and spiritual healing.

Carol

Age at interview: 54

Age at diagnosis: 32

Sex: Female

Background: Carol is a woman living with her husband and children. She has had a difficult childhood and ongoing problems with her parents. She has suffered from depression, paranoia and thoughts of suicide.

Brief outline: Carol has supportive health professionals. She reacted badly to lithium, and is now doing much better on her current medication (currently Quetiapine 200mg/day, Amitriptyline 50mg, Carbamazepine 200mg, Atenolol 25 mg, Raberazole 20mg).

Andrew

Age at interview: 55

Age at diagnosis: 51

Sex: Male

Background: Andrew has two grown children and a new partner with a 12-year-old son. He suffered a manic episode in 2000 at a time he was 'workaholic' and life seemed out of control. He went into hospital voluntarily.

Brief outline: Andrew avoided medication but found help at a mental health 'drop in' centre. He became better informed and used creativity (e.g. computer art and music) to help his recovery.

Sasha

Age at interview: 43

Age at diagnosis: 39

Sex: Female

Background: Sasha is single and works in a security firm. She was bullied at school. The grief over her mother's death in 2002 as well as an ongoing dispute over her mother's will has been very difficult.

Brief outline: Sasha feels her GP is excellent, but decided against medication. She has gained confidence over the years, and has benefited from NHS counselling, but is having trouble accessing further counselling.

Shiad

Age at interview: 39

Age at diagnosis: 32

Sex: Male

Background: Shiad is from an Asian background and was born outside the UK. Shiad felt unsafe at school, and has found it difficult to deal with family issues.

Brief outline: Shiad has not used medication and is not happy with his GP. Nevertheless, he has accessed talking therapies which have helped somewhat. He has also moved away from his family.

Sophia   **Age at interview:** 39

Age at diagnosis: 36

Sex: Female

Background: British-Italian health professional, Sophia has felt like an outsider from an early age. She was bullied at school and also had a termination at the age of 16.

Brief outline: Sophia has had three bouts of depression since 1998 (including a suicide attempt). Main helpful approaches include therapy, Efexor (75mg/day), alternative therapies and writing in a diary.

Ruth   **Age at interview:** 39

Age at diagnosis: 18

Sex: Female

Background: Ruth is a media trainer living in London. There is a history of mental illness in her family. Her bipolar disorder began while studying at Oxford University.

Brief outline: Multiple severe bouts requiring hospitalisation at times. Most helpful approaches include medication (currently depacote 1000mg/day, Efexor 75mg/day), fish oils, talking therapies, social support and cranio-sacral massage.

Marcus   **Age at interview:** 37

Age at diagnosis: 22

Sex: Male

Background: Marcus suffered depression and attempted suicide after leaving university and starting work. He was diagnosed with bipolar disorder in 1989. He is currently employed as a teacher and has had a number of bouts of depression/mania.

Brief outline: Useful approaches include medication, CBT, therapy, hospitalisation and self-help groups. Currently takes Lithium (600mg/day) and citalopram (Cipramil) 20mg/day.

Jill

Age at interview: 33

Age at diagnosis: 23

Sex: Female

Background: Jill was adopted from the US, grew up in London, and is currently a single teacher living with her dog. Diagnosed with depression in 1993, and has attempted suicide.

Brief outline: Jill is currently feeling well after a recent rough patch. Helpful approaches have included talking therapies, Prozac (20mg/day), living in a sunnier climate and exercise.

Derek

Age at interview: 45

Age at diagnosis: 32

Sex: Male

Background: Derek is a Black gay male artist, living with his partner. A difficult family life, he thought about suicide at the age of 14 and again had depression at 32.

Brief outline: Effective approaches have included counselling from his GP, partner support, doing a 'Landmark' course, swimming and finding an authentic and creative expression for himself through his work.

Jenny

Age at interview: 43

Age at diagnosis: 37

Sex: Female

Background: Jenny lives with her husband and six-year-old son in a village. Jenny was diagnosed with severe depression after the birth of her son, and had another episode subsequently.

Brief outline: Helpful approaches have included hospitalisation, venlafaxine (75mg X 3/day), fish oils, individual (CBT) and relationship counselling, support from local women, joining Depression Alliance, and a gradual return to work to build confidence.

References

Anlue, S. L. R. (1998) 'The Medicalisation of Deviance.' In J. Germov (ed.) *Second Opinion: An Introduction to Health Sociology*. Melbourne: Oxford University Press.

Anne Maria, M.-L. (2003) 'The gender gap in suicide and premature death or: why are men so vulnerable?' *European Archives of Psychiatry and Clinical Neuroscience 253*, 1–8.

Anthony, W. (1993) 'Recovery from mental illness: The guiding vision of the mental health service system in the 1990s.' *Psychosocial Rehabilitation Journal 16*, 11–23.

Beck, C. T. (2002) 'Postpartum depression: A metasynthesis.' *Qualitative Health Research 12*, 453–472.

Bensoussan, A. (1999) 'Complementary medicine – where lies its appeal?' *Medical Journal of Australia 170*, 247–248.

Betty, S. (2005) 'The growing evidence for demonic possession: What should psychiatry's response be?' *Journal of Religion and Health 44*, 13–30.

Bluepages (2008) Available at http://bluepages.anu.edu.au/treatments/what_works/, accessed 1 June 2008.

Blumer, H. (1969) *Symbolic Interactionism: Perspective and Method*. Berkeley, CA: University of California Press.

Bochner, A. P. (1997) 'It's about time: Narrative and the divided self.' *Qualitative Inquiry 3*, 418–438.

Bolton, J. (2003) 'Stigma alone does not explain non-disclosure of psychological symptoms in general practice.' *Evidence Based Mental Health 6*, 128.

Borg, M. and Kristiansen, K. (2004) 'Recovery-oriented professionals: Helping relationships in mental health services.' *Journal of Mental health 13*, 493–505.

Bose, R. (1997) 'Psychiatry and the popular conception of possession among the Bangladeshis in London.' *International Journal of Social Psychiatry 43*, 1–15.

Boseley, S. (2006) 'Doctors' letter sparks NHS alternative therapies row.' *The Guardian*, 24 May.

Boydell, K. M., Goering, P. and Morrell-Bellai, T. L. (2000) 'Narratives of identity: Re-presentation of self in people who are homeless.' *Qualitative Health Research 10*, 26–38.

Braddock, C. H. And Braddock, L. S. (2005) 'The doctor will see you shortly: The ethical significance of time for the patient–physician relationship.' *Journal of General Internal Medicine 20*, 1057–1062.

Browne, J. and Minichiello, V. (1995) 'The social meanings behind male sex work: Implications for sexual interactions.' *British Journal of Sociology 46*, 598–622.

Burns, D. (1980) *Feeling Good: The New Mood Therapy*. New York: Avon Books.

Burroughs, H., Lovell, K., Morley, M., Baldwin, R., Burns, A. and Chew-Graham, C. (2006) 'Justifiable depression: How primary care professionals and patients view late-life depression? A qualitative study.' *Family Practice 23*, 369–377.

Chapple, A., Ziebland, S. and McPherson, A. (2004) 'Stigma, shame, and blame experienced by patients with lung cancer: Qualitative study.' *British Medical Journal 328*, 1470.

Charmaz, K. (1983) 'Loss of self: A fundamental form of suffering in the chronically ill.' *Sociology of Health and Illness 5*, 168–195.

Chen, C.-H., Wang, S.-Y., Chung, U.-L., Tseng, Y.-F. and Chou, F.-H. (2006) 'Being reborn: The recovery process of postpartum depression in Taiwanese women.' *Journal of Advanced Nursing 54*, 450–456.

Chew-Graham, C. A., Mullin, S., May, C. R., Hedley, S. and Cole, H. (2002) 'Managing depression in primary care: Another example of the inverse care law?' *Family Practice 19*, 632–637.

Chiu, L., Morrow, M., Ganesan, S. and Clark, N. (2005) 'Spirituality and treatment choices by South and East Asian women with serious mental illness.' *Transcultural Psychiatry 42*, 630–656.

Christensen, H., Griffiths, K. M. and Jorm, A. F. (2004) 'Delivering interventions for depression by using the Internet: Randomised controlled trial.' *British Medical Journal 328*, 265.

Christensen, H., Leach, L. S., Barney, L., Mackinnon, A. J. and Griffiths, K. M. (2006) 'The effect of web based depression interventions on self reported help seeking: Randomised controlled trial.' *BMC Psychiatry 6*, 13 [online] April 5, doi: 10.1186/1471-244x-6-13.

Churchill, R., Hunot, V., Corney, R., Knapp, M. *et al.* (2001) 'A systematic review of controlled trials of the effectiveness and cost-effectiveness of brief psychological treatments for depression.' *Health Technology Assessment 5*, 1–173.

Collins, C. (1998) 'Yoga: Intuition, preventive medicine, and treatment.' *Journal of Obstetric, Gynecologic, and Neonatal Nursing 27*, 563–568.

Connell, R. W. (1992) 'A very straight gay: Masculinity, homosexual experience, and the dynamics of gender.' *American Sociological Review 57*, 735–751.

Craig, C., Weinert, C., Walton, J. and Derwinski-Robinson, B. (2006) 'Spirituality, chronic illness, and rural life.' *Journal of Holistic Nursing 24*, 27–35.

Cuijpers, P. (1997) 'Bibliotherapy in unipolar depression: A meta-analysis.' *Journal of Behavior Therapy and Experimental Psychiatry 28*, 139–147.

Cuijpers, P. and Dekker, J. (2005) 'Psychological treatment of depression: A systematic review of meta-analyses.' *Nederlands Tijdschrift voor Geneeskunde 149*, 1892–7.

Daaleman, T. P., Cobb, A. K. and Frey, B. B. (2001) 'Spirituality and well-being: An exploratory study of the patient perspective.' *Social Science and Medicine 53*, 1503–1511.

Daaleman, T. P., Perera, S. and Studenski, S. A. (2004) 'Religion, spirituality, and health status in geriatric outpatients.' *Annals of Family Medicine 2*, 49–53.

Davie, G. (2007) *The Sociology of Religion.* London: Sage.

Demo, D. H. (1992) 'The self-concept over time: Research issues and directions.' *Annual Review of Sociology 18*, 303–326.

Dinos, S., Stevens, S., Serfaty, M., Weich, S. and King, M. (2004) 'Stigma: The feelings and experiences of 46 people with mental illness.' *British Journal of Psychiatry 184*, 176–181.

Doris, A., Ebmeier, K. and Shajahan, P. (1999) 'Depressive illness.' *The Lancet 354*, 1369–1375.

Dowrick, C. (2004) *Beyond Depression: A New Approach to Understanding and Management.* Oxford: Oxford University Press.

Dumais, A., Lesage, A. D., Alda, M., Rouleau, G. *et al.* (2005) 'Risk factors for suicide completion in major depression: A case-control study of impulsive and aggressive behaviors in men.' *American Journal of Psychiatry 162*, 2116–2124.

Ebmeier, K. P., Donaghey, C. and Steele, J. D. (2006) 'Recent developments and current controversies in depression.' *The Lancet 367*, 153–167.

Editorial (2004) 'Depressing research.' *The Lancet 363*, 1335.

Eisenberg, D., Davis, R., Ettner, S., Appel, S. *et al.* (1998) 'Trends in alternative medicine use in the United States, 1990–1997: Results of a follow-up national survey.' *Journal of the American Medical Association 280*, 1569–1575.

Ellison, C. G. and Levin, J. S. (1998) 'The religion-health connection: Evidence, theory and future directions.' *Health Education and Behavior 25*, 700–720.

Elwyn, G. and Gwyn, R. (1999) 'Narrative based medicine: Stories we hear and stories we tell: Analysing talk in clinical practice.' *British Medical Journal 318*, 186–188.

Emslie, C., Ridge, D., Ziebland, S. and Hunt, K. (2006) 'Men's accounts of depression: Reconstructing or resisting hegemonic masculinity?' *Social Science and Medicine 62*, 2246–2257.

Emslie, C., Ridge, D., Ziebland, S. and Hunt, K. (2007) 'Exploring men's and women's experiences of depression and engagement with health professionals: More similarities than differences? A qualitative interview study.' *BMC Family Practice 8*, 43, doi:10.1186/1471-2296-8-43.

Fenton, S. and Sadiq-Sangster, A. (1996) 'Culture, relativism and the expression of mental distress: South Asian women in Britain.' *Sociology of Health and Illness 18*, 66–85.

Fergusson, D., Doucette, S., Glass, K. C., Shapiro, S. *et al.* (2005) 'Association between suicide attempts and selective serotonin reuptake inhibitors: Systematic review of randomised controlled trials.' *British Medical Journal 330*, 396.

Finucane, A. and Mercer, S. W. (2006) 'An exploratory mixed methods study of the acceptability and effectiveness of mindfulness-based cognitive therapy for patients with active depression and anxiety in primary care.' *BMC Psychiatry 6*, 4, doi: 10.1186/1471/244x/6-14 .

Foucault, M. (1986) *The History of Sexuality.* Harmondsworth: Penguin.

Foucault, M. (2001) *Madness and Civilization: A History of Insanity in the Age of Reason.* London: Routledge.

Fox, N. J., Ward, K. J. and O'Rourke, A. J. (2005) 'The "expert patient": Empowerment or medical dominance? The case of weight loss, pharmaceutical drugs and the Internet.' *Social Science and Medicine 60*, 1299–1309.

Frank, A. W. (1991) *At the Will of the Body: Reflections on Illness.* Boston: Houghton Mifflin.

Frank, A. W. (1995) *The Wounded Storyteller: Body, Illness, and Ethics.* London: University of Chicago Press.

Frass, M., Schuster, E., Muchitsch, I., Duncan, J. *et al.* (2006) 'Asymmetry in *The Lancet* meta-analysis.' *Homeopathy 95*, 52–53.

Gask, L., Rogers, A. D., Oliver, D., May, C. and Roland, M. (2005) 'A qualitative study exploring how general practitioners prescribe antidepressants.' *British Journal of General Practice 53*, 278–283.

Gecas, V. (1982) 'The self-concept.' *Annual Review of Sociology 8*, 1–33.

Gelso, C. J. and Carter, J. A. (1985) 'The relationship in counseling and psychotherapy: Components, consequences, and theoretical antecedents. *Counseling Psychologist 13*, 155–243.

Goffman, E. (1963) *Stigma.* New York: Simon & Schuster.

Gold, R. and Ridge, D. T. (2001) '"I will start treatment when I think the time is right": HIV-positive gay men talk about their decision not to access antiretroviral therapy.' *AIDS Care 13*, 693–708.

Greenhalgh, T. and Hurwitz, B. (1999) 'Narrative based medicine: Why study narrative?' *British Medical Journal 318*, 48–50.

Gunnell, D., Saperia, J. and Ashby, D. (2005) 'Selective serotonin reuptake inhibitors (SSRIs) and suicide in adults: Meta-analysis of drug company data from placebo controlled, randomised controlled trials submitted to the MHRA's safety review.' *British Medical Journal 330*, 385–389.

Happ, M. B. (2000) 'Interpretation of nonvocal behavior and the meaning of voicelessness in critical care.' *Social Science and Medicine 50*, 1247–1255.

Healy, D. (2008) 'Halting SSRIs.' Mind. Available at
http://www.mind.org.uk/NR/rdonlyres/59D68F19-F69C-4613-BD40-A0D8B38D1410
/0/DavidHealyHaltingSSRIs.pdf, accessed 30 May 2008.

Healy, D., Herxheimer, A. and Menkes, D. B. (2006) 'Antidepressants and violence: Problems at
the interface of medicine and law.' *Public Library of Science Medicine 3*, e372.

Holmes, J. (1992) *Between Art and Science.* London: Routledge.

Hopper, K. (2007) 'Rethinking social recovery in schizophrenia: What a capabilities approach
might offer.' *Social Science and Medicine 65*, 868–879.

Hyden, L.-C. (1997) 'Illness and narrative.' *Sociology of Health and Illness 19*, 48–69.

Jackson, P. S. (1998) 'Bright star – black sky: A phenomenological study of depression as a
window into the psyche of the gifted adolescent.' *Roeper Review 20*, 215–221.

Jacobson, N. (2003) 'Defining recovery: An interactionist analysis of mental health policy
development, Wisconsin 1996–1999.' *Qualitative Health Research 13*, 378–393.

Jadhav, S., Weiss, M. G. and Littlewood, R. (2001) 'Cultural experience of depression among
white Britons in London.' *Anthropology and Medicine 8*, 47–69.

Jago, B. J. (2002) 'Chronicling an academic depression.' *Journal of Contemporary Ethnography 31*,
729–757.

Jones, L. and Green, J. (2006) 'Shifting discourses of professionalism: A case study of general
practitioners in the United Kingdom.' *Sociology of Health and Illness 28*, 927–950.

Kabat-Zinn, J. (1990) *Full Catastrophe Living.* New York: Delta.

Kangas, I. (2001) 'Making sense of depression: Perceptions of melancholia in lay narratives.'
Health 5, 1363–4593.

Karp, D. A. (1994) 'Living with depression: Illness and identity turning points.' *Qualitative Health
Research 4*, 6–30.

Keller, M. B., McCullough, J. P., Klein, D. N., Arnow, B. *et al.* (2000) 'A comparison of
Nefazodone, the cognitive behavioral-analysis system of psychotherapy, and their
combination for the treatment of chronic depression.' *New England Journal of Medicine 342*,
1462–1470.

King, M., Speck, P. and Thomas, A. (1999) 'The effect of spiritual beliefs on outcome from
illness.' *Social Science and Medicine 48*, 1291–1299.

Kirkwood, G., Rampes, H., Tuffrey, V., Richardson, J., Pilkington, K. and Ramaratnam, S.
(2005) 'Yoga for anxiety: A systematic review of the research evidence.' *British Journal of
Sports Medicine 39*, 884–891.

Kirsch, I., Deacon, B., Huedo-Medina, T., Scoboria, A., Moore, T. and Johnson, B. (2008) 'Initial
severity and antidepressant benefits: A meta-analysis of data submitted to the Food and Drug
Administration.' *Public Library of Science Medicine 5*, e45.

Kirsch, I., Moore, T., Scoboria, A. and Nicholls, S. (2002) 'The emperor's new drugs: An analysis
of antidepressant medication data submitted to the U.S. Food and Drug Administration.'
Prevention and Treatment 5, 23 [online].

Kleinman, A. (2004) 'Culture and depression.' *New England Journal of Medicine 351*, 951–953.

Klerman, G. L. and Weissman, M. M. (1989) 'Increasing rates of depression.' *Journal of the
American Medical Association 261*, 2229–2235.

Koenig, H. G. (2000) 'Religion, spirituality, and medicine: Application to clinical practice.'
Journal of the American Medical Association 284, 1708.

Koenig, H. G., Larson, D. B. and Larson, S. S. (2001) 'Religion and coping with serious medical
illness.' *Annals of Pharmacotherapy 35*, 352–359.

Koenig, H. G., McCullough, M. and Larson, D. B. (2001) *Handbook of Religion and Health: A
Century of Research Reviewed.* New York: Oxford University Press.

Kohut, H. (1971) *The Analysis of Self.* New York: International Universities Press.

Kokanovic, R., Dowrick, C., Butler, E., Herrman, H. and Gunn, J. (2008) 'Lay accounts of depression amongst Anglo-Australian residents and East African refugees.' *Social Science and Medicine 66*, 2, 454–466.

Lafrance, M. N. and Stoppard, J. M. (2006) 'Constructing a non-depressed self: Women's accounts of recovery from depression.' *Feminism and Psychology 16*, 307–325.

Laing, R. D. and Esterson, A. (1964) *Sanity, Madness and the Family*. Hammondsworth: Penguin Books.

Larun, L., Nordheim, L., Ekeland, E., Hagen, K. and Heian, F. (2006) 'Exercise in prevention and treatment of anxiety and depression among children and young people.' *Cochrane Database of Systematic Reviews*, Issue 3, Art. No.: CD004691.

Lavender, H., Khondoker, A. H. and Jones, R. (2006) 'Understandings of depression: An interview study of Yoruba, Bangladeshi and White British people.' *Family Practice, 23*, 651–658.

Lawlor, D. A. and Hopker, S. W. (2001) 'The effectiveness of exercise as an intervention in the management of depression: Systematic review and meta-regression analysis of randomised controlled trials.' *British Medical Journal 322*, 763.

Lewis, B. and Ridge, D. (2005) 'Mothers reframing physical activity: Family oriented politicism, transgression and contested expertise in Australia.' *Social Science and Medicine 60*, 2295–2306.

Linde, K., Clausius, N., Ramirez, G., Melchart, D. *et al.* (1997) 'Are the clinical effects of homoeopathy placebo effects? A meta-analysis of placebo-controlled trials.' *The Lancet 350*, 834–843.

Linde, K., Mulrow, C. D., Berner, M. and Egger, M. (2005) 'St John's wort for depression.' *Cochrane Database of Systematic Reviews*, Issue 1, Art. No.: CD000448.

Mackenbach, J. P. (1996) 'The contribution of medical care to mortality decline: McKeown revisited.' *Journal of Clinical Epidemiology 49*, 1207–1213.

Maller, C., Townsend, M., Pryor, A., Brown, P. and St Leger, L. (2006) 'Healthy nature healthy people: Contact with nature as an upstream health promotion intervention for populations.' *Health Promotion International 21*, 45–54.

Mallinson, S. and Popay, J. (2007) 'Describing depression: Ethnicity and the use of somatic imagery in accounts of mental distress.' *Sociology of Health and Illness 29*, 857–871.

Mann, M. P. (2004) 'The adverse influence of narcissistic injury and perfectionism on college students' institutional attachment.' *Personality and Individual Differences 36*, 1797–1806.

Markowitz, S. and Cuellar, A. (2007) 'Antidepressants and youth: Healing or harmful?' *Social Science and Medicine 64*, 2138–2151.

Mason, O. and Hargreaves, I. (2001) 'A qualitative study of mindfulness-based cognitive therapy for depression.' *British Journal of Medical Psychology 74*, 197–212.

Matheson, F. I., Moineddin, R., Dunn, J. R., Creatore, M. I., Gozdyra, P. and Glazier, R. H. (2006) 'Urban neighborhoods, chronic stress, gender and depression.' *Social Science and Medicine 63*, 2604–2616.

Matsumoto, D., Kudoh, T. and Takeuchi, S. (1996) 'Changing patterns of individualism and collectivism in the United States and Japan.' *Culture Psychology 2*, 77–107.

May, C., Allison, G., Chapple, A., Chew-Graham, C. *et al.* (2004) 'Framing the doctor–patient relationship in chronic illness: A comparative study of general practitioners' accounts.' *Sociology of Health and Illness 26*, 135–158.

McPherson, S. and Armstrong, D. (2006) 'Social determinants of diagnostic labels in depression.' *Social Science and Medicine 62*, 50–58.

Meares, R. (2004) 'The conversational model: An outline.' *American Journal of Psychotherapy 58*, 51–66.

Medawar, C., Herxheimer, A., Bell, A. and Jofre, S. (2002) 'Paroxetine, Panorama and user reporting of ADRs: Consumer intelligence matters in clinical practice and post-marketing drug surveillance.' *International Journal of Risk and Safety in Medicine 15*, 161–169.

Melbourne Academic Mindfulness Interest Group (2006) 'Mindfulness-based psychotherapies: A review of conceptual foundations, empirical evidence and practical considerations.' *Australian and New Zealand Journal of Psychiatry 40*, 285–294.

Melchior, M., Caspi, A., Milne, B., Danese, A., Poulton, R. and Moffitt, T. E. (2007) 'Work stress precipitates depression and anxiety in young, working women and men.' *Psychological Medicine 37*, 1119–1129.

Meraviglia, M. G. (1999) 'Critical analysis of spirituality and its empirical indicators: Prayer and meaning in life.' *Journal of Holistic Nursing 17*, 18–33.

Metzl, J. (2001) 'Prozac and the pharmacokinetics of narrative form.' *Signs: Journal of Women in Culture and Society 27*, 347–380.

Michaud, C. M., Murray, C. J. L. and Bloom, B. R. (2001) 'Burden of disease – Implications for future research.' *Journal of the American Medical Association 285*, 535–539.

Miller, W. and Thoresen, C. (2003) 'Spirituality, religion, and health.' *American Psychologist 58*, 24–35.

Moller-Leimkuhler, A. M. (2002) 'Barriers to help-seeking by men: A review of sociocultural and clinical literature with particular reference to depression.' *Journal of Affective Disorders 71*, 1–9.

Montgomery, P. and Richardson, A.J. (2008) 'Omega-3 fatty acids for bipolar disorder.' *Cochrane Database of Systematic Reviews 2*, Art. No.: CD005169.

Moore, A. (2007) 'Eternal sunshine.' *The Guardian*, 13 May.

Murphy, J. M., Laird, N. M., Monson, R. R., Sobol, A. M. and Leighton, A. H. (2000) 'A 40-year perspective on the prevalence of depression: The Stirling County Study.' *Archives of General Psychiatry 57*, 209–215.

Murray, J., Banerjee, S., Byng, R., Tylee, A., Bhugra, D. and Macdonald, A. (2006) 'Primary care professionals' perceptions of depression in older people: A qualitative study.' *Social Science and Medicine 63*, 1363–1373.

Myers, S. (2000) 'Empathic listening: Reports on the experience of being heard.' *Journal of Humanistic Psychology 40*, 148–173.

National Collaborating Centre for Mental Health (2004) *Depression: Management of Depression in Primary and Secondary Care.* London: National Institute for Clinical Excellence.

National Institute for Mental Health in England (2005) *NIMHE Guiding Statement on Recovery.* London: Department of Health.

Nelson, G., Lord, J. and Ochocka, J. (2001) 'Empowerment and mental health in community: Narratives of psychiatric consumer/survivors.' *Journal of Community and Applied Social Psychology 11*, 125–142.

NHS Centre for Reviews and Dissemination (2002) 'Homeopathy.' *Effective Health Care 7*, 12.

O'Hara, M. W. (1986) 'Social support, life events, and depression during pregnancy and the puerperium.' *Archives of General Psychiatry 43*, 569–573.

O'Kearney, R., Gibson, M., Christensen, H. and Griffiths, K. M. (2006) 'Effects of a cognitive behavioural Internet program on depression, vulnerability to depression and stigma in adolescent males: A school-based controlled trial.' *Cognitive Behavioural Therapy 35*, 43–54.

O'Sullivan, S. (2006) 'Pragmatics for the production of subjectivity: Time for probe-heads.' *Journal for Cultural Research 10*, 309–322.

Pampallona, S., Bollini, P., Tibaldi, G., Kupelnick, B. and Munizza, C. (2004) 'Combined pharmacotherapy and psychological treatment for depression: A systematic review.' *Archives of General Psychiatry 61*, 714–719.

Patton, M. Q. (2002) *Qualitative Research and Evaluation Methods.* Thousand Oaks, CA: Sage.

Pennebaker, J. W. and Seagal, J. D. (1999) 'Forming a story: The health benefits of narrative.' *Journal of Clinical Psychology 55*, 1243–1254.

Pilgrim, D. (2007) 'The survival of psychiatric diagnosis.' *Social Science and Medicine 65*, 536–547.

Pilkington, K., Kirkwood, G., Rampes, H., Fisher, P. and Richardson, J. (2005a) 'Homeopathy for depression: A systematic review of the research evidence.' *Homeopathy 94*, 153–163.

Pilkington, K., Kirkwood, G., Rampes, H. and Richardson, J. (2005b) 'Yoga for depression: The research evidence.' *Journal of Affective Disorders 89*, 13–24.

Pilkington, K., Kirkwood, G., Rampes, H., Fisher, P. and Richardson, J. (2006) 'Homeopathy for anxiety and anxiety disorders: A systematic review of the research.' *Homeopathy 95*, 151–162.

Plummer, D. C. (1999) *One of the Boys.* New York: Haworth Press.

Pollock, K. and Grime, J. (2003) 'GPs' perspectives on managing time in consultations with patients suffering from depression: A qualitative study.' *Family Practice 20*, 262–269.

Pollock, K., Grime, J. and Mechanic, D. (2002) 'Patients' perceptions of entitlement to time in general practice consultations for depression: A qualitative study.' *British Medical Journal 325*, 687.

Rappaport, J. (2000) 'Community narratives: Tales of terror and joy.' *American Journal of Community Psychology 28*, 1–24.

Reilly, D. T., Taylor, M. A., Campbell, J. H., Carter, R. *et al.* (1994) 'Is evidence for homoeopathy reproducible?' *The Lancet 344*, 1601–1606.

Repper, J. and Perkins, R. (2003) *Social Inclusion and Recovery.* London: Bailliere Tindall.

Richards, T. J. and Richards, L. (1994) 'Using Computers in Qualitative Research.' In N. K. Denzin and Y. S. Lincoln (eds) *Handbook of Qualitative Research.* Thousand Oaks, CA: Sage.

Ridge, D. and Ziebland, S. (2006) '"The old me could never have done that": How people give meaning to recovery following depression.' *Qualitative Health Research 16*, 1038–1053.

Ridge, D., Plummer, D. and Peasley, D. (2006) 'Remaking the masculine self and coping in the liminal world of the gay "scene".' *Culture, Health and Sexuality 8*, 501–514.

Ridge, D., Williams, I. Anderson, J. and Elford, J. (2008) 'Like a prayer: The role of spirituality and religion for people living with HIV in the UK.' *Sociology of Health and Illness 30*, 413–428.

Roberts, G. and Wolfson, P. (2004) 'The rediscovery of recovery: Open to all.' *Advances in Psychiatric Treatment 10*, 37–48.

Roberts, L., Ahmed, I. and Hall, S. (2006) 'Intercessory Prayer for the Alleviation of Ill Health (review).' *Cochrane Database of Systematic Reviews*, Issue 4, Art. No.: CD000368.

Robinson, L. A., Berman, J. S. and Neimeyer, R. A. (1990) 'Psychotherapy for the treatment of depression: A comprehensive review of controlled outcome research.' *Psychological Bulletin 108*, 30–49.

Robson, C. (1993) *Real World Research: A Resource for Social Scientists and Practitioner-Researchers.* Oxford and Cambridge, MA: Blackwell.

Rose, D., Fleischmann, P., Wykes, T., Leese, M. and Bindman, J. (2003) 'Patients' perspectives on electroconvulsive therapy: Systematic review.' *British Medical Journal 326*, 1363–1367.

Rose, D. S., Wykes, T. H., Bindman, J. P. and Fleischmann, P. S. (2005) 'Information, consent and perceived coercion: Patients' perspectives on electroconvulsive therapy.' *British Journal of Psychiatry 186*, 54–59.

Rowe, D. (2003) *Depression: The Way Out of Your Prison*, 3rd edn. Hove: Routledge.

Russell, S. J. and Browne, J. L. (2005) 'Staying well with bipolar disorder.' *Australian and New Zealand Journal of Psychiatry 39*, 187–193.

Salmon, P. and Young, B. (2005) 'Core assumptions and research opportunities in clinical communication.' *Patient Education and Counseling 58*, 225–234.

Scambler, G. (2004) 'Re-framing stigma: Felt and enacted stigma and challenges to the sociology of chronic and disabling conditions.' *Social Theory and Health 2*, 29–46.

Schreiber, R. (1996) '(Re)Defining my self: Women's process of recovery from depression.' *Qualitative Health Research 6*, 469–491.

Schulz, R., Drayer, R. A. and Rollman, B. L. (2002) 'Depression as a risk factor for non-suicide mortality in the elderly.' *Biological Psychiatry 52*, 205–225.

Segal, Z., Williams, J. M. G. and Teasdale, J. D. (2002) *Mindfulness-Based Cognitive Therapy for Depression: A New Approach to Preventing Relapse.* New York: Guilford Press.

Shang, A., Huwiler-Muntener, K., Nartey, L., Juni, P. *et al.* (2005) 'Are the clinical effects of homoeopathy placebo effects? Comparative study of placebo-controlled trials of homoeopathy and allopathy.' *The Lancet 366*, 726–732.

Sheldon, B. (1995) *Cognitive-Behavioural Therapy: Research, Practice, and Philosophy.* London: Routledge.

Shiels, C., Gabbay, M., Dowrick, C. and Hulbert, C. (2004) 'Depression in men attending a rural general practice: Factors associated with prevalence of depressive symptoms and diagnosis.' *British Journal of Psychiatry 185*, 239–244.

Shoshanah Feher, R. C. M. (1999) 'Coping with breast cancer in later life: The role of religious faith.' *Psycho-Oncology 8*, 408–416.

Silvers, K., Hackett, M. and Scott, K. (2003) 'Omega 3 fatty acids for depression (Protocol).' *Cochrane Database of Systematic Reviews*, Issue 4, Art. No.: CD004692.

Sloan, R. P. and Bagiella, E. (2002) 'Claims about religious involvement and health outcomes.' *Annals of Behavioral Medicine 24*, 14–21.

Smith, B. (1999) 'The abyss: Exploring depression through the narrative of the self.' *Qualitative Inquiry 5*, 264–279.

Smith, J., Braunack-Mayer, A. and Wittert, G. (2006) 'What do we know about men's help-seeking and health service use?' *Medical Journal of Australia 184*, 81–83.

Solomon, A. (2002) *The Noonday Demon: An Anatomy of Depression.* London: Chatto and Windus.

Spitzer, R. L. (1981) 'The diagnostic status of homosexuality in DSM-III: A reformulation of the issues.' *American Journal of Psychiatry 138*, 210–215.

Spong, S. and Hollanders, H. (2003) 'Cognitive therapy and social power.' *Counselling and Psychotherapy Research 3*, 216–222.

Stanton, A.L., Danoff-Burg, S. and Huggins, M.E. (2002) 'The first year after breast cancer diagnosis: Hope and coping strategies as predictors of adjustment.' *Psycho-Oncology 11*, 93–102.

Stevenson, F. and Knudsen, P. (2008) 'Discourses of agency and the search for the authentic self: The case of mood-modifying medicines.' *Social Science and Medicine 66*, 170–181.

Stoll, A., Severus, W., Freeman, M., Rueter, S. *et al.* (1999) 'Omega 3 fatty acids in bipolar disorder: A preliminary double-blind, placebo-controlled trial.' *Archives of General Psychiatry 56*, 407–412.

Strauss, C. (1997) 'Partly fragmented, partly integrated: An anthropological examination of "postmodern fragmented subjects".' *Cultural Anthropology 12*, 362–404.

Tasaki, K., Maskarinec, G., Shumay, D., Tatsumura, Y. and Kakai, H. (2002) 'Communication between physicians and cancer patients about complementary and alternative medicine: Exploring patients' perspectives.' *Psycho-Oncology 11*, 212–220.

Teasdale, J., Segal, Z., Williams, J., Ridgeway, V., Soulsby, J. and Lau, M. (2000) 'Prevention of relapse/recurrence in major depression by mindfulness-based cognitive therapy.' *Journal of Consulting and Clinical Psychology 68*, 615–623.

Teasdale, J. D., Segal, Z. V. and Williams, J. M. G. (2003) 'Mindfulness training and problem formulation.' *Clinical Psychology: Science and Practice 10*, 157–160.

Thase, M. E., Greenhouse, J. B., Frank, E., Reynolds, C. F. *et al.* (1997) 'Treatment of major depression with psychotherapy or psychotherapy-pharmacotherapy combinations.' *Archives of General Psychiatry 54*, 1009–1015.

Thoresen, C. E. and Harris, A. H. S. (2002) 'Spirituality and health: What's the evidence and what's needed?' *Annals of Behavioral Medicine 24*, 3–13.

Thorne, S. E., Ternulf Nyhlin, K. and Paterson, B. L. (2000) 'Attitudes toward patient expertise in chronic illness.' *International Journal of Nursing Studies 37*, 303–311.

Timulak, L. (2007) 'Identifying core categories of client-identified impact of helpful events in psychotherapy: A qualitative meta-analysis.' *Psychotherapy Research 17*, 310–320.

UK ECT Review Group (2003) 'Efficacy and safety of electroconvulsive therapy in depressive disorders: A systematic review and meta-analysis.' *The Lancet 361*, 799–808.

US Department of Health and Human Services (1999) *Mental Health: A Report of the Surgeon General – Executive Summary.* Rockville, MD: US Department of Health and Human Services, Substance Abuse and Mental Health Services Administration, Center for Mental Health Services, National Institutes of Health, National Institute of Mental Health.

Walton, J. and Sullivan, N. (2004) 'Men of prayer: Spirituality of men with prostate cancer: A grounded theory study.' *Journal of Holistic Nursing 22*, 133–151.

Warner, L. (2002) *Out at Work: A Survey of the Experiences of People with Mental Health Problems within the Workplace.* London: Mental Health Foundation.

Watkins, E. and Baracaia, S. (2002) 'Rumination and social problem-solving in depression.' *Behaviour Research and Therapy 40*, 1179–1189.

White, H. (1987) *The Content of the Form: Narrative Discourse and Historical Representation.* Baltimore, MD: Johns Hopkins University Press.

Whittington, C. J., Kendall, T., Fonagy, P., Cottrell, D., Cotgrove, A. and Boddington, E. (2004) 'Selective serotonin reuptake inhibitors in childhood depression: Systematic review of published versus unpublished data.' *The Lancet 363*, 1341–1345.

Whitty, M. (2002) 'Possible selves: An exploration of the utility of a narrative approach.' *Identity 2*, 211–228.

Willis, E. M. (1989) *Medical Dominance.* Sydney: Allen and Unwin.

Wilson, J. and Read, J. (2001) 'What prevents GPs from using outside resources for women experiencing depression? A New Zealand study.' *Family Practice 18*, 84–86.

Wink, P., Dillon, M. and Larsen, B. (2005) 'Religion as moderator of the depression–health connection: Findings from a longitudinal study.' *Research on Aging 27*, 197–220.

Winnicott, D. W. (1992) *The Family and Individual Development.* London: Routledge.

Wittink, M. N., Barg, F. K. and Gallo, J. J. (2006) 'Unwritten rules of talking to doctors about depression: Integrating qualitative and quantitative methods.' *Annals of Family Medicine 4*, 302–309.

Woods, T. E. and Ironson, G. H. (1999) 'Religion and spirituality in the face of illness: How cancer, cardiac, and HIV patients describe their spirituality/religiosity.' *Journal of Health Psychology 4*, 393–412.

Young, T. M. (1996) 'Using narrative theory and self psychology within a multigenerational family systems perspective.' *Journal of Analytic Social Work 3*, 137–155.

Recommended Reading

Burns, D. (1980) *Feeling Good: The New Mood Therapy.* New York: Avon Books.

Dowrick, C. (2004) *Beyond Depression: A New Approach to Understanding and Management.* Oxford: Oxford University Press.

Frank, A. (1995) *The Wounded Storyteller: Body, Illness, and Ethics.* London: University of Chicago Press.

Rowe, D. (2003) *Depression: The Way Out of Your Prison,* 3rd edn. Hove: Routledge.

Solomon, A. (2002) *The Noonday Demon: An Anatomy of Depression.* London: Chatto and Windus.

Wolpert, L. (1999) *Malignant Sadness: The Anatomy of Depression.* London: Faber.

Yalom, I. D. (2001) *The Gift of Therapy: Reflections on Being a Therapist.* Piatkus: London.

Subject Index

Author Index